Second Edition

# AGROINDUSTRIAL
# PROJECT ANALYSIS
## CRITICAL DESIGN FACTORS

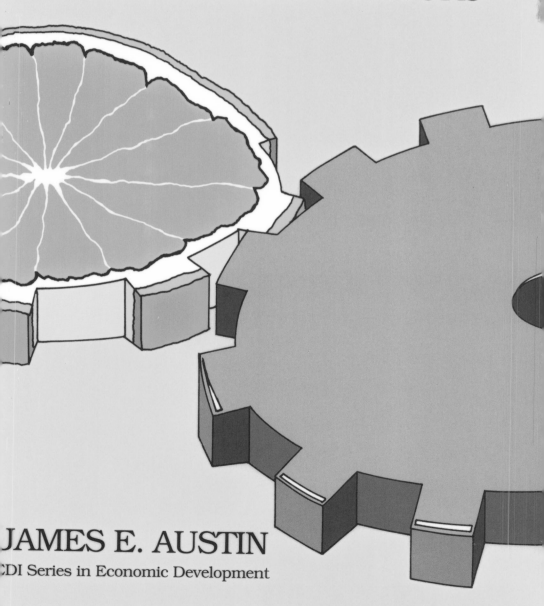

# JAMES E. AUSTIN

CDI Series in Economic Development

# Agroindustrial Project Analysis

EDI Series in Economic Development

**Second Edition**

# *Agroindustrial Project Analysis*

## Critical Design Factors

JAMES E. AUSTIN

*Published for The Economic Development Institute
of The World Bank*

**The Johns Hopkins University Press**

*Baltimore and London*

*Library of Congress Cataloging in Publication Data*

Austin, James E.
  Agroindustrial project analysis : critical design factors / James
E. Austin.—2nd ed.
     p.    cm.
  ''Published for the Economic Development Institute of the World
Bank.''
  Includes bibliographical references and index.
  ISBN 0-8018-4530-0
  1. Agricultural industries.   2. Agricultural development projects—
Evaluation.   I. Economic Development Institute (Washington, D.C.)
II. Title.
HD9000.5.A97   1992
338.4—dc20                                          92-19227
                                                     CIP

# Contents

# Foreword

AGROINDUSTRY—that is, industry based on the processing of agricultural raw materials—is of growing importance in the economics of developing countries. In some instances, the processing is required to prepare a primary product for domestic or foreign trade. In others, agroindustry offers a means of increasing the domestic value added to a raw material through manufacture. With rising incomes and growing urbanization in developing countries, the demand for processed foods in particular tends to increase rapidly. Consideration of these issues led the Economic Development Institute in 1974 to initiate courses in agroindustrial projects for planners from the developing world. The first (1981) edition of this book grew out of training materials prepared for those courses.

During the next ten years this book maintained its position as a leading reference concerning broad considerations of agroindustrial policy and systems. However, times have changed and much experience has been gained and is now integrated into this substantially revised second edition.

This book is intended to be an applied guide to the design and analysis of agroindustrial investments in developing countries. It should be of use both as a tool for national planners concerned with agroindustry and as a training aid for courses on investment analysis. Those responsible for investments in the agroindustrial sector commonly have backgrounds in either agriculture or industry but not both; this book provides an introduction to the subject that encompasses both areas of expertise. It does assume, however, that users have a working knowledge of the economic structure of their country.

This book is one of a number published or in preparation that arise from the training courses of the Economic Development Institute. We hope that making these publications available for wider circulation will help those new to the field and those responsible for training to master relevant analytical techniques that can lead to more efficient investment planning.

AMNON GOLAN
*Director, Economic Development Institute*
*The World Bank*

# Preface

THE PREPARATION OF THIS SECOND EDITION presented a perplexing and stimulating challenge. The first edition was published in 1981 and, to my great satisfaction, was well received by public sector analysts, private practitioners, and academics. The book filled an important void in the literature, and the publication of English, Spanish, and French versions facilitated its international dissemination.

An insidious comfortableness can envelop an author who has produced a useful contribution to the literature. One feels good about the accomplishment and then moves on to the next intellectual challenge. There is a certain resistance to revisiting one's past works and retracing a known path rather than forging a new one. So authors often need a nudge to go backward. Happily, once headed in that direction, they may find themselves jumping forward even further. So it was with this book.

At the urging of J. A. Nicholas Wallis, Agriculture Division Chief at the World Bank's Economic Development Institute (EDI), I agreed to prepare a second edition of *Agroindustrial Project Analysis*. Nick's deft provocation was doubly compelling: Had anything new and important been learned about agroindustry analysis over the past decade? Did I feel any sense of fiduciary responsibility to readers of the first edition? Yes and yes. Intellectually and professionally the second edition became imperative.

The challenge was to bring the book into the 1990s by incorporating new knowledge while preserving that which had proved so useful to readers of the first edition. I believe we have achieved the proper balance. The major change in the second edition is the addition of a new chapter elaborating the systems approach to agroindustrial analysis. This new analytical framework captures the intellectual advances in the field and presents a richer conceptual and technical approach. The three core analytical chapters on marketing, procurement, and processing, which have proved to be of great utility to thousands of practitioners, have been enriched with additional sections, analyses, and field examples. The new analytical framework is applied and illustrated throughout these chapters. Information has been updated wherever possible to capture the latest technological and market trends and advances. Examples and analyses based on older data have been retained when the underlying points or concepts remain valid. Readers of the first edition will be able to capture significant additional intellectual value from this new edition. New readers will be introduced to the conceptual frontier of agroindustrial analysis and will also be given a field-proven methodology.

To broaden both the scope and the depth of materials on agroindustries, the Economic Development Institute has simultaneously sponsored the development of a companion volume to this second edition: *Agroindustrial Investment and Operations*, by James G. Brown with Deloitte & Touche (forthcoming in the EDI Development Studies series from the World Bank, Washington, D.C.). That book builds on the conceptual framework presented here and delves in more detail into the financial and operating dimensions of agroindustries. Although each book is self-contained, readers are strongly urged to use both.

The preparation of this second edition has benefited from the helpful suggestions and continuing support of Nick Wallis and the Economic Development Institute. Professor Sy Rizvi of Cornell University provided thoughtful comments on chapter 5 and invaluable assistance in updating appendix C. Dr. Samuel Young, formerly of the Massachusetts Institute of Technology, helped prepare the original version of appendix C and strengthened chapter 5 by sharing his research on the nutritional effects of various processing technologies. The manuscript also benefited from comments from Jim Brown, Jacques Crosnier, anonymous reviewers in the World Bank's publication review process, and participants in the December 1990 Worldwide Seminar on Agroindustry Development.

I reiterate my appreciation for the support and suggestions of a multitude of people who made the first edition possible: Gunther Koenig, formerly of the World Bank, who pioneered in promoting agroindustry training at EDI; Price Gittinger and Robert Youker, formerly of EDI; Walter Falcon of Stanford University Food Research Institute; Ray Goldberg, Louis Wells, Jr., and George Lodge of the Harvard University Graduate School of Business Administration; Nancy Barry of Women's World Banking; Kenneth Hoadley of Arthur D. Little Management Education Institute; Primitivo Zepeda Salazar of the Banco de Mexico-FIRA; Gustavo Esteva of Mexico; and Ferruccio Accame, Jaime Romero, Frank Meissner, and Hugh Swartz of the Inter-American Development Bank.

The assistance of the Economic Development Institute and the Harvard Business School were invaluable to the development of this second edition. Special thanks go to my former assistant, Leslie Cadwell, who diligently word-processed the manuscript. I am also grateful to the staff of J. E. Austin Associates for their technical and administrative support. Martha V. Gottron edited the manuscript for publication, Cynthia Stock prepared the charts, Kathryn Kline Dahl managed production of the book, and Emily Evershed prepared the index.

To all those whose cooperation made this book a reality, I express my deep appreciation. It is my hope that our collective effort will contribute to the development of more efficient, effective, and equitable agroindustrial projects in the developing world.

# 1 An Overview

THE PURPOSE OF THIS BOOK is to provide an analytical framework for designing agroindustrial projects. It is written for private managers and public sector analysts involved in establishing agroindustries. The framework is tailored specifically to the distinctive characteristics of developing country environments, but the approach is also relevant to the design of agroindustrial projects in more industrialized economies. These food- and fiber-processing businesses constitute a significant and dynamic segment of the private sector and are of high importance to countries' development. This initial chapter defines agroindustry, discusses its importance in developing countries, and describes the organization of the book.

## Defining Agroindustry

An agroindustry is an enterprise that processes materials of plant or animal origin. Processing involves transformation and preservation through physical or chemical alteration, storage, packaging, and distribution. The nature of the processing and the degree of transformation can vary tremendously, ranging from the cleaning, grading, and boxing of apples to the milling of rice to the cooking, mixing, and chemical alteration that create a textured vegetable snack food. As shown in table 1-1, agroindustries can be roughly categorized according to the degree that the raw material is transformed. In general, capital investment, technological complexity, and managerial requirements increase as the degree of transformation rises. Raw food and fiber are transformed to create an edible or usable product, to increase storability, to obtain a more easily or economically transportable form, and to enhance palatability, nutritional value, or consumer convenience.

Agroindustrial projects are unique because of three characteristics of their raw materials: seasonality, perishability, and variability.[1] Each of these main characteristics merits brief discussion.

*1*

**Table 1-1.** *Categories of Agroindustry by Level of Transformation of Raw Materials*

| Level I | Level II | Level III | Level IV |
|---------|----------|-----------|----------|
| | | *Selected processing activities* | |
| Cleaning | Ginning | Cooking | Chemical alteration |
| Grading | Milling | Pasteurization | Texturization |
| Storage | Cutting | Canning | |
| | Mixing | Dehydration | |
| | | Freezing | |
| | | Weaving | |
| | | Extraction | |
| | | Assembly | |
| | | *Illustrative products* | |
| Fresh fruits | Cereal | Dairy products | Instant foods |
| Fresh | grains | Canned or frozen | Textured vegetable |
| vegetables | Meats | fruits and | products |
| Eggs | Spices | vegetables | Tires |
| | Animal | Cooked meats | |
| | feeds | Textiles and | |
| | Jute | garments | |
| | Cotton | Refined vegetable | |
| | Lumber | oils | |
| | Rubber | Furniture | |
| | Flour | Sugar | |
| | | Beverages | |

## Seasonality

Because raw material for agroindustries is biological, its supply is seasonal, available at the end of the crop or livestock-reproduction cycle. Although supplies of raw material are usually available only during one or two brief periods in the year, the demand for the finished product is relatively constant throughout the year. Unlike the nonagroindustrial manufacturer, the food- or fiber-processing factory must contend with a supply-and-demand imbalance and problems of inventory management, production scheduling, and coordination among the production, processing, and marketing segments of the farm-to-consumer chain. Seasonality can also lead to a shortage in the working capital available to handle the bulge in expenses and the heavy financial cost of carrying the inventory; such financial shortages can lead to shortfalls in raw material procurement, causing severe underutilization of the processing plant's capacity.

## Perishability

Unlike the raw material used in nonagroindustries, biological raw materials are perishable and often quite fragile. An automobile manufacturer does not have to worry about its steel rotting. Agroindustrial inputs, however, must be handled and stored with speed and care to preserve their physical traits and, in the case of food products, their nutritional quality. The perishability of raw food and fiber materials, and related characteristics such as fragility (of eggs, for example) and bulkiness (of livestock, for example), often require special and sometimes more costly transportation methods.

## Variability

The final distinctive characteristic of agroindustries is the variability in the quantity and quality of raw materials. Changes in weather and damage to crops or livestock from disease or pests make quantity uncertain. A late monsoon might lead farmers to produce a different crop, abundant rains might permit the planting of a second or third crop, or a drought might eliminate the dry-season crop. Even with good rains and field growth, the harvest could be greatly reduced at the last minute by a pest infestation. Even without these adverse vagaries of nature, quality varies because standardization of biological raw materials remains elusive, despite advances in animal and plant genetics. This variability contrasts sharply with the extensive specifications for and high certainty of standard materials used in other manufacturing industries. Variability exerts additional pressure on an agroindustrial plant's production scheduling and quality-control operations.

## Other Characteristics

Although they are not unique to agroindustry, three other characteristics should be emphasized. First, raw material is usually the major cost component in agroindustries. Thus, procurement operations fundamentally shape the economics of the enterprises. The uncertainty that surrounds agroproduction leads to considerable instability in raw material prices, thereby complicating budgeting and management of working capital.

Second, because many agroindustrial products are necessities or of major economic importance to countries, governmental interest and involvement in agroindustrial activities are often high. Social, economic, and political considerations and government actions become particularly relevant to project analysis.

Third, the same agroindustrial products are produced in many different countries. Therefore, a local agroindustry is linked to international markets, which represent alternative sources of raw materials, competitive imports, and export opportunities. International commodity markets experience considerable price volatility, thereby magnifying the agroindustry's financial uncertainty on the input and output sides. In some instances the climatic conditions of a country give the agroindustry a unique advantage in producing certain export products, such as tropical fruits or off-season vegetables.

Agroindustry's distinctive characteristics call for a special analytical framework that takes these features into account. That framework is described in the following chapter, but first, an examination of agroindustry's high importance in developing countries is in order.

## A Force for Development

Agroindustry contributes significantly to a nation's economic development for four reasons. First, individual agroindustries are essential to the development of a nation's agricultural sector because they are the primary method of transforming raw agricultural products into finished products for consumption. Second, agroindustry often constitutes the majority of a developing nation's manufacturing sector. Third, agroindustrial products are frequently the major exports from a developing nation. Fourth, the food system provides the nation with nutrients critical to the well-being of an expanding population.

### A Door for Agriculture

Most agricultural products, including subsistence products, are processed to some extent. A nation therefore cannot fully use its agronomic resources without agroindustries. A survey of rice milling practices in six provinces in Thailand, for example, revealed that approximately 98 percent of the rice was processed in rice mills rather than hand-milled at home.[2] Similarly, a survey of 1,687 households in four regions in Guatemala revealed that 98 percent of families took their maize to mills for grinding and subsequently made the maize dough into tortillas in the home.[3] Mechanical processing saves consumers time and effort; women in particular benefit, because they traditionally have responsibility for food preparation and their resultant freed time becomes available for other economic production activities.[4] The demand and necessity for processing services increase as agricultural production increases. One cannot occur without the other.

Agroindustries are not merely reactive; they also generate new demand backward to the farm sector for more or different agricultural output. A processing plant can open new crop opportunities to farmers and, by so doing, create additional farm revenue. For example, when an international corn processing company introduced its new starch extraction technology into Pakistan, it created many new product possibilities and stimulated demand for more maize.[5]

Agroindustries sometimes play an important role in disseminating agricultural production techniques that increase farmer productivity. As a result, small or subsistence farmers have sometimes been able to boost their income by selling more in the commercial market. In other cases new production techniques have enabled farmers to cultivate new lands or land unsuitable for traditional crops. In regional development programs, agroindustries have provided the economic justification to build rural infrastructure such as roads that provide access to raw materials, electrical installations for plant operation, or irrigation facilities. Agroindustries can also function as an economic focal point for cooperatives of small farmers and related community-development activities.

The process by which rural industrialization occurs can greatly affect the significance and permanence of the developmental stimulus agroindustries give to rural communities. One critical element appears to be community participation. A United Nations Industrial Development Organization Expert Group concluded that the "formulation of policies and programmes of rural industrialization had to involve a much greater participation of the people in order to be effective."[6] The group recognized that the rural population's lack of resources and limited administrative capacity would require special external assistance to enable fuller participation and effectiveness.

When agroindustry creates a backward demand, farm employment usually increases. That is significant because agriculture remains the primary employer in developing nations, whereas manufacturing employs fewer workers. In Latin America, for example, agriculture absorbs 38 percent of the labor force but accounts for only 15 percent of the gross national product (GNP), while manufacturing absorbs 15 percent of the labor force but accounts for 35 percent of the GNP.[7]

Agroindustries are often more intensive users of domestic rather than imported resources because of the availability of local agricultural raw materials. A study of Costa Rica found that for every 100 colones sold, agroindustries used 45.6 colones of national raw materials, whereas nonagroindustries used only 12 colones.[8]

### A Cornerstone of the Manufacturing Sector

The importance of agroindustries in the manufacturing sector of developing countries is often not fully realized. In most countries food and fiber processing constitute the foundation of the nation's industrial base. In 1987, for example, agroindustries accounted for 72 percent of manufacturing output in Somalia, 53 percent of the value added in Pakistan's manufacturing sector, and 54 percent in Guatemala.[9]

Agroindustries are more important to the industrial sector of lower-income countries and decline in relative importance as industrialization advances. The initial stages of industrialization draw on the countries' natural agricultural endowment and focus on basic necessities. In the 1850s the United States was 85 percent rural, and most food processing was done on farms. Grain and grist mills constituted more than 60 percent of food manufacturing, with alcoholic beverages and cane sugar refining accounting for another 20 percent. With growing urbanization, refrigeration, and rail transport, meat processing emerged to capture 30 percent of the sector's sales. Between 1850 and 1900, agroindustries led the industrialization process, expanding fifteenfold while the rest of the manufacturing sector grew less than sixfold.[10]

Textile production is one of the first agroindustries established in developing countries because it produces a basic good and can take advantage of lower labor costs as well as the agronomic capabilities to grow cotton. As of 1974, 50 percent of all looms and 48 percent of all spindles were installed in developing countries.[11] In 1987 textiles and clothing constituted, on average, 22 percent of the manufacturing sector of twenty low-income countries and 14 percent in forty-four middle-income economies.[12]

As part of the economic development process, countries diversify subsequently into nonagroindustrial products, frequently as part of an import substitution strategy.[13] The shifting pattern is shown in table 1-2: over time and at each higher level of development, agroindustry contributes less to manufacturing value added. Between 1970 and 1987 its share decreased from 66 percent to 63 percent for low-income countries, from 53 percent to 48 percent for lower-middle-income nations, from 37 percent to 32 percent for upper-middle-income economies, and from 25 percent to 23 percent for high-income economies. Agroindustry's share of manufacturing value added averaged 61 percent for thirty-three countries of Sub-Saharan Africa, and for a third of those the contribution was above 70 percent.[14]

Although agroindustries tend to account for a smaller relative share of the manufacturing sector as industrial development advances, other important transformations within the agroindustrial sector occur. As shown in table 1-3, the per capita sales of processed foods and the value added per employee in the developing countries' food and beverage industries appear to increase as incomes rise. That is a result of growing productivity, the expanding urban population, and the

**Table 1-2.** *Agroindustry's Share of Manufacturing Value Added, 1970 and 1987*

(percentage of current prices)

| Country group | Food, beverages, tobacco 1970 | Food, beverages, tobacco 1987[a] | Textiles and clothing 1970 | Textiles and clothing 1987[a] | Total agroindustry 1970 | Total agroindustry 1987[a] |
|---|---|---|---|---|---|---|
| Low-income[b] | 41 | 41 | 25 | 22 | 66 | 63 |
| Lower-middle-income[c] | 37 | 34 | 16 | 14 | 53 | 48 |
| Upper-middle-income[d] | 22 | 18 | 15 | 14 | 37 | 32 |
| High-income[e] | 14 | 15 | 11 | 8 | 25 | 23 |

a. 1987 data were not available for twenty of the eighty-seven countries, so 1984 data were used.

b. Average of twenty countries with a GNP per capita of $545 or less in 1988.

c. Average of thirty countries with a GNP per capita of $545–2,200 in 1988.

d. Average of fourteen countries with a GNP per capita of $2,200–6,000 in 1988.

e. Average of twenty-three countries with a GNP per capita of $6,000 or more in 1988.

*Sources:* Derived from World Bank, *World Development Report 1990* (New York: Oxford University Press, 1990), pp. 188–89; World Bank, *World Development Report 1987* (New York: Oxford University Press, 1987), pp. 214–15.

more complex and diverse types of processed foods demanded by urban consumers as their earning power increases. Because the urban population of 1.6 billion in developing countries in 1988 will grow to 2.1 billion by the year 2000, one can expect a significant growth in the food-processing industries.[15] (A billion equals 1,000 million.) The mix of processed foods will change to favor those requiring higher levels of transformation, as indicated in table 1-1. Population and income growth are increasing faster in developing countries than in indus-

**Table 1-3.** *Value Added and Processed Food Sales in Developing Countries, 1975*

(dollars)

| Country group | Value added per employee in food and beverage industry | Per capita processed food sales Total population | Per capita processed food sales Urban population |
|---|---|---|---|
| Low-income[a] | 667 | 17 | 53 |
| Middle-income[b] | 3,607 | 48 | 112 |
| High-income[c] | 7,504 | 158 | 252 |

a. Developing countries with a GNP per capita of $250 or less.

b. Developing countries with a GNP per capita of $251–1,000.

c. Developing countries with a GNP per capita of more than $1,000.

*Source:* United Nations Centre on Transnational Corporations, *Transnational Corporations in Food and Beverage Processing* (New York, 1981), p. 141.

trialized countries, and these two variables drive food demand. One can continue to expect food processing to be an important source of economic dynamism in developing countries.

A further indicator of the importance of agroindustry within the manufacturing sector is its employment-generating capacity. In developing countries in 1975, almost 14.2 million people were engaged in the food and beverage industries alone; excluding fiber-processing agroindustries, this figure constituted about one-sixth of all the jobs in the manufacturing sector.[16] The annual average growth rate in employment in these jobs between 1970 and 1975 was 6.3 percent, far exceeding the population growth rate of 2.8 percent. The food and beverage industry was particularly important as an employment source in the lowest-income countries, in which the annual average growth rate in these jobs was 7.9 percent between 1970 and 1975.[17] In Venezuela the food-processing sector accounted for 37 percent of the industrial value added in 1987, 20 percent of the direct industrial employment, and 38 percent of the indirect employment of this sector.[18] Food processing had the highest indirect employment multiplier of all Venezuelan industries.

In this regard the significance of small-scale industries is particularly notable: these industries, most of which are agroindustries, generally provide most of the jobs in the manufacturing sector. For example, small-scale industries in Indonesia accounted for approximately 75 percent of manufacturing employment even though they contributed only 16 percent of the sector's value added.[19] Thus, improving the viability of small and medium-size agroindustries appears to be especially important to achieving employment objectives.

A final point on the employment benefits of agroindustries is that they frequently provide major employment opportunities for women. In India, for example, 25 percent of the workers in the food and beverage industry are women, as are 60 percent in the tobacco industry. In Sri Lanka women constitute about 40 percent of the labor force of the food and drink industry; in Cyprus, about 35 percent; in Honduras, about 20 percent.[20]

Although these figures demonstrate the economic significance of the agroindustrial sector, they understate its effect on a nation's other industries. A large percentage of the commercial sector is engaged in distributing agroindustrial products. Agroindustries similarly contribute to the financial sector and other service industries. Finally, enterprises manufacturing materials directly or indirectly for agroindustry, such as packaging, agrochemicals, and farm machinery, depend on the demand for agricultural produce, and this demand in turn depends on a viable food- and fiber-processing industry.

**Figure 1-1.** *Agribusiness Components of U.S. Labor Force, 1989*

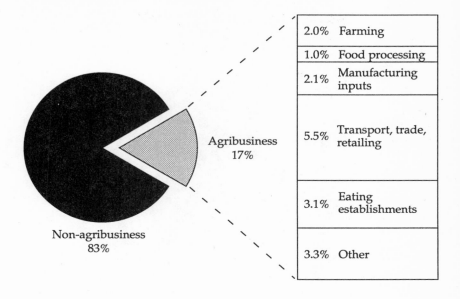

| | | |
|---|---|---|
| | 2.0% | Farming |
| | 1.0% | Food processing |
| | 2.1% | Manufacturing inputs |
| | 5.5% | Transport, trade, retailing |
| | 3.1% | Eating establishments |
| | 3.3% | Other |

Agribusiness
17%

Non-agribusiness
83%

*Source:* U.S. Department of Agriculture data.

Even in the highly industrialized countries where the agricultural sector shrinks in relative importance, the off-farm components become increasingly significant and preserve the overall economic contribution of agribusiness.[21] While farming employs only 2 percent of the total U.S. work force, the rest of the agribusiness system occupies another 15 percent (see figure 1-1). Farm production accounts for 24 percent of the U.S. consumer's food dollar while the rest of the food system adds the remaining 76 percent of the value (see figure 1-2). The overall agribusiness system contributes about 16 percent of GNP in the United States; the makeup of this 16 percent by each of the stages in the system is shown in figure 1-3.

## An Export Generator

The most important natural resource of most developing countries is agriculture. Because agricultural products are demanded throughout the world and because production capacity frequently exceeds local consumption, there is an opportunity to export food and fiber. Such exports have traditionally dominated trade in developing countries,

**Figure 1-2.** *Value Added Components of U.S. Expenditures on Food, 1989*

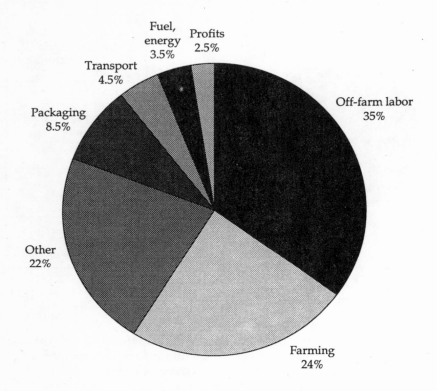

*Source*: Dennis Dunham, *Food Cost Review, 1989*, Agricultural Economic Report 63, Economic Research Service, U.S. Department of Agriculture, Washington, D.C., July 1989.

but the raw material must be processed into a form suitable for export. Even minimal processing, such as drying grain or ginning cotton, adds economic value to the produce and generates more foreign exchange. The value added in agroindustrial products tends to exceed that of other manufactured exports because other exports frequently rely on imported components, and export agroindustries tend over time to increase the domestic percentage of value added by increasing the degree of raw material processing.[22]

For example, ginning operations are expanded to include textile weaving and apparel manufacturing; beef carcasses are processed into portion cuts or canned products; coffee beans are transformed into instant and freeze-dried coffee. Such incremental industrializa-

**Figure 1-3.** *Agribusiness Components of U.S. Gross National Product, 1989*

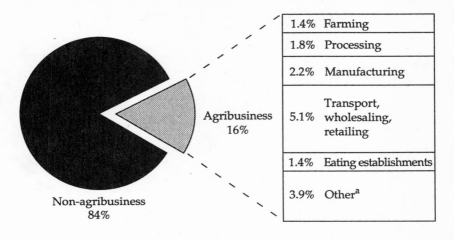

| | |
|---|---|
| 1.4% | Farming |
| 1.8% | Processing |
| 2.2% | Manufacturing |
| 5.1% | Transport, wholesaling, retailing |
| 1.4% | Eating establishments |
| 3.9% | Other[a] |

Agribusiness 16%

Non-agribusiness 84%

a. Other includes mining, forestry, and supporting services other than transport, wholesaling, retailing, and eating establishments.
*Source*: U.S. Department of Agriculture data.

tion not only increases value added but also creates products that are further differentiated, have higher income elasticities, and are more insulated from the price fluctuations of less processed commodities.[23]

Between 1972 and 1981 the average annual change in the export prices of agricultural raw materials was 14.9 percent, while the price variability of more processed food and beverages was 9.1 percent and 10.3 percent, respectively.[24] The proportion of more highly processed products in major food exports from developing countries to industrialized countries increased from 11 percent to 23 percent between 1965 and 1975 (see table 1-4).

Agroindustrial products (including agricultural commodities that undergo minimal transformation) are the dominant export for most developing countries.[25] They account for at least half of the exports in forty developing countries, whereas manufactured goods represent more than 50 percent of the exports in only fifteen developing countries. In eighteen others fuel dominates, and in another thirteen, minerals are primary. In Nicaragua, for example, more than 85 percent of exports between 1960 and 1970 were agroindustrial products.[26] Closer scrutiny reveals another export pattern—heavy reliance on a few principal products. In 1978 cotton, coffee, sugar, and meat products constituted 66 percent of Nicaragua's total exports.

**Table 1-4.** *Change in Share of Raw, Semiprocessed, and Processed Food Exported from Developing Countries to Industrialized Countries, 1965–75*

(percent)

| Export | Raw | Form | |
|---|---|---|---|
| | | Semiprocessed | Processed |
| Meat | −8 | n.a. | 8 |
| Fish | 9 | n.a. | −9 |
| Vegetables | −6 | n.a. | 6 |
| Fruit | −5 | n.a. | 5 |
| Groundnuts | −25 | n.a. | 25 |
| Copra | −27 | n.a. | 27 |
| Palm kernels | −55 | n.a. | 55 |
| Sugar | −32 | 32 | n.a. |
| Coffee | −5 | n.a. | 5 |
| Cocoa | −12 | 11 | 1 |

n.a. Not applicable.

*Source:* United Nations Centre on Transnational Corporations, *Transnational Corporations*, p. 103.

In general, the narrower the product line, the more exposed the nation is to the dramatic fluctuations of international commodity prices. The Nicaraguan statistics reveal the benefits of a diversified export portfolio. In 1960 cotton products accounted for 27 percent of the country's total exports; by 1965 the "white gold" had boomed to 51 percent, but five years later it had decreased by half. During the same ten-year period, processed beef exports rose from $3 million (5 percent of exports) to $27 million (15 percent of exports), thereby largely offsetting the decline in cotton exports.[27] Similarly, between 1977 and 1978 cotton and sugar exports fell $18 million, but beef exports more than compensated for this decline by increasing $30 million. By broadening its agroindustrial export portfolio, a country may be able to obtain some countercyclical protection.

In the international trade of agricultural products a dichotomy emerges between low-value products and high-value products. Low-value products consist mainly of raw materials (rubber, cotton, tobacco) and bulk food products (grains, oilseeds); high-value products exist in unprocessed form (nuts, eggs, fruits), semiprocessed (vegetable oil, meat, flour, sugar, coffee, animal feeds), or highly processed (cheese, spices, cereal preparations, prepared fruits and vegetables, sugar preparations). In 1980 trade in low-value products was valued at $110 billion ($85 billion as bulk and $25 billion as raw materials). Trade in high-value products was $120 billion ($35 billion as highly processed, $60 billion as semi-processed, and $25 billion as unprocessed).[28] The trend is toward higher value products, which means a growing importance for agroindustries in the export arena.

In the trade area, agroindustries also help developing countries save foreign exchange by substituting domestic goods for imports. This local production helps nations increase their level of self-sufficiency and food security.[29]

### The Nutrition Dimension

An estimated 550 million people in developing countries are under-nourished, with 57 percent of these in Asia, 27 percent in Sub-Saharan Africa, 11 percent in Latin America, and 5 percent in the Middle East, mostly living in rural areas.[30] By generating income opportunities for low-income farmers and providing employment to low-income workers, agroindustries can improve a population's diet. If agroindustries stimulate increased food production for the domestic economy, they may contribute to the country's food security. Furthermore, the food-processing industry is particularly important to the nutritional well-being of the urban poor because of their dependence on commercial food channels. In Venezuela, for example, 91 percent of calories come from processed foods.[31]

To the extent that agroindustries can improve storage, transportation, and handling, they may be able to lower the costs of food to consumers by reducing post-harvest losses and making the entire food marketing chain more productive and efficient. Such reductions in food prices have a disproportionately positive impact on the poorest and most nutritionally vulnerable nonfarm groups, who often spend 60–80 percent of their income on food. Food processors may also provide nutritional benefits to the population by improving the sanitary conditions and health safety of the food supply. Additionally, they may enhance the food's nutritional value by fortifying it with needed micronutrients; for example, iodizing salt to combat goiter. Food processors have increasingly been addressing the growing health and nutritional concerns about diet-linked coronary disease, hypertension, cancer, and osteoporosis. New product formulations have reduced or eliminated cholesterol, fat, and salt and increased fiber content and calcium levels.

Agroindustrial projects can, however, have adverse nutritional consequences if they are not carefully designed, and projects must be closely examined to prevent the undesirable nutritional effects they may cause. For example, an agroindustry might cause farmers to shift from producing staples, thus lowering the supply and raising the price. The income from a cash crop may or may not be large enough to improve family diets. In any case, the nutrition of low-income, landless workers or urban consumers may suffer from such a rise in the price of staples. Alternatively, higher prices in the international market can lead to an increase in the export of staples and a decrease in the domestic supply. Finally, some forms of processing can decrease a food product's nutritional value.

### The Growing Importance of Agroindustry

The importance of agroindustry in a nation's development is being increasingly recognized, and financing for agroindustrial projects has grown considerably in recent years. Policymakers have rediscovered that creating a strong agricultural sector is a prerequisite to achieving viable industrialization. Agriculture can only be as strong as its agroindustry, and vice versa. And the vitality of the industrial sector as a whole is affected significantly by the strength of its agroindustry subsector. In 1988 more than a quarter of international aid flows from multilateral agencies—$3.5 billion—was destined for agricultural and agroindustrial projects.[32] Between 1970 and 1990 the World Bank lent $3.9 billion to thirty-six countries for projects in the agroindustry subsector, with the lending volume in the 1980s more than double that of the 1970s.[33] In 1980–81 almost half of the lending from the Arab Bank for Economic Development to Africa was for agroprocessing.[34] The International Finance Corporation's investments in food and agribusiness operations rose from $43 million in 1976 to $257 million by 1990, with another $341 million invested in textiles and $247 million in pulp and paper plants.[35] It should be noted that these investments have not always yielded the expected economic development benefits or financial profitability. The reasons for such shortfalls are often found in flawed design of the projects, which could have been prevented by applying the project analysis methodology laid out in this book.

## Organization of the Chapters

The next chapter presents an analytical framework that is a systems approach to examining and designing agroindustrial projects. The distinctive nature of agroindustry dictates the need for a special perspective. The components of the systems approach are presented conceptually and illustrated with examples.

The systems method of analysis is then applied in the remaining chapters to the three main areas of agroindustrial activity. Chapter 3 addresses marketing: the issues of consumer preference, market segmentation, demand forecasting, product pricing, distribution channels, and competitive forces. Chapter 4, on procurement, discusses the relations between the production and processing stages and methods of managing the critical flow of raw material from the farm to the factory. Chapter 5 examines the processing factor and the related issues of technology selection, plant location, inventory management, packaging, and other inputs; programming, quality control, and by-product considerations follow.

Although each of these three chapters explores a particular operational activity of agroindustries, systems analysis presupposes an underlying recognition of the close interdependence of operations in the entire food and fiber production chain. Consequently, each separate analysis considers one activity's effect on the remaining two. The systems method implies an interactive process whereby the effect of one decision can be traced through the whole system to reveal consequences that, at times, necessitate modifying the original project design.

Each chapter identifies problem areas common to agroindustrial projects. To guide the analyst in evaluating projects, central issues are reduced to question form within each chapter, and these are compiled as a complete project analysis checklist in appendix A at the end of the book. The questions indicate the information needed to analyze thoroughly each particular activity. All the relevant data are seldom available to the analyst, however, and, depending on the size of the project and the capabilities of the personnel, the cost of collecting data may not be justified. Thus, not all questions can be answered, nor need they be to carry out effective project analysis. Project investment and design decisions are always made with imperfect information; nevertheless, it is crucial for the analyst to recognize what information is desirable so that data gaps can be recognized and, if not remedied through new data collection, dealt with by explicit assumptions. It is better to know what questions have gone unanswered than never to have asked—risks can be better judged this way.

The goal of this book is to provide private business people and concerned public sector officials with practical guidelines from actual experience and to distill and translate theoretical concepts into a form useful to practitioners. Many of the examples given are from active agroindustrial projects rather than proposed enterprises. It is hoped that by studying the problems mature enterprises encounter, project analysts can anticipate operational difficulties in the design of proposed projects. But each project is unique, and an analytical framework is ultimately only a guide. The analyst must adapt its concepts to the peculiarities of the specific project and bring his or her critical judgment to bear. The framework's emphasis on the key determinants of project viability, however, helps minimize effort spent reviewing marginal aspects of projects.

Readers wishing to extend and deepen their understanding of agroindustrial project analysis are referred to a companion volume to this book: *Agroindustrial Investment and Operations* by James G. Brown with Deloitte & Touche.[36] That work is based on the conceptual framework presented here, but it provides more specific operating guidelines, including detailed profiles of various types of agroindustries.

Because of its position in the food system, an agroindustry affects the nutritional status of a nation's population. Malnutrition has caused massive human suffering and severe erosion of the human capital in many countries. Although a viable food-and-fiber system is fundamental to dealing with the problem of malnutrition, project analysts have generally paid little attention to the nutritional aspect of agroindustries. Furthermore, the growing nutritional and health awareness among consumers in general is leading private companies and public regulators to scrutinize the marketing opportunities and issues surrounding the nutritional dimension of food processing and products. Consequently, each chapter raises nutritional issues for readers to consider.[37]

Those involved in designing agroindustries may be economists, agronomists, industrial engineers, management specialists, or public policy analysts. This book keeps that diverse audience in mind, providing a broad framework that can be used by different professionals. Highly technical or specialized language and analytics have been intentionally avoided. Some information may be common knowledge to those in certain disciplines but new to others; readers should adapt the framework to their own fields of expertise and the particulars of the project being studied. Again, this adaptation will enrich the analytical process, strengthen the framework, and consequently increase the viability of the agroindustrial project.

# 2 A Systems Approach to Agroindustrial Analysis

THE ANALYTICAL FRAMEWORK presented in this chapter utilizes a systems approach to project analysis, because agroindustry's distinctive characteristics create a set of critical interdependencies. Examining these systemic linkages is essential to designing and operating successful agroindustries. Thus, this agroindustrial project analysis framework views agroindustries as systems and focuses on four types of systemic linkages:

- *Production chain linkages.* These consist of the operational stages that agroindustry materials flow through as they move from the farm through processing and then to the consumer.
- *Macro-micro policy linkages.* These concern the multitude of effects that governmental macropolicies have on an agroindustry's operations.
- *Institutional linkages.* These involve the relationships among the different types of organizations that operate and interact with the agroindustry production chain.
- *International linkages.* These deal with the interdependencies of national and international markets in which the agroindustry functions.

Each of these linkages deals with different dimensions of the agroindustry system, but all are interrelated. The task of the project analyst is to understand how the production chain, macropolicy, institutional, and international linkages interact and affect the viability of the agroindustry. The subsequent sections in this chapter elaborate each of the linkage categories. These analytical components of the systems approach then need to be applied to the analysis and design of agroindustrial projects. This application stage is structured around the three core operating areas of an agroindustry: procurement, processing, and marketing. All agroindustries have to obtain the raw agromaterials, transform them into products, and then distribute them to buyers. The four systemic linkages affect each of these three core operations and so are considered throughout the analyses presented in the following three chapters on marketing, procurement, and processing.

Our analytical framework and its application focus primarily on creating a deeper understanding of the distinctive nature of agroindustrial projects and the design factors critical to success. Complete project analysis requires, of course, financial and economic analysis. Although the financial and economic implications of the various systems design elements are discussed, separate chapters are not allocated to these methodologies. There is an abundant literature on these techniques in general,[1] and James Brown's companion volume to this book, *Agroindustrial Investment and Operations*,[2] covers these aspects in depth as they relate to agroindustry. That volume also provides more specific data on different types of agroindustries and thus allows multiple opportunities for applying the analytical systems approach to particular agroindustry settings. Similarly, this book emphasizes project design, but recognizes that specific management techniques are the vital lubricant to project implementation. Brown's book delves into the management operations dimensions of agroindustries in more detail.

## Production Chain Linkages

Agroindustrial projects have often suffered from an "analytical schizophrenia." Analysts are ambivalent about whether to examine agroindustries as agricultural projects or as manufacturing projects. This ambivalence reflects the dichotomy in the analyzers: ministries are split into agriculture and industry; development banks are specialized as agricultural or industrial; and analysts are categorized as agricultural economists or industrial engineers. For agroindustrial project analysis the dichotomy is false and counterproductive. Agroindustries are inherently intersectoral; it is essential to view the operation as links in a production system. Even though recognizing the importance of the entire system, some analysts focus predominantly on agricultural production and lump everything post-harvest into "marketing," thereby glossing over the analysis of the special demands and characteristics of agroindustries. One must recognize agroindustry's uniqueness but also understand that it constitutes only part of the seed-to-consumer agribusiness system; one's analytical lens must scan the entirety of the chain because of the interdependencies of the links.

This production chain is depicted in figure 2-1 as a flow chart. The system begins with production inputs to the farm, which converts these into agricultural raw materials, a portion of which may be retained for on-farm consumption and the remainder transported to the agroindustry directly or through produce markets. At the processing stage the agricultural raw materials are stored and then trans-

**Figure 2-1.** *Flow Chart for Agroindustry*

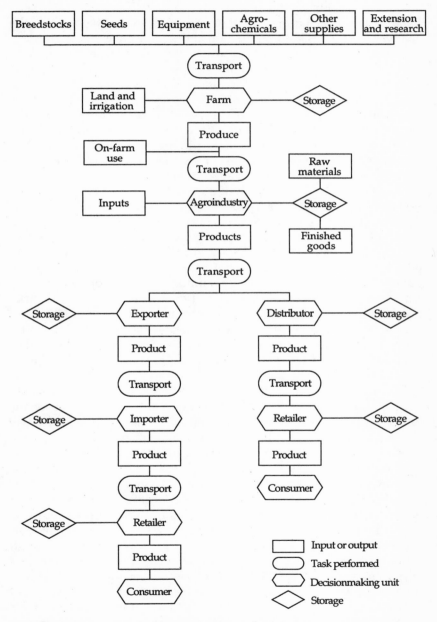

*Note*: Labor and financing inputs occur for each task. Agroindustry products may include by-products or be inputs to other agroindustries including additional processing operations.

formed by industrial inputs and processes into consumer or industrial products, which are stored and then distributed through the wholesaling and retailing channels of the domestic or foreign markets. Labor and financial inputs occur at each stage in the chain. Thus, the chain encompasses both production and service businesses.

The precise structure of the production chain varies for each agroindustry system and setting. For example, for agricultural produce requiring low levels of transformation, such as fresh fruit, the processing stage would be dominated by cleaning, sorting, packaging, and storage. Industrial transformative processes would be minimal. Other agricultural produce might pass through multiple processing stages, with the initial agroindustry producing commodities such as vegetable oil, leaf tobacco, flour, or sweeteners that become inputs into other agroindustries engaged in further processing. In the United States about one-fourth of the food shipments consist of such semiprocessed producer goods.[3]

A companion affliction to analytical schizophrenia is "analytical myopia," in which project design focuses only on parts of the production chain without taking into account all of the links and interdependencies. This risk is illustrated by the experience of a West African government that had adopted an industrial development strategy aimed at maximizing the value added to the nation's agroindustrial products.[4] For many years the country's cotton ginners had been exporting cottonseed, and the local vegetable oil refineries importing unrefined oil. Hence, the government's development bank agreed to finance a private entrepreneur's proposal to set up a cottonseed-oil extracting plant.

The plant was constructed, but it was discovered afterward that not enough cottonseed was available to reach the minimum economic operating level of the plant's equipment. The analysts had focused on the processing stage and had inadequately analyzed the raw material production stage. Such miscalculation can be lethal to an agroindustry. To correct the resultant imbalance, the government launched— with major fanfare—a program to stimulate greater cotton production. The prospect of large cotton supplies prompted another private group to put up a textile plant. Cotton output did increase but was insufficient to meet the textile plant's needs, forcing it to import cotton yarn from Pakistan. There was, however, now more than enough cottonseed to operate the oil extraction plant at capacity. But this output, in turn, exceeded the needs of the local oil refineries. Furthermore, the supply of the resultant cottonseed meal by-product could not be absorbed by the local animal feed industries, which were not sufficiently developed because of the incipient nature of the commercial poultry industry.

An agroindustry system is filled with interdependencies, so an analyst must carefully examine all of the backward and forward linkages. By focusing myopically on the oil extraction operation rather than on the larger set of linked subsystems (fiber, food processing, and livestock), the private entrepreneurs and government planners in the case described above failed to see and plan for problems and opportunities arising from the system's interdependencies. The resultant ad hoc planning was unnecessarily costly to the businesses and the country.

Often the analytical myopia is with the agriculturalists rather than the industrialists. Rare is the developing country that has not watched an agricultural production project succeed in raising output only to falter and perhaps even fail because of bottlenecks or inadequate planning in the downstream agroindustry stages of the production chain. Such problems abound when new production technologies are instituted, as during the "green revolution" years in Asia and Latin America. In the Philippines rice production soared 30 percent with the introduction of the early high-yielding varieties of rice. One agribusiness specialist observed that "along with this development appeared new problems. There were inadequate drying and storage facilities. The marketing system for rice was not able to respond to the demands placed on it by the increased production. Managers in neither the government nor private industry had planned adequately for this eventuality."[5] Similarly, in Pakistan an industry observer noted "the almost complete breakdown in marketing channels. . . . Hundreds of tons of paddy were stored in the open, in piles on the drying floor, and without protection. These same mills had their milled rice storage facilities filled to capacity."[6] In Nicaragua the government funded a project to modernize rice production through the use of irrigated, mechanized farming technology. The government's and entrepreneurs' fixation on production to the neglect of the post-harvest stages in the chain led to costly bottlenecks in storage and milling.[7]

The foregoing examples make clear the importance of viewing agroindustries broadly and recognizing the interdependencies in the production chain. It is equally important to understand the dynamic nature of the production chain. The flow of raw material supplies is vital; it dictates capacity requirements in transport, storage, and processing. That flow may fluctuate, however, because of seasonality and the vagaries of nature. The timing and magnitude of seasonal flows can be affected by production technology; for example, new seed varieties with different growth cycles or irrigation may permit a second or third crop in the off-season. The vagaries of nature are less predictable, but they too can be incorporated into planning. For example, suppliers in different geographical areas can be used so as to reduce the risk of disease or drought, and contingency import plans can be developed.

The interdependent nature of the production chain means that changes at one point often trigger changes elsewhere, significantly affecting the functioning of the entire system. Events in the evolution of the banana business in Central America are illustrative.[8] During the 1950s banana production in this region was threatened by the Panama disease, which was wiping out the Gros Michel variety. Standard Fruit Company shifted to a different variety, which was viewed by importers as too delicate to survive shipment without damage. The variety's fragility led Standard to begin boxing the fruit in the tropics rather than continuing to ship on stems. However, the banana jobbers' ripening rooms were equipped to handle bunches rather than boxes, and they initially resisted switching to boxes. But not only did the boxes protect the fruit from in-transit damage, they also allowed much more accurate grading, standardized maturity, and ease of handling by distributors, particularly retailers, who began insisting on boxes. The advantages were considerable. Within five short years all firms in the industry were boxing in the tropics.

This packaging innovation required major investments in carton plants and a major change in the input cost structure and the handling and packaging operations of the banana companies. While boxing increased packaging costs, the elimination of the stems reduced total bunch weight 15–20 percent and permitted transportation savings. The higher costs of boxed bananas combined with the greater ability to grade more selectively and label the boxed fruit led United Fruit to differentiate its bananas by creating a branded, higher quality product supported aggressively with advertising and selling at a premium price. That further revolutionized the marketing end of the production chain.

Sometimes change occurs at the retail and consumer end of the chain. For example, the emergence and growth of supermarkets increases the bargaining power of the retailer and often forces agroindustries to adjust packaging, delivery, and even product design. The invention and increasing use of microwave ovens in the United States created the opportunity for a multitude of adaptations and new product inventions by food processors to meet the growing consumer demand caused by this technological advance.

A final perspective on the production chain can be gained by examining its value-added components. Each of the direct and indirect productive functions that occur throughout the length of the chain adds value in the cumulative process of creating the final product. The amount of value created will depend on how each function is carried out and how it is linked with the others in the chain. For the designer of an agroindustry this perspective is particularly important in considering which of the functions in the chain it should perform itself (that is, its degree of integration) and how it should relate to its suppliers and buyers to maximize their collective value creation effort.

An example is in the cane sugar production chain, where any number of occurrences might change the value during the critical function of harvesting. When and how the cane is cut and how quickly it reaches the sugar mill and is processed all significantly affect the quantity and quality of sugar that can be extracted from the cane. In one Latin American country the sugar mills were supplied mostly by independent growers operating relatively small farms. Traditionally these farmers individually hired laborers to cut and load the cane onto contracted trucks to be hauled to the mills. During harvest both laborers and trucks often became scarce, causing delays; furthermore, bottlenecks sometimes occurred at the mills as the number of coincidentally arriving trucks created long unloading lines. One of the mills adjusted the configuration of these activities by providing mechanical harvesting services for a fee to the farmers, who individually could not have justified the equipment investment given their small landholdings. The mill then helped organize the local independent truckers into a cooperative and created a logistics schedule coordinated with the harvesting services. As a result, the previous delays were eliminated, harvesting costs were reduced, trucks were used more efficiently, and the sugar extraction rates increased. The farmers, the transporters, and the mill all earned greater profits, and the mill's competitive position in the industry was strengthened by creating a more loyal and cost-efficient procurement system.

This ability to structure creatively the "value activities" in the chain is what author Michael E. Porter sees as a key to gaining and sustaining competitive advantage.[9] He emphasizes the attainment of this advantage through cost leadership or differentiation. Within our systems approach framework the Porter perspective is an important addition to the examination of the production chain linkages because it sharpens our focus on the competitive strategy dimension. The subsequent chapter analyses of marketing, procurement, and processing will examine the implications of activities configuration for cost leadership and differentiation.

## Macro-Micro Policy Linkages

The business environment of an agroindustry is significantly shaped by the government's policies and actions. Given the economic, politi-

Figure 2-2. *Public Policy Impact Chain*

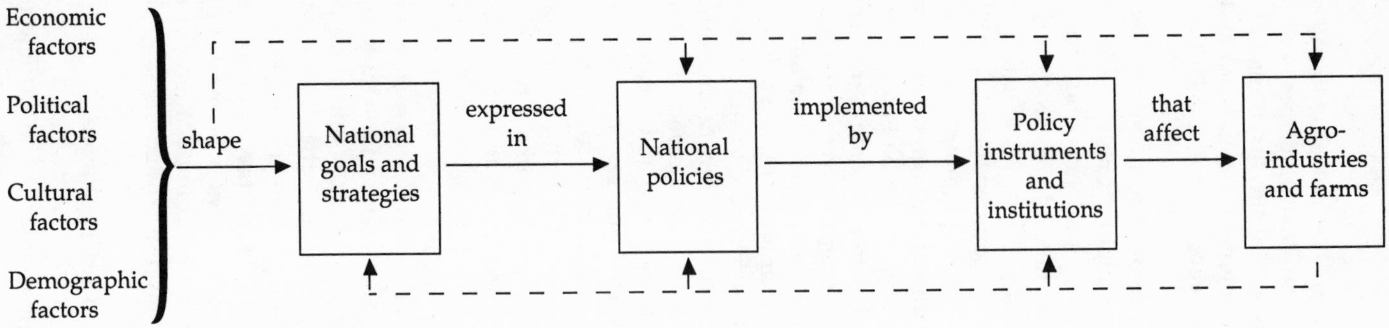

cal, and social importance of food and agriculture, most governments are particularly heavily involved in their nation's agrosystem. Government constitutes a "mega-force" in the nation's food and fiber production chain, and so the systems approach must encompass an examination of the government's role.[10]

One way to envision the linkages between the government's policies at the macro level and the operations of the agroindustry at the micro level is the "public policy impact chain" shown in figure 2.2.[11] National development goals and strategies are expressed through national policies that are implemented by various policy instruments (taxes, credits, subsidies, and so forth) that affect in a variety of ways the production chain and the specific agroindustry. Alternative types of development strategies—for example, import substitution or export promotion—can give rise to distinct policy configurations and have quite different effects on agroindustries. Macropolicies can be grouped into the following categories: fiscal (revenues and expenditures), monetary (credit and interest rates), trade (foreign exchange and import/export controls), and incomes (prices and wages). In addition to these general policies, governments also formulate macropolicies for specific sectors such as agriculture, industry, transportation, education, health, environment, and others.

The task of the analyst is to identify how specifically the macropolicies will affect the agroindustry being examined. They can alter access to inputs and markets, costs and types of inputs, competition, and prices. The effects are pervasive, permeating the procurement, processing, and marketing operations of an agroindustry. Table 2-1 identifies various macropolicies and the points in the production chain they might affect.

For example, under fiscal policy for agriculture the government might provide a subsidy on fertilizers that would reduce farmers' input costs, possibly stimulate greater fertilizer use and higher yields, and result in a larger supply of raw materials at perhaps a lower price for the agroindustry. The removal of a subsidy might have the opposite effect in the short run but lead to a shifting to other crop alternatives for which production was financially sustainable without subsidization. An unsubsidized crop, being less exposed to the political vagaries surrounding subsidies, might represent a more dependable and sustainable supply source but for a different agroindustry. If the original agroindustry wanted to preserve its supply in the face of the subsidy removal, it might have to increase its price to the farmer or provide the subsidized inputs. Thus, the policy analysis of the agricultural production stage in the chain is relevant because of the implications for the agroindustry's procurement operations.

Table 2-1. *Factors Affected by Selected Macropolicy Instruments at Selected Points in the Agroindustry System*

| Macropolicy instrument | Point in agroindustry system | | | | | |
|---|---|---|---|---|---|---|
| | Farm production | Transport | Storage | Processing | Distribution | Exporting |
| **Fiscal policy** | | | | | | |
| Taxes | Land costs | Operating costs | Operating costs | Costs; choice of technology | Costs | Costs |
| Investment | Irrigation; research | Roads; rail; port infrastructure | Public warehousing | Power supplies | Transport infrastructure | Transport infrastructure |
| Subsidies | Input costs | Fuel costs | Operating costs | Costs | Costs | Price competitiveness |
| **Monetary policy** | | | | | | |
| Interest rates | Input costs | Operating costs | Carrying costs | Costs; choice of technology | Carrying costs | Costs |
| Credit supply | Investment | Investment | Investment | Investment | Investment | Investment |
| **Trade policy** | | | | | | |
| Foreign exchange allocation | Access to imported inputs | Access | Access | Access | Sources of imports; competition | Revenue |

| | | | | | | |
|---|---|---|---|---|---|---|
| Foreign exchange rates | Cost of imported inputs | Costs | Costs | Costs; choice of technology | Import prices | Competitiveness |
| Duties | Cost of imported inputs | Costs | Costs | Cost protection | Import prices | Export prices |
| Quotas | Access to imported inputs | Access | Access | Access protection | Competition level | Export volume |
| *Incomes policy* | | | | | | |
| Price controls | Input costs | Freight rates | n.a. | Revenue | Revenue | Export revenue |
| Price supports | Output prices | n.a. | Location; level | Raw material costs | n.a. | n.a. |
| Wages | Input costs | Costs | Costs | Costs; choice of technology | Costs | Costs |
| ***Other*** | Agrochemical restrictions; water usage | Routes; safety standards | Bonding | Safety; health regulations; grading standards; pollution control | Sanitation; grading | Countertrade and bilateral agreements |

n.a. Not applicable.

In the area of monetary policy the government's regulation of interest rates will, for example, affect inventory carrying costs and therefore the agroindustry's profits and perhaps storage policies. In the area of trade policy an overvalued exchange rate will decrease the costs of imported inputs for farmers and processors but increase the competition from imported finished goods with the agroindustry's outputs. Of course, duties or quantitative restrictions could affect access, costs, and competition of imports. In the area of incomes policy, agricultural price supports can directly affect the cost of the raw materials to the agroindustry; at the consumer end, price controls on the processed goods can limit the revenues. In the absence of subsidies the agroindustry might find its margins severely squeezed by government's policies to raise farmers' incomes and lower consumers' food costs. Agroindustries are caught right in the middle of this basic food policy dilemma.[12]

It is evident that the private analyst must carefully analyze the significance of the government's policies and actions because they can directly and indirectly have dramatic effects on the agroindustry's strategy, operations, and viability. It is equally important for the public sector analyst to scrutinize these policy effects in order to avoid unintended consequences in any part of the production chain.

## Institutional Linkages

The previous two elements in this systems approach framework focused on the flow of materials and activities in the production chain and on macropolicies influencing various points in the chain. The third element deals with the institutions operating the system. The structuring and managing of institutional relationships are critical to effective design and operation of agroindustries. Project analysis must encompass institutional analysis.

For any agroindustry the primary operating and bargaining relationships within the production chain are with its suppliers, mainly the farmers, and its buyers. From a competitive perspective the agroindustry interacts with its rival processing companies and faces the threat of potential new competitors and even substitute products (for example, high fructose corn syrup for cane sugar, synthetic sweeteners for natural sweeteners, or synthetics for cotton).[13] From our previous analysis of the macro-micro linkages, it is evident that interaction with the government is also of primary importance. The government's control and regulation of resources can affect all of the other relationships and hence competitive structure and dynamics.

Five main types of economic institutions operate in the production chain: farmers and producer cooperatives, state-owned enterprises,

multinational corporations, local firms, and marketing intermediaries. Some of their salient institutional characteristics are briefly
described here, and the nature of their participation in the production
chain is indicated here and in table 2-2.

## Farmers and Cooperatives

Most farmers operate as independent businesses. Agriculture is char-
acterized by a large number of producers, although farm size varies
widely. This structure often means that an agroindustry has to deal
with many suppliers or their intermediaries. To gain economic or
political power, farmers sometimes organize into cooperatives or
other forms of producer associations. Often governments actively
promote the organization of cooperatives. Cooperatives supply
worldwide about 20 percent of the farm inputs and market about 30
percent of farm production.[14] In Costa Rica, for example, cooperatives produce 45 percent of the coffee, 37 percent of the beef, and 88
percent of the ornamental plants, all of which are important exports
for the country.[15] Sometimes the producer cooperatives integrate vertically into the agroindustry stage of the production chain. Cooperatives in Maharashtra, India, for example, grow and mill almost 90
percent of the white sugar.[16] In Cameroon a cooperative union processes and exports coffee directly to France.[17]

Cooperatives, because of their many members, often have significant political power, and economic size and control over supply give
them increased bargaining power as suppliers. Their organizational
form, however, often slows down their decisionmaking process and
operating responsiveness. Not infrequently, cooperatives lack adequate professional management and have limited capital, leading to
serious operating problems.

## State-owned Enterprises

Governments often choose to intervene in the food and fiber production chain through the use of state-owned enterprises (SOEs), or parastatals. These SOEs are policy instruments, but unlike the others discussed earlier in the macropolicy section, these are organizations
operating directly in the chain and carrying out various productive
functions. Thus, they require explicit attention in the examination of
institutional linkages.

Governments have turned to SOEs for many reasons. Because of the
political explosiveness of food shortages and price instability, it is not
surprising that politicians have created SOEs to give them more direct
control over the food system. SOEs have also been used to gain politi-

**Table 2-2.** *Selected Institutional Roles in an Agroindustry System*

| Role in production chain | Economic institution | | | | | | | | |
|---|---|---|---|---|---|---|---|---|---|
| | *Multinational corporation* | *Farmer* | *Cooperative* | *Marketing intermediary* | *Local firm* | *Financial organization* | *Industry association* | *State-owned enterprise* | *Government* |
| Input supply | ✓ | — | ✓ | ✓ | ✓ | — | — | ✓ | — |
| Farm production | ✓ | ✓ | — | — | ✓ | — | — | ✓ | — |
| Raw material assembly | — | — | ✓ | ✓ | ✓ | — | — | ✓ | — |
| Processing | ✓ | — | ✓ | ✓ | ✓ | — | — | ✓ | — |
| Distribution | ✓ | — | ✓ | ✓ | ✓ | — | — | ✓ | — |
| Retailing | ✓ | — | — | — | ✓ | — | — | ✓ | — |
| Supporting services | ✓ | — | — | — | ✓ | ✓ | ✓ | ✓ | ✓ |
| Regulation | — | — | — | — | — | — | — | — | ✓ |

*Note:* A check mark (✓) indicates performance of a particular role.

cal support by providing economic benefits to favored groups through prices, purchases, protection, payoffs, and positions. Some African nations have used parastatals as vehicles for wresting control of trading channels from ethnic groups who traditionally dominated food distribution. On economic grounds SOEs have been justified as antidotes to noncompetitive, concentrated structures or as providers of needed inputs that the private sector has not supplied adequately, for example, research, technical assistance, storage, or capital. On social grounds SOEs have been used to stabilize consumer food prices, support farmer incomes, generate employment, and promote regional development. International development aid agencies actively promoted the formation of SOEs in the 1960s and 1970s; now they are promoting their dissolution.

SOEs operate at all stages in the production chain and are heavily used throughout the developing world. Table 2-3 reports the prevalence of their use in the food system around 1980 in eighty developing countries. Table 2-4 reveals that the developing countries use SOEs more heavily than the industrialized nations, but even the latter have an abundance of SOEs in their food systems.

SOE performance in terms of economic efficiency and effectiveness has generally been disappointing. Parastatal operations have often imposed a serious financial drain on government budgets. For example, in the 1980s net government transfers to agricultural marketing SOEs reached 27 percent in the Gambia, 12 percent in Zambia, 11 percent in China, and 5 percent in Mexico.[18] In recent years there has been a strong movement toward privatization of government enterprises and increasing market liberalization. Nonetheless, SOEs remain significant actors in the production chain. A new agroindustry might find SOEs providing a wide range of inputs to the farmers growing the agroindustry's needed raw materials. The SOEs might be purchasing, transporting, and storing the farmers' produce and therefore be a possible supplier for the agroindustry. In fact, an SOE might even be operating a competing processing operation. On the marketing side SOEs might be engaged in wholesaling and even retailing foodstuffs. For some products they may be an exporter and even have monopoly control. Clearly, state-owned enterprises should be in the analyst's institutional matrix with the full recognition that their economic behavior will be influenced much more by political forces and considerations than private sector companies.

## Multinational Corporations

The 130 largest multinational food corporations have about 800 affiliates in developing countries and territories and produce about one-

**Table 2-3. Prevalence of State-owned Enterprises (SOE's) in the Food Systems of Eighty Developing Countries, around 1980** (percentage of countries)

| Activity | Africa and the Middle East[a] | | | Asia and Oceania[b] | | | Latin America and the Caribbean[c] | | | Total | | |
|---|---|---|---|---|---|---|---|---|---|---|---|---|
| | SOE monopoly[d] | Mix of SOE and private activity[e] | No SOE activity[f] | SOE monopoly[d] | Mix of SOE and private activity[e] | No SOE activity[f] | SOE monopoly[d] | Mix of SOE and private activity[e] | No SOE activity[f] | SOE monopoly[d] | Mix of SOE and private activity[e] | No SOE activity[f] |
| Credit | 9 | 75 | 16 | 6 | 70 | 24 | 19 | 71 | 9 | 11 | 73 | 16 |
| Insurance | 2 | 23 | 75 | 0 | 13 | 87 | 5 | 14 | 81 | 2 | 19 | 79 |
| Fertilizers[g] | 41 | 43 | 16 | 19 | 69 | 12 | 19 | 43 | 38 | 31 | 48 | 21 |
| Other agrochemicals[g] | 34 | 43 | 23 | 0 | 56 | 44 | 5 | 29 | 66 | 20 | 42 | 38 |
| Water | 0 | 16 | 84 | 0 | 37 | 63 | 0 | 24 | 76 | 0 | 22 | 78 |
| Seed[h] | 45 | 25 | 30 | 0 | 37 | 63 | 0 | 43 | 57 | 25 | 32 | 43 |
| Energy | 0 | 27 | 73 | 0 | 44 | 56 | 5 | 24 | 71 | 0 | 30 | 69 |
| Farm equipment[g] | 30 | 39 | 31 | 0 | 50 | 50 | 5 | 38 | 57 | 17 | 41 | 42 |
| Farm production | 0 | 30 | 70 | 0 | 56 | 44 | 0 | 67 | 33 | 0 | 44[i] | 56 |
| Procurement[i] | 2 | 84 | 14 | 0 | 94 | 6 | 0 | 90 | 10 | 1 | 88 | 11 |
| Storage | 0 | 61 | 39 | 0 | 88 | 12 | 5 | 76 | 19 | 1 | 70 | 29 |
| Transportation | 0 | 66 | 34 | 0 | 69 | 31 | 0 | 48 | 52 | 0 | 62 | 38 |

| | | | | | | | | | | | | |
|---|---|---|---|---|---|---|---|---|---|---|---|---|
| Food processing | 0 | 55 | 45 | 0 | 88 | 12 | 5 | 81 | 14 | 1 | 68 | 31 |
| Export marketing | 2 | 82 | 16 | 0 | 70 | 30 | 10 | 76 | 14 | 4 | 78 | 18 |
| Food wholesaling | 0 | 52 | 48 | 0 | 63 | 37 | 5 | 71 | 24 | 1 | 60 | 39 |
| Food retailing | 0 | 45 | 55 | 0 | 31 | 69 | 0 | 58 | 42 | 0 | 46 | 54 |

a. SOE inventory for Africa and the Middle East includes forty-four countries out of fifty-nine.

b. SOE inventory for Asia and Oceania includes fifteen countries. Excluded are Bhutan, Iran, and the centrally planned economies of China, Democratic Kampuchea, Laos, Mongolia, the People's Democratic Republic of Korea, and Viet Nam.

c. SOE inventory for Latin America and the Caribbean includes twenty-one countries out of twenty-seven.

d. Percentages are obtained by dividing the number of countries that have complete SOE control over the activity by the number of countries surveyed. For example, the number 9 in the first row, first column, means that SOEs completely control credit in 9 percent of the forty-four countries surveyed (four countries).

e. Percentages are obtained by dividing the number of countries that have some SOE presence in the activity by the number of countries surveyed.

f. Percentages are obtained for this default category by dividing the number of countries where no evidence of SOE presence was found by the number of countries surveyed.

g. Produced and/or imported and distributed.

h. Certified or hybrid only.

i. When the government farms at least one crop; when the government farms five crops, the percentage drops to 35 percent.

j. Import and/or domestic procurement.

Source: Global Food Policy Research Project files, Harvard University, Graduate School of Business Administration, Boston, 1983.

**Table 2-4.** *Comparative Use of State-owned Enterprises*

| Activity | Industrialized countries | | | Developing countries | | |
|---|---|---|---|---|---|---|
| | High | Medium | Low | High | Medium | Low |
| Credit | ✔ | — | — | ✔ | — | — |
| Procurement | ✔ | — | — | ✔ | — | — |
| Export marketing | ✔ | — | — | ✔ | — | — |
| Transportation | ✔ | — | — | ✔ | — | — |
| Energy | ✔ | — | — | — | — | ✔ |
| Fertilizer | — | — | ✔ | ✔ | — | — |
| Other agrochemicals | — | — | ✔ | ✔ | — | — |
| Storage | — | ✔ | — | ✔ | — | — |
| Processing | — | ✔ | — | ✔ | — | — |
| Wholesaling | — | ✔ | — | ✔ | — | — |
| Retailing | — | — | ✔ | — | ✔ | — |
| Farm equipment | — | — | ✔ | — | ✔ | — |
| Seeds | — | — | ✔ | — | ✔ | — |
| Insurance | — | ✔ | — | — | — | ✔ |
| Farm production[a] | — | — | ✔ | — | — | ✔ |

*Note:* A check mark (✔) indicates the degree of use. High use is use by more than 60 percent of countries; medium, use by 40–60 percent; low, use by less than 40 percent.

a. Farming five or more crops.

*Source:* Global Food Policy Research Project files, Harvard University, Graduate School of Business Administration, Boston, 1983.

eighth of the processed food output.[19] Multinational corporations have traditionally played a dominant role in the export of many basic commodities. They are highly involved in coffee, cocoa, tea, bananas, canned fruits, vegetable oils, and specialty fish, and moderately involved in exports of beef, fresh fruits and vegetables, and sugar.[20] In the domestic markets multinational corporations have concentrated on branded rather than staple foods, especially dairy, canned fruits and vegetables, refined oils and margarine, soft drinks, coffee, tea, and poultry (see table 2-5). Multinationals are often the technological and marketing leaders in their segments. In some products— for example bananas and pineapple—these corporations are partially vertically integrated into production and processing. Multinationals are also important suppliers of farm and factory inputs such as equipment.

The presence of multinational food processing companies in developing countries will likely increase because they are seen as strategic growth markets, as evidenced by the following comment by the Heinz company's chairman:

In 1980, we conducted an internal company review of global investment potential. Our first unsettling discovery was that at

**Table 2-5.** *Involvement of Multinational Corporations in Food Processing Industries in Developing Countries, Mid-1970s*

| Food | Degree of involvement |
|---|---|
| *Branded foods* | |
| Coffee (extracted) | High |
| Confectionery | High |
| Dairy products (processed; ice cream) | High |
| Fruits and vegetables (canned) | High |
| Refined oils and margarine | High |
| Soft drinks (syrup) | High |
| Tea | High |
| Beer (nonlocal) | Moderate |
| Breakfast foods | Moderate |
| Cookies and crackers | Moderate |
| Biscuits | Moderate |
| Soft drinks (bottled) | Moderate |
| Meat (processed) | Low |
| Wines and spirits | Low |
| | |
| *Staples* | |
| Animal feeds | High |
| Poultry | High |
| Vegetable oils (crude) | Moderate |
| Wheat (milled) | Moderate |
| Bakery goods | Low |
| Corn (dry milled) | Low |
| Dairy products (fresh; cheese) | Low |
| Fish (fresh; dried) | Low |
| Fruits and vegetables (fresh) | Low |
| Meat (fresh slaughtered) | Low |
| Beer (local) | None |
| Pulses and roots | None |
| Rice (milled) | None |
| Sugar (noncentrifugally milled) | None |

*Note:* Data pertain to involvement in domestic markets only.

*Source:* Derived from United Nations Centre on Transnational Corporations, *Transnational Corporations in Food and Beverage Processing* (New York, 1981), p. 98, table 56.

that time 85 percent of the world's population had not been exposed to the Heinz brand. We also found—and it remains true today—that in the mature markets of Europe and the North American continent food consumption was not growing by more than one percent. If we wanted significant expansion in volume, we would have to look beyond the industrialized West.[21]

## Local Firms

Most agroindustries are indigenously owned companies, although sometimes local firms enter into joint ventures with multinationals as a means of accessing technology, brands, or foreign markets. Often the agroindustry is part of a local "business group." These groups are large multicompany organizations usually operating in different businesses but under common financial and management control, often with some degree of family ownership. Agroindustries such as beer companies are likely to be part of these groups because they are solid cash generators and were frequently the dominant type of industry in the country in the early stages of industrialization and business group formation. Some of the business groups have their origin in the agricultural sector and have vertically integrated into agroindustries. The large size of business groups often increases their access to information, capital, and managerial resources and strengthens their bargaining power with suppliers, buyers, and the government.

## Marketing Intermediaries

This institutional category refers to those groups performing the commercialization functions in the production chain. Although these functions can be performed by farmers or agroindustries themselves, generally independent marketing intermediaries are involved. They are often the key actors in moving agricultural produce from the farm gate to produce markets or to the agroindustry. Critics tend to blame intermediaries for exploiting small farmers and increasing marketing costs. Such suspicions often lead to the government's use of food-marketing SOES. Although exploitation may sometimes occur because of market imperfections and uneven bargaining power, in many cases the crop assembly function is efficiently carried out by small marketers, who are able to locate and rapidly transport small amounts of geographically dispersed production quantities. In some countries the food-marketing channels may be dominated by certain ethnic groups, who may gain certain advantages and efficiencies from their social network.[22]

In addition to the aforementioned types of institutions, the agroindustry will undoubtedly have linkages with other organizations. Managing the business-government relationship will involve interactions with a variety of public entities, some of which may be particularly important, for example, the public health and food standards department or the customs bureau. Other private entities such as financial institutions and industry associations may be important to

the firm. The critical task for the analyst is to identify the most significant institutions in the production chain, understand the nature of
those organizations, and design relationships that strengthen the
agroindustry.

## International Linkages

The final analytical element in this systems approach framework is
the international dimension. Agroindustries do not operate in isola-
tion; they are connected in various ways with the international economy. Technological advances in transportation have shrunk the
globe; all markets are increasingly accessible quickly and economically. Similarly, advances in electronic information and financial institutions have led to the emergence of highly integrated international
capital markets. These, in combination with floating exchange rates,
have created close links between the international financial and commodity markets. Shifts in currency values introduce greater instability in commodity prices. The analyst must identify and examine
these various international linkages, which can be viewed as existing
on the input and output sides of the agroindustry.

On the input side the firm may be dependent on or have the option
of using external suppliers of raw materials, packaging, chemicals,
equipment, capital, technology, and services. How the firm utilizes
the international market on the supply side can significantly affect
risks, costs, and competitive differentiation. Our discussion of macropolicies revealed that trade policies, particularly exchange rates and
import controls, can be quite relevant to these international input
linkages.

On the output side the international markets are outlets for agroindustry exports and sources of potential competition. Many agroindustries are part of global industries, in which production and markets are spread across many countries and are interdependent.
Actions or conditions in an industry in one country can have an effect
on firms in that same industry in another country. For example, lowering taxes on banana exporters in Ecuador adversely affects the cost
competitiveness of Guatemalan banana exporters. A bumper rice
crop in Thailand might push international prices downward, and its
exports to another country could put severe competitive pressure on
local rice mills forced to buy national rice at higher support prices. A
devaluation in one exporting country might create a cost advantage
for its exporting agroindustry relative to its counterpart in a neighboring country.

The existence of huge agricultural subsidies in the European Economic Community, for example, has led to overproduction and the

dumping of surpluses onto the world market at greatly reduced prices, thereby causing considerable disruption and damage to unsubsidized exporters. Disputes over the elimination of such practices, which are driven by domestic political and income support concerns and policies, led to the 1990 collapse of the GATT (General Agreement on Tariffs and Trade) negotiations. Their resumption in 1991 signals significant change in agricultural trade dynamics in the 1990s.

International markets possess threats and opportunities for agroindustries. The analyst needs to identify the possible international nexus points for the agroindustry and assess their implications. This international perspective has become even more important as governments increasingly peel away the protective insulation of import substitution strategies and turn more toward promoting exports and becoming internationally competitive.

# 3 *The Marketing Factor*

THE VIABILITY OF AN AGROINDUSTRIAL PROJECT requires soundness in each of the project's three basic component activities—procurement, processing, and marketing. Although this is the operational sequence of the materials flow in the production chain, the marketing factor is the logical starting point for project analysis: unless there is adequate demand for a project, it has no economic basis.

## Primary Elements

A marketing analysis examines the external environment's possible or actual response to a firm's product by analyzing consumer characteristics and the competition. Such information helps the firm to construct a comprehensive marketing plan and, recognizing the production chain linkages, to design appropriate procurement and processing strategies. The marketing analysis also draws further on the systems approach by considering the effects of both government policies and international markets (see figure 3-1).

In addition to adequate market demand, an agroindustry's viability is determined by the agronomic capacity to produce its raw material supplies. The agroindustrial system obviously requires both markets and supplies for project success. A production bias, however, has historically dominated agricultural and agroindustrial project analysis, and markets were considered secondary issues. Yet Say's Law is not always reliable; supply does not necessarily create its own demand.[1] Too often projects have failed because of a mismatch of production and marketing.[2] There is no sense growing something if it cannot be sold. But, of course, it cannot be sold if it cannot be grown. Clearly, this is an iterative process, but because agronomic feasibility testing consumes significant time and resources (such as land, inputs, and research), it is often economical to identify market needs first. In addition, land has multiple crop or livestock usages, and market information can help an analyst choose among such alternatives. Furthermore, a market analysis can identify a product need that is agronomically feasible but has not been considered. For example, based on a study of export market needs, the producers in one Cen-

Figure 3-1.  *Marketing Analysis in Agroindustry Analysis*

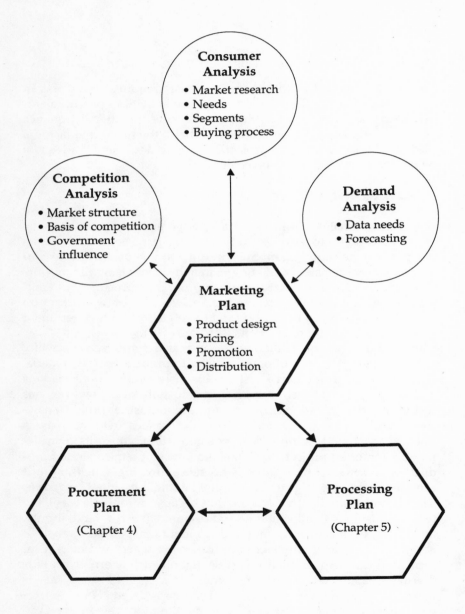

tral American country began growing okra, even though it had never been produced there and was not locally consumed. Agroindustrial project design must be market-focused.

As indicated in chapter 1, agroindustrial products differ from other products in the unique characteristics of their raw materials (perishability, seasonality, and variability in quantity and quality) and in their frequent status as necessities, which often attracts political attention to, and government control of, prices, quality, and distribution. The marketing of agroindustrial products consequently differs in many aspects from the marketing of nonagroindustrial goods.

The primary elements to be considered in the marketing analysis of an agroindustrial project are:

- *Consumers.* The analyst examines consumer needs, market segmentation, the purchasing process, and market research.
- *The competitive environment.* The analyst examines market structure, the basis of competition, and governmental influence.
- *The marketing plan.* The analyst defines the elements of product design, pricing, promotion, and distribution that constitute the firm's marketing strategy.
- *Demand forecasting.* The analyst examines the data needs and forecasting techniques for projecting sales.

## Consumer Analysis

To define the project's potential consumer, the analyst must identify the needs the product will satisfy, the market segments the product will serve, and the method of purchase. Market research is needed to obtain this information. If the agroindustrial product is a common one, the amount of new consumer analysis needed may be minimal. A new product, however, will require a thorough analysis.

### Consumer Needs

The purpose of marketing is to define and meet consumer needs. Socially responsible marketing does not create needs but responds to needs existing within a cultural context. Needs include not only absolute necessities but also wants.

Consumer needs are created by a complex interaction of physiological, sociological, and psychological motives. For processed foods, which constitute the bulk of agroindustrial products, consumer needs are frequently expressed as preferences for a product's taste, smell, color, texture, appearance, and convenience for users. More fundamentally, the needs relate to nutritional requirements and appetite satisfaction. For fiber products such as cotton, jute, or wood, consumers are industrial buyers (often from another agroindustry) whose main interests are price and physical qualities.

Another motive affecting consumer purchasing is social status. For example, the Yucatán region of southern Mexico has a plant called *chaya* that grows wild and is rich in protein. It was eaten by the ancient Maya along with maize and beans in a nutritionally sound diet. Over the years, *chaya* became known as a "poor person's" food, and it was consumed less and less, even though the people's diet was short of protein.

Consumer preferences also depend on several needs in addition to intrinsic product qualities, including such usage conveniences as packaging or cooking ease. To develop an appropriate product and an effective marketing program, an analyst should examine consumers' motives for purchasing a product.

## Market Segmentation

To match a product with the needs of consumers, it is necessary to divide consumers into groups or market segments. Numerous variables categorize consumers and define segments—for example, geographic location. In a country as large as India, there are considerable differences in language and culture among states, and an agroindustry attempting to market its products nationally would have to adjust its communication and products to these differences.[3] Geographic location often reveals ethnic or regional taste differences: consumers in northern Thailand prefer glutinous rice, whereas consumers in central and southern regions prefer nonglutinous varieties. Age and sex of consumers are two other common segmenting variables—for example, weaning foods are targeted to infants and protein- and calorie-rich foods to pregnant or lactating women.

Another differentiating variable is income level because effective demand and food preferences change as income levels rise. This variable clearly affects product pricing and can easily affect other product characteristics. Consider, for example, the market-research data presented in table 3-1, from a study to determine the feasibility of marketing nutritionally fortified cookies and crackers in Guatemala. These data are stratified by income level and indicate the size of the package most frequently bought. The table reveals a difference between high- and low-income consumers: the low-income purchasers prefer smaller packages, probably because these consumers have reduced incomes and cash flow. To service the nation's large, low-income market segment, the product's packaging would have to be adjusted accordingly.

**Table 3-1.** *Preferred Form and Size of Packaging for Cookies and Crackers in Guatemala*
(percentage of purchasers polled)

| | Income of purchaser | | |
|---|---|---|---|
| Package form and size | Low | Medium | High |
| *Can* | | | |
| Small | 5 | 9 | 5 |
| Medium | 12 | 27 | 20 |
| Large | 15 | 25 | 36 |
| Total preference | 32 | 61 | 61 |
| *Box* | | | |
| Small | 7 | 8 | 4 |
| Medium | 6 | 6 | 4 |
| Large | 9 | 8 | 13 |
| Total preference | 22 | 22 | 21 |
| *Other small package* | 34 | 10 | 14 |
| *No preference* | 12 | 7 | 4 |

*Source:* MARPLAN, Guatemala City, 1972.

Another market differentiation is between domestic and export consumers—the latter frequently demand higher product quality and different packaging. (See chapter 5 for further discussion of packaging.) Some export markets are seasonal due to climatic differences; an example is the winter fresh fruit and vegetable market in the United States and Europe when local production is dormant. The quality demanded in these export markets is significantly greater than that demanded in local markets, and more affluent consumers are willing to pay premium prices for this quality. Since 1974 Chile pursued this market opportunity aggressively, developing the requisite production, selection, packing, and logistics system needed to meet the markets' quality standards. By 1990 the country had become the Southern Hemisphere's number one fruit exporter, surpassing New Zealand, Australia, Argentina, and South Africa. An integral part of this success was a continual search for and penetration of new product and market segments; Chile created, for example, the winter market for fresh raspberries in the United States and Europe, of which it held nearly a 100 percent share.

In addition to being defined by socioeconomic or demographic characteristics, market segments can also be defined by user type—for example, industrial consumers, institutional consumers, wholesale or retail businesses, and end consumers. Finally, market segments can

**Figure 3-2.** *Illustrative Subsegmentation Process*

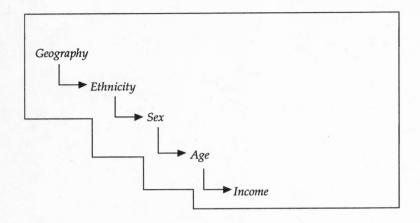

develop around product types: necessities, status items, convenience goods, or specialty items. This distinction will influence the pricing, promotion, and distribution of the product. For example, a market segment is emerging for organically grown fresh and processed foods, reflecting U.S. consumers' rising health consciousness and concern about pesticides. Tapping this segment requires adjustments from distribution channels all the way back through production and farm inputs.

Market segments should be viewed dynamically because they change over time in response to a multitude of social and economic forces. For example, U.S. consumers increasingly spend more of their food dollar on away-from-home expenditures (purchased meals and snacks); that amount rose from 20 percent in 1960 to 27 percent in 1980.[4]

Market segmentation is used to identify potential consumers because an appropriate marketing strategy cannot be determined until the market has been defined. The consumer groups can be sequenced into subsegments according to various descriptive characteristics, as in figure 3-2, or organized into matrixes, as in figure 3-3.

Because market segmentation limits the agroindustrial project's options, the analyst should select a segment based on the competitive environment and the strengths and weaknesses of the company. Once the segment is selected, the analyst can use the consumer profile to develop the marketing plan.

Because of the characteristics of the raw material, agroindustrial projects have many product-processing options. For example, man-

**Figure 3-3.** *Illustrative Segmentation Matrixes*

Income

|  | A | B | C | D |
|---|---|---|---|---|
| 20–29 |  |  |  |  |
| 30–39 |  |  |  |  |
| 40–49 |  |  |  |  |
| 50+ |  |  |  |  |

*(row label: Age)*

Income and sex

|  |  | A | | B | | C | | D | |
|---|---|---|---|---|---|---|---|---|---|
|  |  | M | F | M | F | M | F | M | F |
| South | Indian |  |  |  |  |  |  |  |  |
|  | Mestizo |  |  |  |  |  |  |  |  |
| West | Indian |  |  |  |  |  |  |  |  |
|  | Mestizo |  |  |  |  |  |  |  |  |
| North | Indian |  |  |  |  |  |  |  |  |
|  | Mestizo |  |  |  |  |  |  |  |  |

*(row label: Region and ethnicity)*

goes are sold in the following forms: fresh, frozen halves, dried, slices, in syrup, nectar, puree, juice, soda drink, jam, candy, pastries, ice cream flavoring, liquor, and chutney.[5] When deciding on the degree of processing, the project analyst must consider the sometimes considerable marketing differences for each product segment. One West African nation, seeking to increase the value added in its exports, decided to make cocoa butter rather than export the beans whole. However, the entrepreneurs did not carefully examine the market segment for cocoa butter. It was smaller than the segment for whole beans and more susceptible to erosion by substitute products, and tariffs were higher on butter than on beans. As a result, the nation and the investors put themselves into a narrower and more competitive segment that left them with an underutilized and unprofitable plant. Value was lost rather than added.

## The Buying Process

Understanding the buying process can guide the project analyst in designing the marketing plan. The buying process can be examined by looking at who decides to purchase the product, how they decide, and when and where they make the purchase.

The *who* is often more than one person. To know where to direct promotion, it is important that the project analyst identify all those in the decisionmaking unit. Individual members (for example, parent and child) might be reached by different methods. Because the end consumer is often not the buyer, the processor is more interested in the buyer than the consumer. For example, infants consume baby food, but parents purchase it. Baby-food manufacturers therefore choose flavors based on parents' preferences.

Consumers make purchasing decisions in a variety of ways. *How* they make these decisions influences a marketing plan's promotion, pricing, and distribution. Low-price items are often purchased on impulse; hence, consumer accessibility, product display, and packaging are determining factors. One Mexican snack food manufacturer put its products in small bags and mounted a direct delivery system to a multitude of small stores, where the products were placed on readily accessible display racks, thereby maximizing availability.[6] Expensive items are frequently planned purchases that, because of the cash outlay, require greater information for the consumer. For planned purchases, such as major items of clothing, brand image and sales advice are significant factors. Brand is also important in food purchasing because certainty of results—known taste, preparation procedures, appearance—is desired.

*When* people buy involves frequency and seasonality. Staple products such as rice are bought often, whereas luxury products are purchased occasionally. Purchasing frequency affects several marketing issues, pricing among them. A manufacturer, for example, can sell rice at a low price because it is purchased frequently, but a product such as palm hearts requires a high price to offset its low sales volume. The demand for some agroindustrial products, such as ice cream and hot breakfast foods, is seasonal. Seasonality poses additional questions for inventory management, cash flow, and diversification of product line—questions that will be examined further in chapter 5.

*Where* people purchase varies by segment and product. High-income consumers tend to use supermarkets or specialty stores, whereas low-income consumers shop at small, neighborhood stores or public markets. Although buyers are willing to travel for planned purchases, they buy impulse items according to what is available. When designing a distribution system, manufacturers should consider where the targeted consumers shop. For example, when the Mexican government's food-marketing agency, Compañía Nacional de Subsistencias Populares, built a network of low-price retail stores in the 1970s, it took care to situate them in low-income neighborhoods. Note that as countries develop, transportation means improve and consumer mobility increases, thereby broadening the purchase locus.

### Market Research

Market research attempts to identify consumer needs, market segments, and the buying process to facilitate sound marketing decisions. The process consists of four steps: data specification, source identification, data collection, and data analysis.[7]

DATA SPECIFICATION. The private or public marketer must define his or her specific requirements for market information on consumer needs, market segments, and buying process. The data required will vary according to the type of agroindustrial project, the marketer's familiarity with the product's market, and the financial risks.[8]

SOURCE IDENTIFICATION. After identifying the information needed, a marketer should locate primary and secondary sources of the information. Primary sources include potential consumers, producers, distributors, and field experts. Secondary sources—such as government feasibility reports, industrial publications, loan analyses, census data, and international agency studies—can also be useful.[9]

DATA COLLECTION. Data can be collected formally or informally. Formal data collection techniques consist of an explicit research design, a statistical sampling, and standardized information-collection procedures such as telephone, mail, or direct interview surveys. Direct surveys and interviews may be the most feasible methods in developing nations, given the sometimes limited coverage and other deficiencies of postal and telephone services.[10] Informal collection methods can include talking to a few consumers or distributors or examining company data or competing products. Sometimes marketers conduct controlled experiments to test such aspects of a marketing plan as price or promotion. Econometric modeling—which will be discussed later in the chapter—is a research tool used to forecast demand. The financial and managerial resources of agroindustrial small-scale industries are often too limited to conduct thorough market research, and this function may have to be carried out through government assistance to the entire industry or sector.

DATA ANALYSIS. Data analysis requires interpretation of the information to fit specific informational needs—for example, the testing of product concepts, characteristics, pricing, or promotion. Before making the final analysis, however, marketers and project analysts should verify all sources and collection methods because the quality of the findings depends on the reliability of the data.

The value of market research information should be weighed against its cost so that an adequate amount of good quality data is collected at the lowest cost possible to ensure acceptable validity. Such data should enable better decisionmaking, which will in turn generate economic benefits that exceed the cost of collecting and analyzing the data. Locating the point of lowest cost and maximum benefit requires judgment. The decisionmaker must consider the cost of more market research and the probable effect on sales, and weigh the risk of misjudgment in the absence of more and better data. Perfect information is never possible, and decisionmaking always takes place under uncertainty. Market research is intended to reduce this uncertainty at a reasonable cost.

For example, the manager of a vegetable oil plant was considering switching from a plastic can to a polyethylene bag for a shortening product because of the cost savings, estimated at $0.01 a container or $10,000 a year for an output of 1 million units. The marketing director proposed spending $5,000 for a consumer survey and a panel to test the new packaging concept. The manager was not enthusiastic about spending half a year's savings on market research, but he was uncertain about how the new packaging would affect sales. He suspected that there was only a 50 percent chance that sales would fall by more than 10 percent, but the marketing director pointed out that with the profit margin of $0.10 a unit, a 10 percent drop of 100,000 units would negate the cost savings. He thought that market data would provide information by which the manager could estimate the effect of the change in packaging.

The research was conducted and indicated that one-third of the consumers would not buy the product in the new package because after they consumed all the shortening, they recycled the plastic containers to other uses. As a result, the manager estimated, with 90 percent certainty, that sales would drop by 25 percent and generate a loss of $22,500 (1 million units × 25 percent sales loss × 90 percent certainty × $0.10 margin), which would negate the cost savings of the new packaging and result in a net loss.

Consumer analysis is essential to ensuring that a project will be directed toward and tailored to real market needs, but consumer analysis alone does not guarantee business success. Competitive realities must also be confronted.

## Analysis of the Competitive Environment

Agroindustrial projects do not exist in a vacuum. They enter a marketplace crowded with agroindustrial firms and products, and their success partly depends on their ability to compete with other firms. Accordingly, a marketing analysis should examine the structure of the market and the basis of competition. It is also important to examine how the government's macropolicies and actions affect the competitive environment.

### Market Structure

Market structure has been a traditional focal point for economists studying the competitive environment. A structural examination of a market can begin by identifying the competitors operating in each of the high priority market segments specified by the marketing analysis. These rivals can be public or private enterprises, regional, national, or multinational companies. The likelihood and significance of new entrants (future competition) in the market must also be assessed, and analysts should consider competition from substitute products (for example, synthetics for cotton or soft drinks for fruit juices) as well. Products should be identified with their broad industrial classifications: the textile mill is in the fiber business instead of the cotton business, and the juice processor is in the beverage business instead of the fruit juice business. The interdependent nature of agroindustries implies that they must further broaden the concept of competition. Suppliers of raw material who can integrate forward to process their own product are potential competitors—a dairy farmers' cooperative, for instance, could add a processing plant for its milk. Similarly, large buyers may integrate backward to produce a product they use—a supermarket chain, for instance, might construct a vegetable cannery. In effect, one is looking at Michael E. Porter's five sources of competition within the market's structure: rivals, potential entrants, substitutes, suppliers, and buyers.[11]

A structural analysis should also identify the number of competitors to determine the oligopolistic tendencies in the market. The location of other firms' markets and raw materials also carries implications for competition. Finally, the size of competing firms in net worth (assets), sales volume, and market shares should be examined. Market share is an indication of industrial concentration and suggests the market power of the firms. Data across years are useful for revealing competitive trends in the market.

The next task for the new agroindustry intending to operate in a given market is to assess the barriers to entry. Can the proposed agroindustry get in? How likely are other competitors to enter? A discussion of five common entry barriers in agroindustry follows.

ECONOMIES OF SCALE IN PROCESSING.  In a capital-intensive processing enterprise with significant economies of scale, an ongoing producer with a large share of the market has a lower cost structure than a new, low-volume company does. A new company in this market would have difficulty competing with the price of the established, high-volume company. In addition, the limited purchasing power in developing countries lessens the effective demand and reduces the possible number of economically viable manufacturers. Excess capacity is another entry deterrent in agroindustries. Finally, given the scarcity of capital in developing countries, capital requirements may impede entrants. Agroindustries tend to be less capital intensive than many types of manufacturing businesses and therefore pose lower economic barriers to entry. However, there is a wide range of capital requirements among different kinds of agroindustries. For example, a sugar mill in Bangladesh required an investment of $17.7 million while a cassava pellet factory in Thailand needed only $75,000.[12] Even within the same type of commodity system, investment levels can vary greatly depending on scale and range of products processed: a Korean 16,000–ton maize processing plant producing starch, syrup, flour, and fructose represented an investment of $16.5 million, while a 1,600–ton Ugandan maize flour producer entailed a $580,000 investment.

ABSOLUTE COST DISADVANTAGE.  A firm may possess a patented or proprietary formula or production technique that creates a lower cost structure regardless of the scale of its operation. An example is a manufacturer of dehydrated potatoes, whose manufacturing process can only be approximated by a newcomer through extensive research and development.

VERTICAL SYSTEM CONTROL. Barriers to market entry in agroindustry can arise because firms integrate vertically to control the raw material inputs or the distribution channels. That can prohibit new operations or put them at an absolute cost disadvantage. An example of vertical control is the multinational banana companies that control production, packing, transport, and marketing operations.

BRAND FRANCHISE. Existing products may have strong consumer loyalty. In this case, a new company must price its product significantly lower than the original product or advertise heavily to attract consumers from their usual brand. Similarly, imported or foreign food brands frequently enjoy higher prestige and thus create a barrier to local producers.

SWITCHING COSTS. For some buyers switching to a different product, usually a substitute, will be impeded by additional costs for changing equipment or procedures, by perceived quality risks, or by traditional preferences. For example, a new corn starch plant in Peru encountered great resistance to change from industrial users who preferred the white imported (but technically equivalent) starch, from the consumers who used sweet potato and potato starch, and from the confectioners who used flour.[13] In another country a new plant producing high fructose syrup was unable to get the international soft drink bottlers to switch from sugar to their 42 percent syrup because the licensors only permitted the use of the higher concentrated 55 percent syrup in the United States.

The project analyst should weigh the entry barriers because an otherwise attractive project may not be viable if the barriers to entering a market are severe. Public policymakers may wish to take actions to remove these barriers. But assuming the barriers are surmountable, the analyst then should examine the basis upon which the company will compete in the industry.

### Basis of Competition

Competition occurs simultaneously along several parameters, but they all focus on best meeting consumers' needs. Marketplace advantage will be captured by those companies that provide buyers with greater value. Such value creation and competitive superiority is achievable if a company can attain cost advantage or product differentiation.[14] Cost advantage permits more effective price competition, and product differentiation enables more effective quality competition. The price-quality interplay yields the ultimate consumer value. The mix guides the marketing strategy.

COST ADVANTAGE. Cost gains come through either better control or more efficient combination of resources and activities in the production chain. A critical starting point is to identify the cost structure throughout the chain and then focus analysis on those cost elements. Because most agroindustries are transformation operations, raw materials are the major cost, although in some instances packaging can loom large (see chapter 5). Consequently, priority focus should be on the procurement operations. Whereas purchasing activities for non-agroindustries are often deemed relatively less important than manufacturing operations, for agroindustries they are primary. Superior procurement can readily produce cost advantage (see chapter 4).

Economies of scale can be an important source of cost reduction for some agroindustries, but perhaps even more critical is capacity utilization, given the seasonality and variability of agricultural supplies. Those firms able to manage storage, broaden product lines, or expand usage may be able to achieve better balance of supply and demand and fuller use of facilities. For example, one vegetable processor added different vegetables that were harvested sequentially, thereby extending his canning season and plant usage. Another food company evened out production by promoting year-round consumption of its product as a snack and a cooking ingredient rather than just a traditional holiday food.

Geography also plays a part in cost advantages. For example, Philippine mango exporters were paying $0.72 per kilogram for air shipment to Tokyo but $5.49 per kilogram to Los Angeles; relative to Mexican mango exporters they had a cost advantage in the Japanese market and a disadvantage in the United States.[15] Large food processors can sometimes lower distribution costs by integrating forward and taking over the wholesaling functions, thereby shortening the distribution channels and getting economies of scale in storage and transport. In the United States, major meat packers reduced transportation and labor costs by relocating in rural livestock production areas.

DIFFERENTIATION. Differentiation as a source of competitive advantage can come from actions taken at a multitude of points in the production chain. For example, genetic engineering can be used to create agricultural raw materials with different processing or content characteristics—oilseeds with varying oleic acid levels, for example—

resulting in distinct agroindustry products (and costs). Beers can use special yeasts or soft drinks special ingredient formulas to create distinct flavors and special consumer preference. Through genetic breeding the British agribusiness entrepreneur Bernard Matthews developed a 4–6 pound turkey that was small and cheap enough so that British consumers began to consume it regularly rather than just at holidays. Processing innovations extended the differentiation. His company later invented a technology to produce deboned, extruded turkey roasts and, later, sliced, breaded turkey steaks.[16]

The Netherlands' flower growers supply about 70 percent of the world market and Colombia's growers are second. Most of Colombia's competitive advantage stems from lower costs and more favorable climatic conditions, but the Netherlands has maintained its dominance through continual investment in research and development for product innovation, providing 4,000 different varieties of cut flowers to the U.S. market.[17] The banana companies' use of cartons, cited in the last chapter, was an example of creating value for distributors and retailers through more efficient handling. The boxing of individual bunches also enabled United Fruit to improve its quality control and to brand its fruit, thereby differentiating its product sufficiently to gain premium prices.

Because quality is subjective, market segments can evaluate it differently. Sometimes price alone is presumed to indicate quality, and a low price will create consumer resistance because the quality is perceived negatively. It is important to recognize the difference between the intrinsic and perceived quality of a product: brand and image creation is a strategy of perceived quality competition, whereas packaging, product content, and service are means of intrinsic quality differentiation. Value is in the eyes of the buyers; it is vital to understand what is important to them and how they perceive worth. The consumer must remain foremost in the analyst's mind.

New products go through a product life cycle during which their market experience changes. (Although this pattern is worth noting, it is less applicable to food products than to other manufactured items.) A model of the product life cycle is presented in figure 3-4.[18] When a new product enters the marketplace, there are few competitors, and the product's newness insulates it from price competition. As the product's success grows, it attracts competition that stimulates primary demand, expands the entire market, and may also introduce price competition. As the product matures, and differences among brands decrease, the basis of competition shifts more to price. Improvements in the production processes or economies of scale lead to reductions in production cost that allow more aggressive price cut-

**Figure 3-4.** *Product Life Cycle*

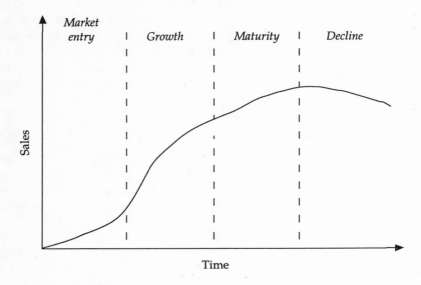

ting. The product, perhaps modified or promoted differently, may extend the maturity stage, but its sales eventually decline because the market is satiated or captured by new products.

Some commodities, such as cereal grains, avoid the final decline because they are necessities. As incomes rise, however, consumers prefer further processed forms of the staple—for example, instant or flavored rice or filled pastas. Manufacturers benefit by identifying the stage of the life cycle at which their particular product will enter the market. Different possibilities arise for attaining cost advantages and differentiation as a product moves through its life cycle, but in all cases the analyst should consider the cost of achieving differentiation and whether the added benefits to the buyer justify the incremental cost.

### Governmental Influence on Competition

Competitive structure and dynamics are also affected by the "megaforce" of government. Analysts need to examine how governmental macropolicies and actions affect the competitive environment.

DUTIES AND QUOTAS. In their trade policy, governments often use duties or quotas to shield a domestic market from import competition. The level and longevity of tariffs should be evaluated in terms of their effects on the proposed product's competitive position. Some possible ramifications are indicated by the following example. A flour mill in the Philippines was established during a time of high import duties. Because the tariff created a barrier to entry, the firm had a large market share and high profits and grew complacent in its attitude toward marketing. When the government subsequently reduced the import tariff, the company was unable to compete effectively with imported flour because its production and marketing system had not been sufficiently well developed.

The United States has used seasonal tariffs, which are raised during the summer months to protect local produce growers from import competition. It also places strict quotas on some imports, such as sugar, to protect domestic farmers whose sugar costs more. Japan does the same with rice, for example.

EXCHANGE RATES. Exchange rates are another part of trade policy. Where the exchange rate is overvalued, imports are made cheaper relative to locally produced agroindustrial products (unless offset by import duties). Such overvaluation is common: by 25–30 percent in the Philippines during the 1970s, by 35 percent in Jamaica and about 25 percent in Colombia in the early 1980s, and by 44 percent in Nigeria during 1980–84.[19] In some countries preferential exchange rates are given to food imports in an effort to keep food prices lower for urban consumers. If these imports are final goods, they place locally processed foods at a competitive disadvantage. If the imports are intermediate or raw materials, such as unrefined vegetable oil, they increase the bargaining power of the agroindustry relative to its local farmer suppliers. Agroindustries utilizing a higher percentage of imported inputs also would be at a competitive advantage relative to a rival using more locally produced inputs.

A devaluation would reverse these advantages. When the currencies of western European countries appreciated in the late 1980s relative to the U.S. dollar, for example, food products from those countries became less competitive than those from Hungary, whose currency did not appreciate and whose exporters were able to increase their penetration of the U.S. market in the areas of packed hams, bacon, and concentrated strawberry, raspberry, and cherry juices.

SUBSIDIES. In the area of fiscal policy, subsidies can create competitive advantage. These are often used, albeit in indirect and somewhat disguised forms, to enhance the price competitiveness of agroindustrial exports. In the case of the Philippine flour mill cited above, soon after the government imposed high duties on flour imports, the

U.S. government decreased its export subsidy levels for wheat and increased them for flour. That move increased the cost of the Philippine mill's raw material imports and decreased the price at which U.S. flour exporters could sell in the Philippines, which was their second largest flour export market.

In one country a high-fructose syrup plant was built on the premise that it would be able to significantly underprice sugar, which was supported by government price supports. When the government subsequently reduced those producer subsidy levels, sugar prices plummeted and the high-fructose syrup's cost advantage evaporated. Consumer subsidies for local foodstuffs are also common and will be discussed in a subsequent section on prices.

STATE-OWNED ENTERPRISES. As was indicated in chapter 2, sometimes governments use state-owned enterprises (SOEs) as intervention vehicles in the food system. In some instances the SOEs will be food processors and therefore direct rivals of the proposed new private agroindustry. That, however, is not necessarily bad from a competitive standpoint. One manager of an Indian agroindustry complained that his problem was that "there is no SOE in my industry." In other agroindustries SOEs were relatively less efficient than their private sector competitors and so negotiated with the government for higher prices, which then acted as a price umbrella under which the private firms could attain higher margins or increase market penetration through lower prices.

Sometimes the government requires the agroindustries to sell to a food-marketing SOE. For example, in several states in India the rice millers were obligated to sell more than half of their output to the government.[20] In Thailand the rice exporters were forced to sell—at below market prices—a certain portion of their exports to the government's Public Warehouse Organization, which then resold the rice to selected retail shops.[21] This control over the flow of the agroindustries' output may have varying competitive effects. It may intensify competition among the private firms for the remaining uncontrolled and presumably higher-priced segment of the market. It may help the private firm by creating a de facto segmentation of the market, in which the SOE serves the poorer, lower-priced, more costly-to-reach consumer groups, and the private firms sell primarily to the more affluent segments.

REGULATORY MEASURES. Governments use a variety of regulatory mechanisms in the food industry. Sanitary and environmental protection standards administered by governmental health or agricultural agencies affect investment and operating costs and can act as entry barriers. They can also act as trade barriers; for example, countries in which hoof-and-mouth disease is endemic are not permitted to export fresh meat to the United States—Argentine beef exporters, for instance, cannot compete in this market unless their beef is cooked. Similarly, foreign meat processing facilities must pass U.S. standards before imported meat can be sold in U.S. markets.

The Philippine mango industry was threatened with the loss of its largest export market in 1987, when the Japanese government banned the import of mangoes fumigated with ethyl di-bromide to eliminate fruit flies.[22] The Japanese government was concerned about the possible carcinogenic effects of the fumigant. Although these possible effects were known in the 1980s, no ban occurred until the Japanese had invented an alternative vapor heat treatment method. The ban proved advantageous to the Japanese equipment manufacturers, as the Philippine mango exporters were forced to buy the equipment to preserve their market.

Governments often manage industrial development through licensing, thereby giving them control over the number of firms entering an industry, their capacity, and often their technology. That control can have a direct impact on market structure and the intensity of rivalry. The Brazilian government used its regulatory power to create the gasohol industry. It promoted the development of fuel alcohol from sugarcane as a substitute for petroleum-derived gasoline. To overcome the switching costs involved, the government required automobile manufacturers to modify their engine designs to permit use of the new agroindustrial fuel source.

Patents and antitrust measures are other legal and regulatory mechanisms that can affect competition. The agroindustry analyst needs to be alert to the broad range of competitive effects that these and other government policies can produce. Often they are decisive in determining a new project's viability. In a highly regulated environment, the real competition may be for administrative preference.

## The Marketing Plan

The data from the analyses of the consumer and the competitive environment are the basis for a project's marketing plan. The purpose of the plan is to position the firm's product most advantageously in relation to its consumers and competition. The elements of the plan are product design, pricing, promotion, and distribution. These constitute the company's "marketing mix," the core of the marketing strategy.

## Product Design

Most products have several design options. Even staples such as rice can assume various forms (for example, enriched, parboiled, long- or short-grain) and packaging (for example, cardboard box, poly-ethylene or cloth bag). Among the design considerations for agroin-dustrial products are taste, texture, cooking ease, color, odor, form, nutritive value, convenience, size, and packaging.[23] These charac-teristics should be matched with consumers' expectations of quality and usage yet kept within the market segment's price range. Costly product improvements must therefore be weighed against the prod-uct's resultant price.

The product, including prototypes for field testing, should be de-signed by the project's marketing and production personnel, with marketing staff identifying the needs the product must meet. When the final design adjustments have been made, full-scale production and marketing begins (see figure 3-5).[24] Market research should con-tinue throughout the life of the product so that the product's design can be modified to fit consumers' changing needs and to achieve competitive advantage through cost reductions or product differen-tiation. One U.S. food processor, Stouffer's, achieved leadership in

**Figure 3-5.  *Product Design Process***

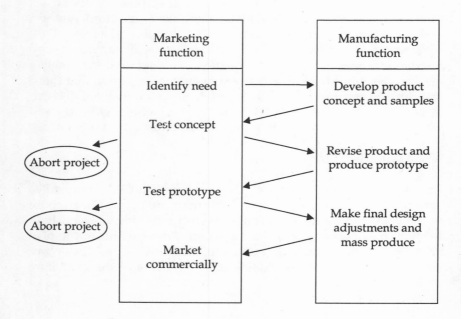

the frozen entree segment by continual development of extensive and distinctive menus, a superior sauce technology, careful ingredient selection, and more attractive packaging.[25]

Analysts should recognize that what consumers prefer is not always in their best interests. For example, polished white rice is treated with talc and glucose because consumers prefer white rice with luster. But the talc and glucose coating must be washed away prior to consumption, a process that increases costs and depletes the rice of vitamin B. Moreover, talc contains asbestos, which may be carcinogenic if ingested in sufficient quantities. For nutritional and economic reasons, the production of treated white rice should be discouraged, but consumer preferences counter this.

## Pricing

The forces of supply and demand in the market set prices for most agroindustrial commodities. Internationally, most developing countries are price takers, and leading export countries are price makers. For example, the prices of wheat and corn (maize) on the Chicago Board of Trade serve as reference points for those commodities. For rice, however, Thailand is the leading exporter, and Bangkok prices are the international reference point. But even for relatively undifferentiated products, there are multiple prices to account for the numerous grades, shipment points, and destinations of agroindustrial products. To reduce some of the uncertainty of market-price variability, some firms have initiated contracts either fixed or tied to futures-market prices.[26] The market imperfections that characterize developing countries—informational deficiencies, infrastructural impediments to mobility, concentrated industry structures, and government interventions—often create considerable room for price variance.

A firm should choose its pricing strategy according to its competitive environment and market segment. That strategy will be influenced by the extent to which the firm is able to achieve cost advantages or product differentiation, as discussed previously in the competitive analysis section. Seven types of pricing strategy are described below.

Cost-Plus Pricing. In cost-plus pricing, the firm adds a margin to its costs for nonmanufacturing costs and profit. For example, if a pair of shoes costs $6 to produce and sells for $10, the markup is 40 percent ([selling price − costs] ÷ selling price). As a percentage of costs, the markup is 66 2/3 percent ([selling price ÷ cost] − cost).[27] A more refined approach is to calculate a markup that will generate a selected return on investment at an expected sales volume. The cost-plus strategy is feasible when there is little or no competition—for example, in price-regulated commodity systems.

PENETRATION PRICING. Penetration pricing is the setting of prices at levels lower than the competition's in order to enter an existing market. Pricing is used to overcome barriers to market entry or to reach a market segment that would be closed at higher prices. This strategy is intended to capture a larger market share and establish a firm market position. It is often not sustainable without a significant cost advantage.

PREDATORY OR PREEMPTIVE PRICING. Predatory pricing is an aggressive approach that underprices existing competitors to erode their market position severely. Preemptive pricing underprices the product to prevent new firms from entering the market. This latter strategy, although it creates only a temporary entry barrier, is equally aggressive. These pricing methods can exert excessive market power that may require public regulation. They are likely to elicit competitive retaliation.

LOSS-LEADER PRICING. The loss-leader strategy prices one product below cost to attract consumers in the hope that they will purchase other products in a company's line. This practice is common in supermarkets.

SKIMMING. In contrast to the previous strategies, skimming sets high prices to attract or "skim off" the price-insensitive segment of the market. This method is often possible early in the product life cycle, when differentiation is high and competition low, or when duties are high or imports prohibited.

PRICE LEADERSHIP. With price leadership, the prevailing price is determined by one firm and followed by others. Coordination among sellers often exists without a formal cartel organization when oligopolies market undifferentiated products. In this case there is a high risk that market shares will change with price changes. Tacit collusion in price leadership is usually subject to public monitoring.

ADMINISTERED PRICES. Prices are administered in regulated industries or industries with cartels. The successful initial efforts of the Organization of Petroleum Exporting Countries (OPEC) cartel to increase oil prices led to attempts to organize agroindustrial cartels for products such as bananas and sugar. These attempts failed because of the large number of producers, the less essential nature of the products, and the existence of substitute products.

CONTROLLED OR SUBSIDIZED PRICES. Because of the social and political importance of food prices, governments frequently use price controls and subsidies, often together, to achieve price stability, to increase food availability for poor, nutritionally vulnerable families, or to benefit politically important groups such as government employees. These government interventions can have a substantial effect on prices; for example, interventions reduced the prices of wheat, sugar, and beans in Egypt and edible oil in the Philippines by more than half.[28] A 10 percent decline in food prices can produce the equivalent of a 6–8 percent increase in real incomes of the poorest decile of the population.[29] Egypt's annual food subsidies in the early 1980s amounted to about $2 billion or 17 percent of the national budget;[30] India's totaled $700 million.[31] As a share of government budgets, food subsidies reached 27 percent in Bangladesh, 26 percent in China, and 14 percent in Peru and Sri Lanka in the early 1980s.[32] Sometimes these interventions have succeeded in achieving greater price stability. For example, between 1967 and 1980 the variance in wholesale rice prices in Bangkok was only a third of the variance in rice export prices.[33]

Economic austerity during the 1980s in many developing countries has led to cutbacks in subsidies and price decontrols, but such policy reversals can be disruptive, or worse, as the following example reveals.[34] The Zambian government in 1986 moved to reduce its maize subsidy. It decontrolled the retail price for higher-grade maize for breakfast meal and doubled the price that the private millers then had to pay to the government food marketing corporation for raw maize. The retail price for lower-grade maize flour was to remain unchanged, and the government's intention was to subsidize the millers in order to keep this flour price down. However, these subsidization arrangements were not firmed up, and so the private millers stopped producing the maize flour and just sold the breakfast meal at the new higher prices. The flour shortages and the higher meal prices led to widespread riots leaving fifteen people dead and hundreds injured. The government then nationalized all the major mills. The incident reveals the highly political nature of pricing in the agroindustrial area and the importance to agroindustries of carefully managing their relationships with government.[35]

To avoid such political problems and the financial difficulties arising from price controls imposed in inflationary environments, the agroindustry analyst should examine the feasibility of producing goods whose prices are not controlled. For example, one South

American dairy shifted its product line away from milk production, which was subject to price controls, to yogurt, ice cream, and cheese, which were not.

When the commodity is tradable internationally, it may be sold at two different prices, with the international price exceeding the domestic. This price differential may cause the firm to divert production into the international market, which may lead the government to impose a domestic quota system. For example, in one Latin American country with price controls and quotas, sugar processors resisted efforts to fortify sugar with vitamin A because the government would then inspect production flows more carefully and detect extralegal shipments made to a neighboring country with higher sugar prices. As long as local prices are significantly less than those prevailing in neighboring countries, cross-border flows, even though illegal, are likely to occur. These can have a significant impact on prices in that market (as well as create shortages in the home market), and so agroindustries should scrutinize the price policies and price levels (and exchange rate effects) of their products in neighboring countries. These price-induced cross-border flows are an example of the international linkages discussed in chapter 2; the agroindustry analyst must view the venture as part of a global industry where actions abroad, including government pricing policies, can affect domestic operations.

### Promotion

Almost all products are promoted to some extent in that consumers are provided with product information (price, quality, and so on) to use in the buying decision. Even a superior product will not reach its sales potential unless consumers are aware of its advantages. Food products are generally among the more heavily promoted consumer products. In the United States food processors spend about 3 percent of their revenues on advertising, which amounts to about 1.5 percent of the consumer's at-home food expenditures.[36] Advertising expenditures tend to increase as a percentage of GNP as countries' incomes rise and communication infrastructure develops. Stouffer's differentiation strategy, cited earlier, was greatly strengthened by the company's decision to increase its advertising expenditures to create a gourmet image, which not only distinguished the Stouffer's meals from the quick meals of its competitors, but also allowed the company to charge premium prices.[37] The promotional requirements for staples and undifferentiated commodities traded internationally are less than those of other, more processed products, but they still exist. The primary tasks in formulating a promotional strategy are deciding whom to reach, what to say, and how to say it.

AUDIENCE. The consumer analysis identifies the decisionmaking unit that is the target of the firm's promotion and specifies differences among members of the unit (for example, differences in sex, age, and position within the group). But because the end consumer is not always the decisionmaker, firms must often design promotion for both the purchaser and the end consumer.

Promotion directed toward the end user is a critical component in a "pull" strategy—stimulating consumer demand so that end users pull the product from the producer through the distributors to the consumers. Promotion can also be directed at wholesale and retail distributors in a "push" strategy in which the firm attempts to convince distributors of the product's advantages so that they will move the product through to the consumer.

Promotional strategies should be designed to avoid adversely affecting low-income groups. Some researchers assert that advertising directed toward marginal consumers creates a disincentive to save and thus diverts scarce resources from needed investments to consumption goods. However, promotional activities can contribute to greater market efficiency and consumer choice by reducing information imperfections. Advertising and modern promotion techniques can also be effective in "social marketing" projects that address various social problems; campaigns have been launched to promote child immunization and to stimulate the use of in-home oral rehydration packets to counter the life-threatening effects of dehydration from infant diarrhea.[38]

Firms should avoid stimulating excessive demand through promotion when a product is nutritionally unsound for consumers or when there is a high probability of product misuse. The analyst should assess the effect of increased product consumption on the nutritional well-being of low-income groups. If the product can displace others, the analyst should estimate the relative costs to consumers in caloric or protein content if nutritional intake might be decreased.

Consider infant formulas, which have replaced breastfeeding in some developing countries (even though breast milk is cheaper, of superior nutritional value, and more sanitary).[39] Media advertising and other sales techniques that appealed to convenience and status consciousness were among the factors that led many low-income women to view bottle feeding as a superior method of nourishing infants.[40] The relatively high price of the formula led some mothers to stretch the formula by diluting it, thus greatly reducing its nutritional value. Furthermore, because of the low level of education and the lack of potable water, hygienic cooking facilities, and adequate fuel in poor communities, sometimes the formula was mixed with polluted water, with dire consequences for some infants. The infant formula companies and the World Health Organization, in conjunction with concerned social advocacy groups, ultimately developed a code of conduct to regulate promotional and other marketing practices in developing countries.[41]

MESSAGE. The promotional message should be derived from an evaluation of consumers' information needs and from the analysis of the competitive market. Because consumers' information needs vary, there may be numerous promotional objectives, including supplying factual product information, generating product awareness, creating product image, stimulating immediate purchase, and providing reinforcement after purchase.

Some promotion is intended simply to stimulate primary demand for a category of product, especially when the product is new or there is little other advertising. Branding is used to stimulate selective demand for a particular company's product and is more effective when the product can be physically differentiated from those of competitors. The Peruvian corn starch processor mentioned earlier shaped its messages to educate potential consumers that the company's corn starch was technically equal to other starches traditionally used. After several years of slowly but successfully getting customers to switch, the company's message shifted toward creating brand loyalty. Kiwi fruit producers in New Zealand spent several years educating distributors and consumers about this "new" product, but they succeeded in creating a significant export market.

It is often difficult for agroindustries to differentiate their products, particularly when the processing is minor. Nevertheless, agroindustries have achieved product differentiation by instituting rigorous quality-control programs. Libyan groundnuts at one point sold at prices 25 percent above the prevailing world market price because of such control methods. Bananas and Colombian coffee have been branded with similar success. The Dutch leadership in the international flower industry has been strengthened by promotional efforts arranging trade fairs and flower exhibits, providing educational programs, and advertising; this effort is carried out by the Flower Council of Holland and supported by levies on growers and traders.[42] In the United States Perdue has achieved premium prices for its branded poultry products. Branding, however, places a significant responsibility on quality control at the processing and procurement stages because poor quality in a branded product can greatly hurt its image and future sales. Finally, promotional messages should be designed to meet the audience's capacity to understand and follow instructions on usage.

VEHICLE. Promotional messages can be communicated to audiences by direct or indirect methods. Direct methods are face-to-face encounters or telephone selling through salespeople. Direct techniques are generally more costly and have a lower breadth and coverage than indirect methods but a stronger effect on consumer behavior. Although telephone contact may achieve as broad and frequent coverage as some mass methods, such as mailings or advertising in periodicals, in many developing countries telephone ownership is limited and service defective, thereby diminishing this method's applicability. Low-income countries average 5 telephones per 1,000 people and upper-middle-income countries average 160 per 1,000.[43]

Indirect promotional vehicles include television, radio, film, newspapers, periodicals, billboards, posters, and leaflets. The distinctions among them reflect differences in the characteristics of the target audience. For example, if the audience has a low literacy rate, a firm would choose oral rather than written media. Likewise, lower-income segments in rural areas might be more readily reached by radio advertising rather than television advertising. Mass media vehicles can cover broad audiences at frequent intervals. Particularly in large urban areas, food companies make heavy use of television and radio advertising.

Direct and indirect techniques of promotion are not mutually exclusive—if it is cost-beneficial to use both techniques, they can be mutually reinforcing. Both techniques can be used with push or pull strategies. In general, if the product is new, complex, expensive, and not easily differentiated, the consumer buying process is complicated and risky, and personal selling is more effective.

## Distribution

Distribution is important in the marketing mix because it links the processor to the marketplace. It should be examined by looking at the structure and functions of the distribution system to assess integration and outlet options.

STRUCTURE. The structure of the distribution system can be described by the length of its channels—that is, the number of intermediaries between the manufacturer and the consumer. It can also be described by the breadth of the system—the number of wholesalers and retailers at each level. Finally, it can be described by the nature of the institutions operating it. At the wholesale level, these institutions can be full-line, limited-line, or specialty wholesalers who buy and resell goods. Agents and brokers also operate as wholesalers, but as commissioned sales agents for the manufacturer rather than as buyers of merchandise. Government marketing boards can also serve as wholesalers, particularly for major export products. Retail stores can be categorized according to the kind of goods offered—for example, convenience, shopping, or specialty.

Turning again to the Stouffer's example, its distribution strategy further strengthened its differentiation. It created value for the retailers by using a strong direct sales force and food brokers to provide rapid restocking and removal of damaged goods. These services and high attention to the client gained it relatively attractive shelf space.[44] Distribution relationships are what give life to the structure, and managing those relationships is one of the keys to competitive advantage.

FUNCTIONS.  Many functions must be performed to move the product from the processor to the consumer—including logistical operations (transport, assembly, repackaging, storage, and inventory management), financing, promotion, and information collection. These intermediary functions and services must be performed regardless of whether the system is free market or centrally planned. The more economically developed the country, the more sophisticated and higher quality the marketing services become. In the United States about 28 percent of the consumer's food dollar goes to the farmer while 72 percent goes for the processing and marketing functions.[45] Almost the inverse is true in many developing country commodity systems. For example, in Ghana in 1977, farmers received 71 percent of the retail price of rice, processors 12 percent, assemblers and wholesalers 12 percent, and retailers 5 percent.[46] As distribution functions grow more complex, greater value is added in the downstream activities in the production chain. Figure 3-6 shows that of the postharvest expenditures in the United States, processing absorbed 33 percent, while transportation, wholesaling, retail foodstores, and retail food services accounted for the rest.

The nature of agroindustrial products often requires specialized transportation capable, for example, of carrying refrigerated, bulk, or live goods. Transport reliability and efficiency is of major importance, especially when the product is both perishable and for export. For example, a Central American exporter of fresh vegetables had a transport network that moved produce from farm to packing plant by pickup truck, from plant to port by refrigerated trailer truck, from port to port by ferry, from port to distributor by trailer truck, and from distributor to retailer by truck and train.

**Figure 3-6.   *Shares of Post-harvest Food System Expenditures in the United States, 1989***

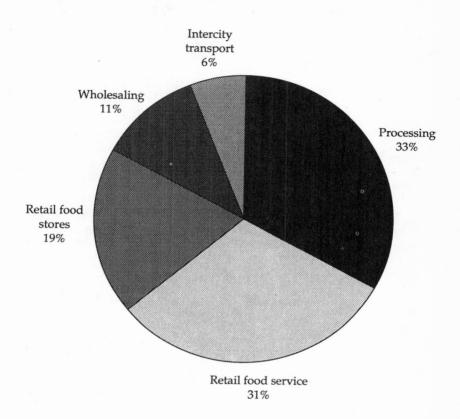

Intercity transport 6%

Wholesaling 11%

Processing 33%

Retail food stores 19%

Retail food service 31%

*Source*: U.S. Department of Agriculture data.

With such complex networks, it is often difficult to obtain the necessary vehicles, transport services, or managerial logistics. In a project's early stages these deficiencies can create serious and costly bottlenecks. In Central America's early attempts to export nontraditional fruits and vegetables to the U.S. market, transport service was uncoordinated and, at times, represented one-third of total costs (see table 3-2). The successful development of Colombia's cut flower industry required the establishment of a refrigerated air transport and warehousing system. In Turkey, a ferry system was developed to bypass the land route to Europe because exports of fresh produce suffered from slow overland transport. Transportation technology improvements can also expand a firm's market coverage. For example, milk distribution used to be confined to markets within 30 miles,

**Table 3-2.** *Cost Structure of Selected Central American Exported Fresh Produce, 1971–72*

| | Cucumbers, Guatemala | | Melons | | | |
| | | | El Salvador | | Honduras | |
| Cost item | Export cost (dollars per box) | Percentage of total cost | Export cost (dollars per box) | Percentage of total cost | Export cost (dollars per box) | Percentage of total cost |
|---|---|---|---|---|---|---|
| Production | 1.29 | 16.6 | 1.96 | 31.8 | 3.52 | 41.3 |
| Packing | 1.41 | 18.1 | 1.20 | 19.5 | 1.10 | 12.9 |
| Transport | 1.67 | 21.5 | 1.96 | 31.8 | 2.87 | 33.6 |
| Tariffs | 1.42 | 18.3 | 0.45 | 7.3 | 0.55 | 6.5 |
| Handling and repacking | 1.18 | 15.1 | n.a. | n.a. | 0.25 | 2.9 |
| Commissions | 0.81 | 10.4 | 0.59 | 9.6 | 0.24 | 2.8 |
| Total | 7.78 | 100.0 | 6.16 | 100.0 | 8.53 | 100.0 |

n.a. Not available.

*Source:* Direct survey by James E. Austin, cited in Ray A. Goldberg, *Agribusiness Management for Developing Countries—Latin America* (Cambridge, Mass.: Ballinger Publishing Co., 1974), p. 180.

but with refrigerated bulk tankers market access has expanded to 2,000 miles. It should be noted that transportation rates and services are often highly regulated by government, thus revealing yet another impact point of the "mega-force."

In most developing countries food wholesaling tends to be highly fragmented and relatively small-scale. However, many governments have modernized wholesaling facilities for fresh produce such as fruit, vegetables, grains, and meat. This investment can be highly desirable because it reduces waste, preserves product quality (including nutrients), shortens the length of the distribution channel, and increases transport and handling efficiencies. As of the mid-1980s, twenty of fifty-nine major cities throughout Latin America, Asia, and Africa had developed new wholesale markets, eighteen were planning them, and twenty-one remained saddled with obsolete ones.[47]

The success of modern facilities depends, however, on ensuring the patronage of buyers and sellers. One new wholesale market in an Asian nation had trouble getting wholesalers to use the facility because it was located on the outskirts of the city and was difficult for the wholesalers' retail customers to reach, although it was easily accessible to producers and processors supplying the wholesalers. Furthermore, people operating the booths were forbidden to sleep overnight in the new facilities, a proscription that conflicted with social traditions.

Which segment of the distribution chain undertakes the storage functions is affected by economics. The capital investment in physical facilities can be a barrier to entry and is what sometimes leads governments to develop public markets as described above. But storage economics are driven primarily by carrying costs. Consequently, government macropolicy affecting interest rates directly affects the cost of working capital tied up in stored inventories.

Prices of agricultural raw materials and processed goods should reflect these carrying costs by rising from the end of one harvest until the beginning of the next. However, if the government imposes price ceilings on the product to keep prices down for urban consumers, then private merchants will store the goods only until they can no longer cover their carrying and other costs when they sell at the controlled price. After that point in the year, the government will either have to take over the storage function or pay the private merchants to do it. If rural prices are not controlled, merchants might even buy the price-controlled goods in the urban centers and resell them in the rural areas at higher prices (agroindustries supplying the merchants might similarly shift their sales to nonprice-controlled areas in the country).[48]

OPPORTUNITIES FOR INTEGRATION. A processor must decide between using the distribution services of the existing institutions and undertaking distribution itself. To develop its own distribution services, a firm must integrate forward. Vertical integration is a question of degree. A processor does not necessarily have to assume all the functions of a wholesaler or even retailer. Rather, the analyst should scrutinize each of the activities in the postprocessing production chain to determine whether cost advantages could be gained or value created if the processor took over various of the activities currently done by others.

Cost advantages might be gained from economies of scale in handling, storage, or transport. Efficiencies might arise from shortening the channel, reducing transport time, and decreasing handling frequency. Differentiation might be obtained by vertical integration that enables the agroindustry to become closer to, more knowledgeable of, and more responsive to its buyers. One snack food manufacturer in Mexico vertically integrated by mounting a direct sales force that delivered the snacks directly to small retail stores. This strategy ensured maximum outlet coverage and gave high delivery frequency to the stores, thereby minimizing their inventory carrying requirements, which were constrained by their small physical facilities and limited capital. It also ensured freshness of the merchandise, high control over point-of-purchase displays, and a rapid and efficient collection system for accounts payable. As the country's single largest purchaser of trucks, the company also gained bargaining power with its vehicle supplier.

Another factor relevant to the integration decision is channel control. The locus of power in the distribution system is often indicated by structural concentration—for example, a few processors who supply many distributors or many processors who supply a few distributors (a large supermarket chain, for instance). When structural concentration occurs, the power lies with the few because many organizations are dependent on them. Power may also be derived by controlling a central function such as storage or transport. If the distribution system's power is highly concentrated and the risk to the processor is high, the processor should consider forward integration.

Increased control, however, increases fixed and working capital requirements and the need for more and different managerial and technical skills. In addition, the relatively fixed investment in distribution facilities may decrease the firm's flexibility in responding to the new distribution requirements of a changing market. Integration can be precluded if the government has introduced a marketing board as a monopsonistic wholesaler.[49]

Forward vertical integration is also difficult because of the strength of distributor-retailer relations. This point can be illustrated by the Filipino flour mill, described earlier, that had neglected its marketing system when protected by an import tariff. When the tariff was removed, the company had no sales force and relied entirely on wholesalers who gave preference to imported brands. The mill considered organizing a sales force and selling directly to the bakeries, but the bakeries resisted because they had developed loyalties to the distributors. The wholesalers gave credit to the bakers (often to meet personal needs), had long-standing friendships with them, and sometimes were even related by family and ethnic ties. These social bonds created barriers to forward vertical integration.

OUTLET OPTIONS. If the analyst decides to use existing distribution channels, he or she must then choose wholesalers and retailers. As discussed above, wholesalers can be selected according to cost, quality, dependability, and control. Retail outlets, however, must reflect the product, the market segment, and the prospective consumers' buying process. It is necessary to choose retailers even when processors vertically integrate through the wholesaling level.

The retail options are intensive, selective, or exclusive, and they differ in breadth. The intensive strategy maximizes breadth and consumer coverage and is appropriate for low-priced, undifferentiated, high-use products such as sugar. Because consumers will not shop around for these products, coverage is critical to intensive retailing. The selective strategy employs a few chosen stores and is appropriate for expensive and differentiated products that people will selectively shop for and that can be sold through direct personal selling—for example, a suit of clothes. With exclusive distribution, one outlet is given the franchise for the product within a competitive area. This is appropriate for specialty goods that are either highly complex, costly items, or luxury, low-use items such as caviar. In all cases, the analyst should review the proposed distribution system to ensure an appropriate product-distribution fit.

### Integrating the Mix

The elements of the marketing mix should be designed to be internally consistent and mutually reinforcing. For example, it would not be consistent to combine an extensive distribution system with a skimming price strategy, or an exclusive distribution system with a broad, mass media promotional program.

The marketing mix for a particular product must also relate to the company's entire line so that sales will not be diverted from another of the company's products. If sales are diverted, such "cannibalization" can make an individual product appear highly successful without significantly benefiting the company as a whole. Sometimes the marketing mix can be adjusted so that consumers will remain with the company and "trade up" from one product to a higher-priced, more elaborate product—for example, from canned peas to frozen mixed vegetables. The marketing approach must also be related to a company's financial, organizational, production, and procurement operations.

The integration of the marketing components into an internally consistent whole that is compatible with the company's product line and the other managerial functions constitutes the marketing plan.[50] Based on the enterprise's marketing objectives, this plan should guide the project through the competitive market environment.

Responses by the competition to the marketing plan will vary according to the product's market position. For example, there will be little reaction when the product is patented, when it captures a low market share, when it is not comparable to competing products, when it is only modestly profitable, or when competitors are financially weak.

Even small-scale industries should have explicit marketing plans, which will be relatively simple because of their narrow product lines and small size but which will serve as a check to ensure attention to the necessary marketing activities. More often than not, it is marketing problems that cause small-scale industries to fail or stagnate.

## Demand Forecasting

Demand forecasts are needed to estimate the economic implications of the marketing plan and are used to project profitability, financial and raw material needs, and plant capacity. Although final demand projections are dependent on a final marketing plan because it sets the parameters of the market segment, the demand forecasts and marketing plans must be developed simultaneously. For example, the expected market size should be estimated early and compared with the minimum economical size for the plant or with the availability of raw material. If market demand does not support this production scale or exceeds raw material supply, the study need go no further. Similarly, the firm would benefit in selecting elements of the marketing mix by projecting the effect of each at various sales volumes.

Forecasting involves collecting and analyzing past data to understand future market behavior and to reduce the uncertainty of decisionmaking. The analyst should carefully examine the forecasting data and techniques, which can be placed in three main categories: judgmental estimates, time-series analyses, and causal models.

### Data Considerations

Before using data for forecasting, an analyst should consider the kind of data he or she needs—including sources, reliability, and underlying assumptions.

TYPE OF DATA. Forecasts should be made in physical and monetary values, and units of measure should be standardized to facilitate comparisons. One agroindustry's rosy sales forecast was based on a steadily upward industry trend. However, these historical figures were in current values; their conversion to constant dollars revealed a historical deterioration in real terms. Unfortunately, this procedural weakness was not discovered until after the project had been launched with unexpectedly disappointing results. Different types of prices—wholesale, retail, and international (free-on-board [f.o.b.] or cost-insurance-freight [c.i.f.])—should not be mixed. Distribution markups represent these price level differences. Manufacturer-level prices are the most relevant for agroindustrial demand projections unless the strategy is to integrate vertically forward into the wholesaling level.

Analysts also must decide what time period the data should encompass. One agroindustry project's demand forecasts turned out to be erroneous because they looked only at the most recent year's prices, which were at a historical peak. The time frame decision should consider how representative the prior years have been in relation to the projected period and which years have used consistent methods of data collection.

Data are most useful when they can be disaggregated to correspond to product categories and market-segment characteristics. This disaggregation is usually not published, and analysts may have to calculate it themselves.

DATA SOURCES. Market sales data can be gathered from primary or secondary sources. Primary sources include reports by trade associations, research studies by educational institutions and international agencies, and company analyses. Data collection from primary sources requires market-research techniques described in the "Consumer Analysis" section of this chapter. Secondary sources include government documents (such as customs statistics, national income-accounts data, industry studies, family budget surveys, or census data) and private sector studies.

DATA RELIABILITY. Analysts should verify the accuracy of the data to ensure reliable projections by reviewing the data-collection techniques, and they should retain a skeptical attitude toward published statistics because erroneous statistics tend to perpetuate themselves. For example, one country's production of wheat flour was estimated in 1960 from a nonrandom sample of wheat mills. The 1970 statistics were still based on the 1960 data, although increased by a factor for the annual population growth. Analysts should be suspicious of historical data that increase uniformly because agroindustries have a significant factor of variability.

In reviewing the data for reliability, analysts should make sure that the data sample was representative and that no historical aberrations occurred. That can be a difficult process. For example, in table 3-3 the historical data for the consumption of tinned milk in Ghana is shown in support of the country's consideration of a tinned milk factory project. An inspection of the statistics might indicate that 1961 was a nonrepresentative year. Further investigation, however, reveals that 1962 and 1963 were actually the nonrepresentative years because the government then had imposed foreign exchange controls and import

**Table 3-3.** *Tinned Milk Consumption in Ghana, 1955–63*

| Year | Total consumption (containers) | Per capita consumption (fluid ounces)[a] |
|------|-------------------------------|------------------------------------------|
| 1955 | 67,949 | 20.81 |
| 1956 | 76,549 | 22.63 |
| 1957 | 95,015 | 27.37 |
| 1958 | 104,126 | 29.23 |
| 1959 | 124,968 | 34.17 |
| 1960 | 131,130 | 34.93 |
| 1961 | 176,920 | 45.93 |
| 1962 | 162,676 | 41.16 |
| 1963 | 168,945 | 41.67 |

a. One fluid ounce = 29.573 milliliters.

*Source:* EDI (Economic Development Institute), *Tinned Milk Market Forecast,* EDI Case Study and Exercise Series IE-5218-5 (Washington, D.C.: World Bank, June 1976; revised September 1979), p. 7.

restrictions. In developing countries, statistics on "apparent consumption" do not necessarily reflect true demand because expenditures can be skewed by import restrictions or other government regulations such as industrial licensing.

DATA ASSUMPTIONS. The preceding example also reveals the importance of examining the assumptions underlying the projections. It is useful to test both the quantity and price assumptions of projections. For example, suppose a prospective spice manufacturer projects sales on the assumption that historical industrial trends will continue (see table 3-4). If prices or volume are 10 percent lower than expected, however, profits will fall by 25 percent. If prices and volume are both 10 percent under forecast, profits (and return on invest-

**Table 3-4.** *Sensitivity Analysis for Spice Sales*

| Sales item | Sales scenario | | |
|------------|----------------|---|---|
| | Historical trend holds | Prices or volume fall 10 percent | Prices and volume fall 10 percent |
| Unit price (dollars) | 0.05 | 0.45 | 0.45 |
| Total volume (units sold) | 10,000,000 | 10,000,000 | 9,000,000 |
| Total revenue (dollars) | 500,000 | 450,000 | 405,000 |
| Costs (dollars) | 300,000 | 300,000 | 300,000 |
| Profits (dollars) | 200,000 | 150,000 | 105,000 |
| Change in profits (percent) | 0 | 25 | 47.5 |

*Source:* Author's calculations.

ment) will drop by 47.5 percent. Changes in price or volume are magnified when translated into profit. Accordingly, this prospective manufacturer should reevaluate sales assumptions because of their extensive financial consequences.

### Forecasting Methods

There are three principal forecasting methods—judgmental estimating, time-series analysis, and causal modeling—each with its own characteristics, uses, and limitations.

JUDGMENTAL ESTIMATES. Some degree of judgment is implicit in all estimates, but when statistical data are limited, the opinions of knowledgeable observers must be the basis for the forecast. Opinions are derived from experience, which is itself a form of historical data, and the experiences of operators in the industry to be entered (for example, manufacturers, distributors, salespeople, bankers, consultants) often provide a reasonable basis for projecting market dynamics. Experience is even more valuable when taken from a systematic sampling of experts on the targeted segment. The most common judgmental forecasting methods are the following:[51]

- *Sales-force composite.* The sales estimates of individual salespersons are pooled into an aggregate sales forecast.
- *Executive jury.* The managers from different functional areas of the enterprise (for example, marketing, production, finance) jointly prepare sales estimates.
- *Panel consensus.* A group of industrial experts discusses and develops a common opinion and prediction.
- *Delphi.* The opinions of experts are gathered by questionnaires, and the results are returned to the experts iteratively until convergence is approximated.
- *Cross-impact analysis.* The forces that are likely to affect the forecast are identified, and experts systematically assess the effects of these forces on each other and on the forecast.

TIME-SERIES ANALYSIS. Time-series methods relate sales to time rather than to causal factors that may underlie sales performance. Using historical data to identify and project past patterns and trends, these methods involve fitting a curve to the data and include freehand, semi-average, least-squares, and trend-line projections.

In projecting trends, analysts should note the seasonal, secular, cyclical, and random variations. These factors are particularly important for agroindustries, which often face considerable price variability both seasonally and across years. Historical statistics can be adjusted to be more representative. For example, sales for a particular period can be estimated by using a moving average of preceding months. Time series can be separated into seasonal or cyclical trends. Similarly, data can be weighted differently through exponential weighting—for example, by assigning higher weight to years that are thought to be more representative of future trends. These methods all represent various kinds of moving averages and may be defined as follows:[52]

- *Free-hand projection.* The analyst plots the historical time-series data and projects them linearly.
- *Semi-average projection.* The analyst divides the series in half, calculates the average of each, and connects the two averages on the graph.
- *Least-squares curve fitting.* The analyst fits a curve to the time-series data by minimizing the squared error between the actual observations and the estimated curve.
- *Mathematical trend curve projection.* The analyst fits a known mathematical curve (with established properties) to the time-series data.
- *Simple moving average.* The analyst weights past observations by $1/n$, where $n$ is the number of observations; as new observations are made, they replace older ones in the calculation of revised averages.
- *Weighted moving average.* This method is the same as the simple moving average, except that the analyst attaches different weight to different observations based on their expected predictions.
- *Exponential smoothing.* This method is the same as the weighted moving average, except that the analyst uses a set of weights that decreases exponentially, thereby giving more recent observations more weight.
- *Box-Jenkins method.* The analyst uses an autoregressive, moving-average linear model to express forecasts as a linear combination of past actual values (or errors).
- *Classical decomposition.* With this method the analyst decomposes a time series into seasonal, cyclical, trend, and irregular elements.

CAUSAL MODELS. Causal techniques attempt to identify those variables that predict sales behavior. Regression analysis is one example of a causal technique that improves the accuracy of estimating. Simple regression uses one variable to predict sales, whereas multiple regression uses several—for example, population, growth, income,

**Table 3-5.** *Alternative Estimates of Per Capita Tinned Milk Consumption in Ghana, 1964–68*
(ounces)

| Year | Consultant's judgment | Regression analysis |
|------|----------------------|---------------------|
| 1964 | 44.75 | 45.97 |
| 1965 | 46.75 | 48.72 |
| 1966 | 48.50 | 51.48 |
| 1967 | 50.25 | 54.24 |
| 1968 | 52.00 | 56.99 |

*Note:* Estimates are projected from consumption data in table 2-3; 1 fluid ounce = 29.573 milliliters.
*Source:* EDI, *Tinned Milk Market Forecast*, p. 7.

and price. The relations between the variables and sales can be plotted, and the points can be connected by a regression line. The relations can be calculated mathematically by the least-squares technique, which minimizes the sum of the squared deviations of the points from the line. Although regression analyses can be performed manually, inexpensive computer-program packages are also available to facilitate the task.

It can be seen from the data in table 3-3 that future sales of the proposed Ghanaian tinned milk factory could be estimated by eye (judgmentally) or by using a formal regression analysis. These alternatives can be compared in table 3-5, which presents a consultant's estimates and those of regression analysis. The difference of approximately 10 percent in the 1968 projected volumes could have a significant effect on the firm's finances and capacity requirements.

Regression analysis is commonly used to determine demand, with price or income changes, by deriving elasticity coefficients. The concept of price and income elasticity is particularly important in demand analysis for food and fiber projects. Elasticity estimates can be calculated from cross-sectional data from family expenditure surveys. The elasticity coefficient, $e$, is expressed mathematically as $e = (\Delta Q/Q) \div (\Delta P/P)$, where $Q$ is quantity demanded and $P$ is price. The change in sales resulting from a change in price is an indicator of consumer price sensitivity. When the percentage change in demand is greater than the change in price (a coefficient greater than 1.0), the demand is elastic. When the reverse is true (a coefficient less than 1.0), the demand is inelastic. When the two changes are equal and produce a coefficient of 1.0, there is unitary elastic demand. The concept of elasticity is also applied to demand changes that result from income changes.

For example, in rural Java in 1976 the overall price elasticity for rice was found to be −0.6; that is, if rice prices rose 10 percent, consumption would fall 6 percent. But consumer behavior for the same product varied by income level. For low-income consumers the income elasticity for rice was about 1.0; that is, a 10 percent change in income would lead to an equivalent consumption change. In contrast, the income elasticity for high-income households was zero or slightly negative.[53] Clearly, pricing strategy can have very different effects across different income groups. Consequently, demand forecasting needs to be disaggregated and tailored to the socioeconomic market segments identified in the marketing research and analysis. It is also important to recognize the cross-price elasticities; the price of one product may lead consumers to switch to substitute products.[54]

Econometric methods attempt to measure the relations between several variables assumed to be demand determinants and to specify the degree of confidence that can be placed in those relations. Several sets of regression equations are used. Econometric demand models have three aspects: identifying the variables, specifying the relations, and making the projections. These models integrate the relations of multiple variables in the estimate; thus, they more accurately reflect reality. The main causal methods may be defined as follows:[55]

- *Simple regression.* The analyst statistically relates one possible explanatory variable to sales.
- *Multiple regression.* The procedure is the same as above, except that more than one explanatory variable (with intercorrelations) is used.
- *Simultaneous equation systems.* The analyst uses a set of interdependent regression equations.
- *Input-output analysis.* The analyst uses a system of linear equations that indicates which inputs are needed to obtain certain outputs.

EVALUATION OF TECHNIQUE. The project analyst should evaluate the forecasting technique because each method is appropriate to different circumstances. The marketing manager should balance the cost of the technique against the desired accuracy to select the forecasting method. The requirement for accuracy is derived from factors such as the amount of capital being used, the firm's familiarity with the market, the uncertainty of demand factors, and the degree of risk decisionmakers are willing to take. (An entrepreneur might be satisfied with lower accuracy than might the banker considering a loan to the project.)

The success and accuracy of any forecasting method is dependent on the reliability of the data. Sophisticated econometric models and mathematical techniques cannot correct weaknesses in the original

## Table 3-6. *Evaluation of Forecasting Methods*

| Method | Cost | Accuracy | Skill requirement | Data requirement | Speed |
|---|---|---|---|---|---|
| *Judgmental* | | | | | |
| Sales-force composite | L | L | L | L | H |
| Executive jury | M | M | M | M | M |
| Panel consensus | M | M | H | M | M |
| Delphi | M | M | H | M | L |
| Cross-impact analysis | H | M | H | H | L |
| *Time-series* | | | | | |
| Free-hand | L | L | L | L | H |
| Semi-average | L | L | L | L | H |
| Least-squares | L | L–M | L | L | H |
| Mathematical curve | L | L–M | L–M | L | H |
| Simple moving average | L | L | L | L | H |
| Weighted moving average | L | L | L | L | H |
| Exponential smoothing | L | L–M | L | L | H |
| Box-Jenkins | H | H | H | H | M |
| Decomposition | M | M | H | M | M |
| *Causal* | | | | | |
| Simple regression | M | M | M | M | M |
| Multiple regression | M | M–H | H | H | M |
| Simultaneous equation | H | H | H | H | L |
| Input-output | H | H | H | H | L |

L, low; M, moderate; H, high.

*Note:* These rankings and the weights of the criteria can vary with the specific situations of individual firms or projects.

data. For example, econometric models may be no more accurate than time-series analyses when structural changes are occurring in the economy.[56] Project analysts who are not economists should not be intimidated by demand equations. Rather, they can examine data and assumptions and let the mathematical analysts verify the estimating technique. Finally, analysts should recognize that different forecasting techniques may need to be employed at different points in the product life cycle and that forecasting should be adjusted accordingly.[57]

Thus, the criteria for selecting a forecasting method are several and depend upon the particular needs, resources, and data and product situation of the specific user. Among the likely criteria are the method's cost, accuracy, skill and data requirements, and speed. These criteria are used in table 3-6 to rank the various forecasting methods discussed in this section.

A final comment on forecasting: It is important to emphasize the need for sensitivity analysis. Market prices, especially of commodity-type goods selling in or affected by the international markets, are often quite volatile. Year-to-year price swings of 25 percent are not unusual. Financial projections should test the impact of such revenue variations on profitability. In ascertaining the likelihood or magnitude of such volatility, one should look beyond historical patterns and examine possible competitive responses. High international prices are likely to stimulate additional supplies. One should analyze the structure of the global industry to determine which countries have the capacity and need to expand or begin production. For example, one cotton production and ginning project was established in the Caribbean in 1981 with expectations that the prevailing strong price of $0.84 per pound would continue. However, China increased its production, and prices plummeted to $0.47 by 1985. Similarly, if the agroindustry is opening up a new business line in domestic markets, it is likely that imitators will follow, especially if barriers to entry are relatively low, thereby causing pressure on prices or volume. If an agroindustry is entering an existing market, established competitors may lash back with serious price discounting in order to hold on to their market share. Consequently, demand forecasts must incorporate competitive response into the analysis.

## Summary

Consideration of the marketing factor is vital to project analysis because it provides the market information to assess a project's viability. Too frequently, a firm's substantial efforts and investments are focused on procurement and processing operations—the other two of agroindustry's three main areas of activity—only to have the expected benefits never materialize because of an inadequate marketing analysis. Systems analysis views these three main activities of an agroindustrial project as closely interdependent.

Because projects enter existing markets, it is essential that firms know the market environments. Accordingly, marketing analysis should examine consumers and competitors. A consumer analysis should identify consumer needs, potential market segments, and the buying process. For this analysis, the firm must conduct market research. A concomitant analysis of the competitive environment should analyze the market structure, the basis of competition, and the government policies and actions affecting competition.

From analyses of the consumer and competition, a firm formulates its project's marketing plan. The plan should set out the project's marketing strategy for product design, pricing, promotion, and distribution. These elements of the marketing mix should be integrated in a comprehensive strategy that will place the product in an optimal marketing position relative to consumers' needs and competing products. The marketing plan should also consider the rest of the company's product line as well as the company's organizational, financial, production, and procurement operations to ensure the cohesion of the project's strategy. The marketing plan should anticipate the competitive reaction and formulate a response that will maintain the project's viability in a dynamic market environment.

The marketing analysis uses and is developed with the demand forecast. Analysts should consider the type, sources, reliability, and underlying assumptions of the data used in the forecasts. Each of the various forecasting methods—judgmental estimating, time-series analysis, and causal modeling—is appropriate to particular conditions. The analyst should determine how much accuracy is desired of the forecasting and balance this finding with the cost of using more sophisticated estimating techniques. Although project decisionmaking is never free from uncertainty, sound forecasting can reduce the ambiguity. Skill and data requirements and the speed with which the forecast can be made are additional considerations in selecting appropriate methods.

## The Marketing Factor: Salient Points for Project Analysis

A project analyst should consider the following questions when reviewing the marketing dimensions of an agroindustrial project.

### Consumer Analysis

*Who are the potential consumers?*
- Socioeconomic, cultural, demographic characteristics?
- Market segments?
- Possible forms of processed product?
- Positioning options for the product?

*Why would consumers buy the product?*
- Physiological, sociological, psychological needs?
- Expressed reasons for purchasing: sustenance? sensory appeal? status? convenience? necessity?
- Relative importance of needs and reasons?
- Implications for the marketing plan?

*How would consumers buy the product?*
- Decisionmaking unit?
- Impulse or planned purchase?

- Purchase frequency?
- Seasonality?
- Purchase location?
- Credit or cash?
- Implications for the marketing plan?

*What market information and methods of data collection are needed?*
- Data needs?
- Data sources?
- Methods of data collection?
- Reliability?
- Cost?
- Value of additional information?
- Capacity of enterprise to gather data?

### Competition Analysis

*What is the product's market structure?*
- Existing competitors?
- Possibilities of new entrants and potential substitutes?
- How many competitors?
- Location relative to markets and raw material?
- Size of sales, assets, market share?
- Changes in market shares?
- Seriousness of barriers to entry?
- Significance of economies of scale, absolute cost advantages, vertical system control, brand franchises, and switching costs?

*What is the basis of competition in the industry?*
- Nature of cost advantages?
- Cost control possibilities?
- Efficiency gains through activity or resource reconfiguration?
- Cost advantage opportunities in procurement operations?
- Economies of scale and capacity utilization?
- Cost effects of location?
- Competitive pricing implications of cost advantages?
- Nature of differentiation?
- Differentiation through raw materials or manufacturing ingredients?
- Innovations through product design, processing technology, packaging?
- Product life cycle implications for cost advantages and differentiation?
- Buyers' perception of value?
- Cost of achieving differentiation?

*How do government policies and actions affect the competitive environment?*
- Effect of duties and quotas?
- Impact of overvalued exchange rates?
- Implications of subsidies to consumers, producers, exporters?
- Role of state-owned enterprises?
- Consequences of regulatory measures: food safety standards? capacity restrictions? licensing? patents? antitrust laws?

### The Marketing Plan

*Was the product adequately designed?*
- Characteristics desired by consumers?
- Cost of quality improvements?
- Product's concept and prototype tested?
- Results and design adjustments?
- Final product market-tested?
- Design fit with consumer needs?

*Was the appropriate pricing strategy adopted?*
- Cost-plus pricing feasible?
- Basis for markup?
- Penetration pricing's effect on entry barriers, market size, and share?
- Legal or ethical acceptability of predatory or preemptive pricing?
- Volume effect of loss-leader pricing?
- Feasibility of skimming?
- Industry price leader?
- Effects of following or deviating from price leader?
- Basis of administered prices?
- Futures markets or long-term contracts as pricing mechanism?
- Existence and effects of controlled or subsidized prices?
- How to manage price negotiations with government?
- Feasibility of nonprice-controlled products?
- Implications of price policies, levels, and exchange rates in neighboring countries?

*Was the right promotional strategy formulated?*
- Audience identified?
- Consumers' information needs specified?
- Information supplied about competitors?
- Purpose of message?
- Impact of branding?
- Adequacy of quality-control procedures?
- Form of communication consistent with audience's capacity to receive?

- Chance of misinterpretation or misuse?
- Share of audience reached?
- Frequency of reach?
- Cost of promotional vehicle?
- Cost-effectiveness of combined direct and indirect promotional techniques?

*Will the distribution system effectively link the manufacturer to the marketplace?*
- Length of channels?
- Number of distributors at each level?
- Types of wholesalers and retailers?
- How logistical functions performed?
- What other service functions performed?
- Locus and basis of controlling power in channel?
- Effect of power distribution on project viability?
- Control, economic, and managerial implications of forward vertical integration?
- Cost advantages or differentiation via integration?
- Social, political, or legal barriers to forward integration?
- Cost, quality, and dependability of existing services and facilities?
- Distributor's managerial capabilities and customer orientation?
- Intensive, selective, or exclusive retail-outlet strategy?
- Consistency of outlet intensity with market segment and buying process?

*Are elements of the marketing mix integrated in a viable marketing plan?*
- Elements of mix internally consistent?
- Effect on other products in company's line?
- Compatibility with company's financial, organizational, production, and procurement operations?
- Likely competitive reaction?
- Adjustments in marketing strategy?

### Demand Forecasting

*Are the forecasts based on sound data?*
- Price data consistent?
- Units of measure standardized?
- Data disaggregated by market segment?
- Primary data generated?
- Secondary sources used?
- Data collected reliably?
- Data sample representative?

- Data verified?
- Underlying assumptions of data?
- Sales and profit sensitive to changes in assumptions?

*Are the forecasting methods appropriate?*
- Source of judgmental estimates?
- Basis of source's expertise?
- Other opinions possible?
- Time-series data representative?
- Consideration of seasonal, secular, cyclical, and random variations?
- Regression technique?
- Estimates of price and income elasticity?
- Variables used in econometric model?
- Causal relations assumed in model?
- Rationale for variable selection and causal assumptions?
- Acceptable level of accuracy?
- Cost and value of increasing accuracy?
- Applicability of previous forecasting methods?
- Data and skill requirements of methods?
- Speed of conducting forecast?

# 4 *The Procurement Factor*

BEFORE AN AGROINDUSTRY COMPANY INVESTS in a processing plant, the procurement of raw material inputs must be studied as carefully as the marketing activities. Agroindustries transform inputs; if those inputs are defective, processing and marketing will suffer accordingly. In addition, because raw materials are the dominant cost for most agroindustries, the procurement system is a major determinant of the project's economic feasibility and competitive advantage. Procurement is also critical to the project's effect on rural development because it links the industrial and agricultural sectors: by transmitting market stimuli to the farmer, the procurement system directly affects rural families.

## Primary Elements

An effective agroindustrial procurement system has five characteristics that provide a solid foundation for the processing operation: sufficient quantity of inputs, adequate quality of inputs, time-sensitive operation, reasonable cost, and efficient organization. In short, a well-organized procurement system is able to supply enough raw material of acceptable quality at the appropriate time and at a reasonable cost. This chapter examines each of the five characteristics of an agroindustrial procurement system, focusing on the following questions:

- *Quantity.* What factors determine how much raw material is produced? How do competing uses for the raw material affect supply?
- *Quality.* What quality is demanded by the market? What factors affect quality? How is quality controlled?
- *Time-sensitivity.* How do seasonality, perishability, and availability constrain the procurement of raw materials?
- *Cost.* What affects the cost of raw materials? What pricing mechanisms are feasible and desirable?
- *Organization.* How is the procurement system structured? How do power relationships affect procurement? How can vertical integration and producers' organizations affect procurement?

Furthermore, because government involvement in agriculture is often heavy, the linkages between procurement activities and government policies and actions are identified throughout the chapter.

## Adequate Quantity of Raw Materials

Agroindustries frequently end up with excess capacity because they fail to ensure an adequate supply of raw materials. Analysts should examine the factors determining the output of raw materials and consider competing uses for those materials that may reduce supply.

### Determinants of Raw Material Output

The first step in analyzing the supply of raw agroindustrial materials is to examine the principal determinants of production—the area to be planted and crop yields. (Herd size and procreation rates are the analogous production determinants for livestock.) For current crops, field surveys and trade sources give indications of the land area and yield. To discover supply trends, production statistics should be examined by region over several years, and the forces affecting area and yield variables should be considered. The analyst can then judge whether the historical production trend is likely to continue and what the implications are for project design. If the land is virgin or the crop new to the land, then extensive testing of soils, water, and climatic conditions is imperative, followed by pilot production. Supply projections should assume wider bands of variability for such new production.

AREA. One of the factors affecting land area is the prevailing and expected land-use pattern. The analyst should calculate the amount of both actual cultivated land and unused land that is "economically arable"—that is, capable of cultivation with the economic resources likely to be available. Trends in land expansion should be examined because increases in the amount of land cultivated can be the source of significant growth in supply. In Brazil from 1947 to 1965, yields increased little, if at all, but outward migration in frontier areas almost doubled crop area.[1] In Thailand the government allowed farmers to use free public forest land for agricultural expansion; between 1967 and 1977 more than three-fourths of the growth in rice production was due to these increased plantings.[2] The analyst should recognize, however, that new land may be of marginal quality and may produce lower, more variable, and less sustainable yields. One agroindustry was left without suppliers when the newly settled farmers abandoned production because of soil and water deficiencies.

The analyst must consider not only how much land is available for planting, but how often it can be planted. In Malaysia the establishment of a publicly funded irrigation and drainage infrastructure permitted double cropping, which by 1983 accounted for 40 percent of the country's rice production.[3] Irrigation also can reduce some of the uncertainty in supply caused by variability in rainfall. Analysts should carefully assess the actual and potential use of irrigation because of its large effect on production quantity.

Expanding the amount of land cultivated or the number of times a crop is planted puts increased demand on labor supplies. More mechanization, especially greater use of tractors, is one way to overcome labor shortages.[4] In many land-abundant and labor-short Latin American countries, mechanization has become almost a necessity; however, the use of tractors is growing even in land-short, labor-abundant Africa and Asia. Evidence indicates that tractors do not enhance yields, but rather displace labor or animal power.[5] This apparent contradiction to the "induced technological innovation" hypothesis may be partially explained by government policies—such as below-market interest rates, overvalued exchange rates, or subsidized fuel prices—that make owning/acquiring tractors profitable for farmers.

Land, the basic asset in agriculture, has multiple uses; hence a farmer has several options for what crops (or livestock) to produce. Analysts should examine the extent to which farmers switch among crops (or livestock) to gauge yearly variations in the supply of necessary raw material inputs for the processing plant. The less farmers switch, the more reliable the supply will be. There are barriers to switching, including soil or rainfall conditions, tradition, the nature of the crop (perennial versus annual), and specialized crop-specific fixed investments. The most powerful determinant , however, is profitability; farmers will shift to alternative crops if the profits exceed the switching costs. Government policies can affect this potential for profit. When the government in one Latin American country removed a production subsidy from vegetables, farmers shifted to other crops, leaving the processor short of raw materials. Farmers' opportunity costs (that is, what they could earn producing other crops) must be carefully assessed.

The analyst should consider the nutritional consequences for consumers and for the country when farmers change crops to supply the processing plant. For example, switching from maize to a condiment crop might decrease the national supply of a staple, thus increasing its price (assuming no imports), decreasing consumption by low-income consumers, and requiring the farmers to buy what they once grew. Replacing a food crop with a cash crop requires careful analysis. Sometimes the switch is beneficial. For example, in the 1970s in the savanna of Bogotá, Colombia, farmers began growing cut flowers for export, rather than the traditional staple, maize. A hectare planted with maize produced 1.3 tons with a profit of $52; planted with flowers for export, the hectare yields $48,000 profit a year, has a higher return on investment, gives more employment (mainly to low-income women) than maize, and generates foreign exchange and tax revenues.[6]

In areas surrounding major urban centers, agroindustries may have to compete with urbanization and industrialization projects for use of the farmland. Industrialization not only absorbs land but also bids away labor. For example, one fruit and vegetable processor found that farmhands and farmers began to change their occupations after an automobile manufacturing plant located in the area. Between 1949 and 1967 the number of farmers declined by 28 percent. By 1970 far more land was in the hands of part-time farmers than full-time farmers (see table 4-1). These changes decreased the amount of vegetables and fruits grown and thus had a significant effect on the processor's supply of raw material. Furthermore, the accompanying fragmentation of land prevented economies of scale in production.

The Colombian flower growers encountered similar pressures as Bogotá expanded and the value of land in the savanna appreciated significantly. Consequently, several producers moved their production to Ecuador and Costa Rica where land was more affordable.

In addition to anticipating industrialization and urban expansion, the analyst should examine any agrarian reform projects being planned for the producing regions under consideration. Some reforms can significantly affect processors, and it is advisable for land-

**Table 4-1.** *Ownership of Farmland after Start-up of Automobile Manufacturing Plant in Baden-Württemberg, Germany, 1970*

| Owner | Farms | | Acreage[a] | |
|---|---|---|---|---|
| | Thousands | Percent | Thousands | Percent |
| Full-time farmers | | | | |
| 100 percent of income | 12 | 4 | 930 | 22 |
| Part-time farmers | | | | |
| More than 50 but less than 100 percent of income | 121 | 42 | 2,420 | 57 |
| Less than 50 percent of income | 156 | 54 | 867 | 21 |
| Total | 289 | 100 | 4,217 | 100 |

a. 1 acre = 0.405 hectares.

*Source:* Otto Strecker and Reimar von Alvensleben, "The Unterland Corporation (B)," Case Study 4-372-252, Harvard University, Graduate School of Business Administration, Boston, 1972.

reform planners to coordinate the market-outlet benefits of their project with agroindustrial development. Conversely, agroindustries should try to support reform efforts to ensure an adequate supply of raw material.

YIELDS. When analyzing yields, the other determinant of output, the analyst should concentrate on quality of land, use of farm inputs, and techniques of cultivation (or animal husbandry). In general, yield-enhancing inputs are used more intensively where land expansion is no longer possible.[7] For example, during 1960–75 agricultural production in Thailand grew by more than 5 percent annually, primarily because of land expansion and irrigation. As the land supply was used up, growth dropped to 3.5 percent a year, and the government and farmers turned toward intensified use of inputs as the source of future growth.[8]

The quality of the land is an important yield determinant—the better the soil and the water, the higher the yield. Irrigation, too, can enhance the quality of the land and make it possible to plant more often. For an agroindustrial project that involves producers using new land or farming a new crop, the soil and water resources should be thoroughly analyzed. One project to set up a cotton gin in a new cotton-producing area relied on yield data from some existing farms and soil tests of only a few of the potential suppliers. Subsequent production results showed high variability in the yields from farm to farm, and additional soil analyses revealed large quality differences even between contiguous farms. Proximity does not guarantee uniformity. The gin fell far short of its raw material requirements and suffered the economic consequences of low capacity utilization.

The analyst should also determine the extent to which farmers use agrochemicals and improved seeds, what the results are for yields, and what barriers might exist to increased usage. For example, agrochemical or seed distribution channels might be limited in geographical coverage, or financing to help farmers purchase these inputs might be unavailable. Such barriers are common when raw material suppliers are small, traditional farmers.

By identifying barriers, the analyst can explore potential solutions—for example, improving the existing input supply channels, having the processing plant provide inputs to farmers, or organizing farmers to acquire needed inputs collectively. Sometimes the farmers remove the barriers themselves, as an anecdote from Malaysia reveals.[9] In one rice-growing area in Malaysia the research officers at a government station refused to release a new, but not fully tested, high-yielding variety that required less fertilizer and other inputs. Some farmers broke into the station, stole some bags of seeds, and planted them. Within two years almost two-thirds of the area was planted with the new variety, to the amazement of the researchers and extension workers.

The cost of inputs is a fundamental barrier to their use. The adequacy of rural infrastructure significantly affects costs. Deficient roads and transportation services raise input marketing costs. For example, the marketing costs for fertilizer are about $35 per ton in Asia, where population density is high and input delivery systems are relatively developed, but in many African countries with weaker transport systems, the costs have exceeded $100 per ton.[10] These weaknesses in infrastructure also impede farmers from taking their products to market and thus reduce their economic incentive to increase output. Government investment in rural roads can be of major importance to agroindustries' procurement systems.

Other government actions can also affect input costs. In Thailand a government tax on rice exports reduced the price that millers were willing to pay farmers, thereby lowering the farmers' incentive to buy inputs. The Thai government subsequently tried to increase input usage by subsidies. Subsidies can increase usage, but that can have perverse effects. For example, the Indonesian government's 80 percent subsidy on pesticide led to a 35 percent increase in usage. This excessive application made fish cultivation in the rice paddies unsustainable, poisoned coastal breeding grounds for shrimp, and caused the evolution of new pesticide-resistant biotypes of insects, which in turn threatened the rice crop.[11] The risk of such environmental degradation should be carefully assessed by the analyst.

Government trade policy can also affect input costs. Overvalued exchange rates, for example, might make imported inputs cheaper, but government import substitution strategies often lead to protection for domestic industries, including agricultural input manufacturers. For example, the net effective rate of protection for manufacturing in the Philippines was 15 percent; for agriculture it was −13 percent.[12] The result often is that the rural-urban terms of trade work against the farmers and create a disincentive to acquire costly yield-enhancing inputs. Sometimes it is not the price of an input that impedes usage but the lack of foreign exchange to acquire imported inputs. In one country, foreign exchange shortages hindered the import of production inputs, causing a serious deterioration in yields.

Lack of knowledge has also been a major barrier to farmers' use of inputs. A national survey of small farmers in Mexico revealed that the primary reason a majority did not use agrochemicals and improved seeds was uncertainty and lack of knowledge about these inputs (table 4-2). In general, small farms receive little technical advice, whereas larger farms heavily use agrochemical inputs and technical

**Table 4-2.** *Use and Primary Reasons for Nonuse of Agrochemicals and Improved Seeds by Small-scale Farmers in Mexico, 1973*
(percent)

| | | Reason for nonuse | | |
| | | Uncertainty and lack of | | |
| Input | Use | knowledge | High cost | Other |
|---|---|---|---|---|
| Fertilizer | 26 | 53 | 37 | 10 |
| Herbicides | 13 | 66 | 18 | 16 |
| Improved seeds | 16 | 74 | 19 | 7 |
| Insecticides | 23 | 61 | 25 | 13 |

*Source:* Compañía Nacional de Subsistencias Populares (CONASUPO), Mexico City.

assistance. For example, in the Mexican study only 4 percent of the traditional farmers received formal technical assistance, a figure that reflects the dichotomy between modern and traditional agriculture, the dichotomy between commercial and subsistence agriculture, and inequalities in land and income distribution. If an agroindustrial processor is to increase its supply of raw material by improving farm technology, it may have to stimulate government agencies or input suppliers to provide farm assistance or it may have to offer technical assistance independently.

Farmers using new techniques or inputs require a learning period. The analyst should not expect the full attainment of productivity gains immediately. The farmers need time to move down the learning curve, and supply projections should assume gradual increases and variability in the initial years.

Government policies that affect farm prices can also have a substantial effect on farm yields. Support prices, marketing boards, price and import controls, and export taxes can significantly affect farm prices. Often these are kept below international prices to protect powerful urban consumers or to provide a source of fiscal revenue. One study revealed that in several countries, domestic prices for various crops averaged 49 percent less than the international border prices.[13] As a result, the study estimated, banana production in Jamaica was reduced by 11.3 percent, sugar by 5.9 percent, and cocoa by 1.2 percent; in the Philippines copra production was reduced by 52.5 percent, sugar by 38.1 percent, and rice by 7.2 percent; and in Nigeria cotton production declined by 12.5 percent. One government's increased support price for basic grains induced farmers to shift out of vegetable production, leaving a canner short of raw materials. Gathering estimates of the price elasticity of supply and the effects of government policies is an important task in calculating the quantity of raw materials available to the agroindustry.

BIOTECHNOLOGY. For agroindustries, emerging developments in biotechnology hold significant potential for affecting agricultural production and therefore procurement operations. Biotechnology is "any technique that uses living organisms (or parts of organisms) to make or modify products, to improve plants or animals, or to develop microorganisms for specific uses."[14] (Appendix B at the end of this book provides a glossary of biotechnology terms.) Traditional biotechnology in the forms of plant and animal breeding and the use of microorganisms such as yeast in brewing, baking, and cheese making have long existed. What is now significant are new techniques that allow genetic makeup to be altered in specifically directed ways. Advances in molecular biology (genetic engineering) and cell biology (in vitro horticulture) are superior to traditional whole plant biology (conventional breeding) in that they can operate at the cellular and molecular levels, bypass sexual reproduction, and move genes among completely unrelated organisms, thereby targeting desired traits and eliminating time consumed by the multigenerational grow-out process of backcrossing used in traditional breeding.[15]

Molecular, cell, and whole plant biologies operate at different levels and use quite different techniques, but they are interrelated and may all be involved in the sequence of steps required for the ultimate creation of usable products. (Biochemistry is also used to help identify and regulate these processes.) Molecular biology identifies the specific gene with the desired characteristics, isolates the corresponding DNA (the genetic code), multiplies it (molecular cloning), and transfers it (gene splicing) to recipient crop cells through vectors such as plasmids or viruses or by microinjection or fusion, thereby joining DNA from different organisms in a process known as recombinant DNA (rDNA). Cell biology is involved through various tissue-culturing techniques in the laboratory, which regenerate the cells altered by molecular biology into whole plants expressing the targeted gene.

Plant and cell tissue culturing can also work independently of molecular biology processes. The first way is by clonal propagation, which is the asexual duplication of an existing desired species that cannot reproduce sexually or, like a hybrid, cannot reproduce sexually without losing its valued traits. Tissue culture is used to preserve varietal stability, that is, it creates replicas of the variety from a piece of tissue snipped from the original variety and cultured in a suspension of nutrients and hormones in a laboratory container. A second way cell tissue culturing works is through somaclonal variation, whereby mutations that may have desirable characteristics occur in the tissue-culturing process. A third way is by creating hybrids through the fusion of protoplasts (cells with their walls removed); this process uses chemically or electrically induced reactions to join different cells growing in suspension culture.

**Figure 4-1. *Biotechnology Processes and Relationships***

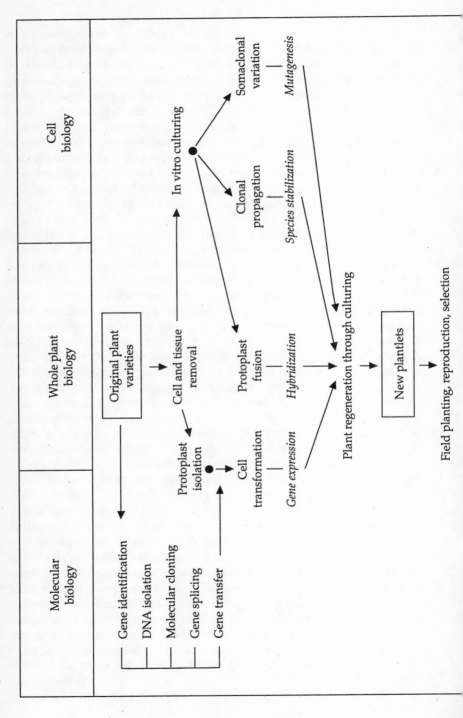

Whatever the alteration method, tissue culturing regenerates cells that are potential plants, and in a single six-square-inch petri dish, a scientist can work with 3 million to 5 million cells. To examine the same number of plants, traditional breeding technology would need, for example, about 2 acres for wheat or about 160 acres for corn.[16] Thus, tissue culturing is able to quickly produce massive numbers of plantlets, which are then grown by conventional plant breeding techniques.[17] Figure 4-1 depicts the relationships of molecular, cell, and whole plant biology.

Clearly, the potential of this technology is high, but the techniques and processes are still evolving. Locating the gene or gene complex (that is, specifying the DNA sequences) that give rise to desirable traits remains a demanding task. Nonetheless, considerable progress has been made. Using molecular biology combined with cell biology and plant breeding, scientists have been able to produce virus resistance in tobacco, cucumbers, and tomatoes. Field tests demonstrated effective protection against infection and yield loss.[18] Clonal propagation has been used to replicate elite palm oil trees. Another company uses tissue culture to produce disease-free sugarcane plantlets, which are then raised at quarantine farms. The stalks are cut and sold as planting material to growers who benefit from a 20 percent yield enhancement over the three-year crop cycle.[19]

Because cultured cells can be sterilized to remove plant bacteria, pathogen-free plant strains can be obtained, and have been for forage grasses and legumes.[20] Brunei is developing pathogen-free mushrooms as well as attempting to culture wild mushrooms obtained from its biologically rich forests. Similar progress has been made on developing plants resistant to insects. One company "immunized" a plant against caterpillars by inserting into the plant leaf a gene from a bacterium known to be lethal to caterpillars but nontoxic to humans, other mammals, fish, birds, and other wildlife.[21] Once fully developed, this approach could eliminate the need for farmers to purchase insecticide or fungicide or invest in spraying equipment, reduce the number of purchased inputs, create an ecologically safer environment, and provide more certain yields. Immunological biotechnology using monoclonal antibodies has given rise to diagnostic kits for pregnancy, ovulation, and many infectious diseases that afflict domestic animals; more recently it has led to detection methods for crop diseases, pest populations, and mycotoxins.[22]

In addition to enhancing yields, making them more certain, and reducing the costs of inputs, biotechnology is also being used to create raw material characteristics preferred by the agroindustries. For example, in response to the preferences of the millers and processors for a high-protein hard endosperm maize (corn), one seed company launched a research effort to track down the desired traits from exotic genes. It succeeded in producing hybrids that have 25 percent more crude protein, 22 percent more methionine, 33 percent more lysine than regular hybrids, and more hard endosperm than other hybrids (63 percent compared with 54–58 percent).[23] Many food processors are undertaking, directly or through contracts, biotechnology research to achieve distinctive features in their raw materials that will allow them to gain competitive advantage either through cost reductions or product differentiation.

An even more dramatic goal is to replace agricultural production of the raw material with industrial production of it through tissue culture. With existing methods this substitution would be economically feasible only for plant products worth $250–500 a kilogram.[24] Japan's Mitsui Petrochemicals Industries has successfully produced the plant dye shikonin using industrial plant tissue culture. This highly valuable red pigment comes from the root of a perennial herb native to China, Japan, the Republic of Korea, and the People's Democratic Republic of Korea. The tissue-culturing technique is estimated to be 800 times more productive than the traditional plant-culturing technique; takes less than a month to grow, compared with four years for the plant, and has a dye content fifteen times greater than the plant.[25]

In developing countries the development of biotechnology faces significant constraints. Existing research has taken place mostly in industrialized nations and has not been oriented toward the specific environments of developing countries, where scientists and research facilities are scarce and government policies toward biotechnology have not been fully formulated. Genetic materials are often deemed a public good and not patentable, thereby reducing private companies' desire to invest in producing or marketing biotechnology products. Nonetheless, progress is being made. The international agricultural research centers are all engaged in biotechnology research and their results are being disseminated. Multinational corporations are increasingly entering into biotech activities in developing countries. The potential of biotechnology to affect positively the food systems and the poor is significant, but biotechnology's impact will depend to a great extent on how it is applied. As with most technologies, biotechnology could have adverse consequences.[26] Because of the potential human and environmental risks inherent in genetic manipulation, it has come under close government regulatory scrutiny in the United States. This scrutiny slows down the introduction of new products and raises the costs of entry. Increased regulation can also be expected in the developing countries. The analyst should assess carefully who will be affected by the technology and how.

SUPPLY SENSITIVITY ANALYSIS. The supply of raw material is uncertain not only because of technical and economic factors but also because of the biological variables inherent in agronomic production. The project analysis should, therefore, include a supply sensitivity analysis to measure the effect that changes in area planted and crop yields have on total output. To determine the probable size of future crops, the analyst should use historical planting and yield variations adjusted for shifts in technologies or production economics. The newer the crop, the land, or the farmers, the greater the expected variability band. The wider the production range, the greater the project risk. The analyst should consider ways to reduce these agronomic risks. Irrigation might lower some weather risks, for example, and price contracts or other services to suppliers might stabilize technology use.

It is worth noting that the adoption of new technologies does not necessarily increase stability. Studies suggest that the use of high-yielding seed varieties may increase rather than decrease production variability.[27] This may occur because farmers vary their use of the agrochemical inputs needed to grow these seeds as the price and availability of those agrochemicals fluctuates.

The sensitivity analysis can also be used to evaluate methods of increasing the supply of raw material. The following example illustrates how a proposed cucumber-pickling plant in the Caribbean could compute the amount of cucumbers it would require. The plant capacity, calculated on market-demand estimates, is 60,000 10-ounce jars a day for 250 working days, with each jar containing 8 ounces avoirdupois or 0.5 pounds of fresh cucumbers.[28] During the pickling process, the firm expects 15 percent of the cucumbers to be damaged during processing. Therefore, if

$Q_p$ = unit quantity of final product processed each day,
$Q_r$ = quantity of raw material contained in each processed unit,
$Q_d$ = number of production days,
$L$ = percentage of raw material lost during processing, and
$R$ = total raw material requirement,

then the total raw material requirement can be computed as

$$R = (Q_p \times Q_r \times Q_d) \div (100 - L).$$

Substituting the particulars of the pickling plant [$R$ = (60,000 jars × 0.5 pounds a jar × 250 days) ÷ 0.85], the plant figures it will need 8,824,000 pounds of cucumbers a year. However, the area planted in cucumbers has been fairly steady for several years, at 1,200 acres (±5 percent) with an average yield of 6,000 pounds an acre (±10 percent annually).[29] The expected average output is thus 7.2 million pounds, 1.6 million pounds less than the 8.8 million pounds the plant needs. If the shortfall cannot be eliminated, the plant will have to operate at 18 percent below capacity, a decrease that could significantly affect the plant's profit and the project's viability.

Assuming that equipment design cannot be adjusted to reduce capacity, the alternatives are to increase the area planted in cucumbers or to improve the yields on the existing area. To compute how much more land must be planted, or yields increased, to overcome the shortfall, assume that

$R$ = total raw material requirements (8.8 million pounds),
$A_a$ = actual area planted (1,200 acres),
$Y_a$ = actual yield (6,000 pounds an acre),
$A_d$ = desired area planted, and
$Y_d$ = desired yield.

Then the desired area for planting can be calculated as $A_d = R \div Y_a$.

Performing the mathematical operations (8.8 million pounds ÷ 6,000 pounds) obtains 1,470 acres. The desired yield from the actual area can be computed as $Y_d = R \div A_a$. Thus, to obtain 8.8 million pounds of cucumbers from 1,200 acres, each acre must yield 7,333 pounds. In other words, plantings will have to increase by 22 percent (to 1,470 acres) or yields will have to improve by 22 percent (to 7,333 pounds) to cover the deficit in raw materials.

These figures do not point to a clear solution because each alternative assumes the same rate of improvement. The next step, then, is for the analyst to estimate the cost of each approach. To increase plantings, the firm will have to offer a higher price for the cucumbers to entice other farmers to cultivate the crop. To improve the yields, the firm will have to provide inputs such as improved seeds, agrochemicals, or technical assistance from an agronomist.

To compare the cost of each alternative realistically, the analyst must also consider the uncertainty of each method; that is, the analyst must estimate the probability of achieving the output by the alternative methods of increased acreage or increased yield. Evaluating the uncertainty is important because it can reverse a decision based on cost comparison. A cost comparison that did not take uncertainties into account would proceed as follows. Assume that

$C_a$ = incremental price per pound to induce increased planting (assumes price elasticity of supply and other crop profitability are known) ($0.02 a pound),
$C_y$ = cost per acre of inputs needed to raise yield ($175 an acre),

$TC_a$ = total cost of increased planting, and
$TC_y$ = total cost of improved yield.

Using R (or 8.8 million pounds) from the previous calculations, then the cost of increased planting can be determined by $TC_a = C_a \times R$. Substitution ($0.02 × 8.8 million pounds) obtains a total cost for increased planting of $176,000. Alternatively, the total cost of improved yield can be calculated, using $A_a$ (or 1,200 acres) from the previous calculations, by $TC_y = C_y \times A_a$. Substitution ($175 × 1,200 acres) obtains a total cost of $210,000. These calculations indicate that the firm should choose the increased planting alternative because it will cost less.

The elasticity of the cucumber supply, however, is unclear: the firm does not know how responsive farmers will be to the price increase. Having consulted the historical statistics on farmer price sensitivity, the analysts are only 60 percent sure that the price increase of $0.02 per pound will stimulate increased plantings. They are more certain of achieving the desired yield of 7,333 pounds, because that is the average yield in the United States, where climate is less favorable, and because domestic experiments have already shown that small plots can produce—under field conditions with the proposed inputs—consistent yields of more than 8,000 pounds an acre. With this knowledge, the analysts attach a 0.9 probability to achieving an actual yield of 7,333 pounds. They thus inflate the total costs of both alternatives accordingly:

$TC_a$ = $176,000 ÷ 0.6 = $293,333, and
$TC_y$ = $210,000 ÷ 0.9 = $233,333.

Similarly, one can obtain a cost per pound of the cucumbers expected to be procured:

$TC_a$ = $176,000 ÷ (8.8 million pounds × 0.6) = $0.033, and
$TC_y$ = $210,000 ÷ (8.8 million pounds × 0.9) = $0.027.

Both calculations that incorporate the uncertainty factor favor the yield-improvement alternative, exactly the reverse of the conclusion based on cost alone.

Probability estimates are a rudimentary method of handling uncertainty factors in supply. More sophisticated analyses can be done with Bayesian probability theory and econometric modeling techniques. The demand forecasting techniques discussed in chapter 2 are, to a great extent, applicable to supply forecasting. Regardless of the technique used, the analyst should consider the uncertainties surrounding supply procurement. Failure to extract judgments about uncertainty is common in agroindustrial project analysis; too often

**Figure 4-2.** *Increase in Output as a Result of Increases in Area Planted and Yield*

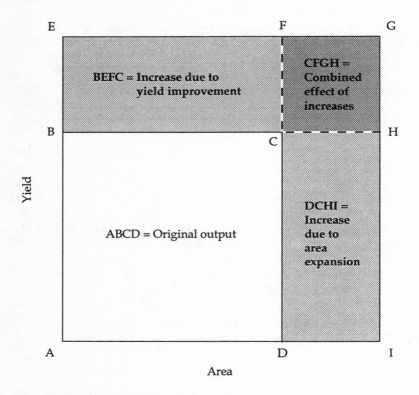

these uncertainties remain hidden, are treated unsystematically in the analysis, or are simply forgotten.

Increasing the area planted and the yields are not, of course, mutually exclusive options. Supply sensitivity analysis should assess the combined effects of changes along both dimensions, a combination illustrated in figure 4-2. In examining projections of increased production, the analyst should ascertain the likely response to each alternative because the feasibility of each can vary dramatically. If land is abundant and traditional farmers resist new agronomic technologies, the desirable strategy would be to increase supply by increasing crop acreage. If land is scarce, the analyst might choose to increase yields.

In any case, the inherent variability in supply means that sensitivity analysis projections should consider the financial effects of large swings in supply quantities. Contingency plans should be formulated to import or purchase raw materials from other regions of the country in the event of a shortfall in the local supply. Contacts and procedures should be established in advance to minimize delays in activating them if the need arises. Supply shortages can be deadly to agroindustries; one cannot afford to be unprepared.

Agroindustries that depend on other industries for their raw materials cannot use the methods described above to increase their raw material supplies. For agroindustries such as leather processors and shoe manufacturers that purchase hides from slaughterhouses, or vegetable-oil processors that obtain cottonseed from gins, the raw material supply responds not to the leather or oil processors but to the market demand for the primary products, beef and cotton. Consequently, the supply sensitivity analysis must focus on the productive capacity and market trends of the primary products. A deteriorating primary market often lowers production, creating a supply shortage for the by-product processor beyond its control. The processor should anticipate shortages and consider substitute raw materials or external sources.

### Competing Uses of Raw Material

After examining the factors that affect the production of raw material, the second step in analyzing supply of raw material is to estimate the amount that will be available for the project's use. To do that, the analyst first must identify the competing uses for the raw material—on-farm consumption, fresh consumption, animal consumption, other industrial use, and use by competitors—and quantify the amount each will absorb. The analyst can then compute the net amount available to the processor by taking gross production and subtracting the quantities consumed for other uses and the quantity lost because of damage or spoilage.

ON-FARM CONSUMPTION. The first deduction from total production is the quantity of the crop that does not enter the commercial market but is consumed on the farm. In general, the more important the raw material to the diet of the rural population and the smaller the farm, the greater the proportion of on-farm consumption. And if the harvest is poor, the family comes first. This priority accentuates supply shortages processors may experience during bad crop years. A subsistence farming pattern, however, may simply reflect the lack of a ready cash market outlet; in Bangladesh, India, and Pakistan even the holders of two hectares or less use 15–20 percent of their land for cash crops.[30] Farmers need cash to pay rents, buy inputs, cancel debts, and acquire nonfarm staples. But they also seek profit opportunities from the cash crop. The possible nutritional consequences for farm families who switch land from staple to cash crops depend on the increased sales, the family's income, the elasticity of demand for food and nonfood items, and the prices of these goods. Accordingly, the analyst should project and monitor the effects of the processing plant's raw material requirements on the population's nutritional intake.[31]

CONSUMPTION OF FRESH VERSUS PROCESSED CROPS. Another deduction is made for the portion of the crop that is consumed in fresh, rather than processed, form. Some agroindustries must compete against a market for fresh produce, and the analyst should assess the intensity of the competition and its variation according to consumer preferences. In Mexico, for example, 90 percent of tomato production is consumed fresh. Half of that is sold in the domestic market and half is exported to the U.S. winter market, where tomatoes command a premium price.[32] In the United States, however, 83 percent of the domestic tomato crop is processed into ketchup, tomato paste, canned whole tomatoes, tomato juice, and other products because consumer demand is greater for processed tomato products than for the fresh produce. In addition, processing eliminates perishability and allows the large U.S. summer crop to be sold throughout the year.

For some crops, the fresh and processed markets are complementary rather than competitive. This is the case for tomatoes that are damaged in appearance; they could not be sold fresh but could be processed for tomato paste. Such complementary uses maximize a crop's recoverable economic value.

ANIMAL VERSUS HUMAN CONSUMPTION. An alternative use for some raw material is its conversion into animal feed. In some countries maize, wheat, or soybeans are used in this way. Using grain calories and protein to produce meat is nutritionally inefficient, however; because of losses in the biological conversion process, fewer calories and protein are available in the meat than were consumed in the grain.[33] Meat-processing agroindustries should be sensitive to this nutritional deficit and recognize that governments may have to give priority to direct human consumption of grains, especially in the face of widespread caloric shortages.

MULTIPLE INDUSTRIALIZATION. Some raw material can be used in more than one processed end product. Maize, for example, can be used to produce animal feed, oil, starch, margarine, mayonnaise, noodles, detergent, flour, and dextrose. A single processor often makes several of these derivative products but may have to compete for supplies of the raw material with processors making different derivatives. The analyst can foresee this dilemma by documenting and quantifying the alternative end uses of the raw material.

COMPETING PROCESSING FIRMS. The most direct competition for raw materials is among processing companies in the same business, whether foreign or domestic. The following combination of events, which occurred in a Central American country, illustrates why the analyst must assess the strength of competition for raw materials.[34] At the same time that a decline in international cotton prices caused the country's cotton crop to level off, the construction of a new cottonseed-oil processing plant increased demand. Japanese oil mills seeking raw supplies also increased the demand for cottonseed. The result of the stable output and growing demand was an 18 percent jump in the price of cottonseed, from $2.80 to $3.30 a hundredweight.[35] The Japanese were able to pay premium prices because they could generate additional revenue by extracting extra linters from the Central American cottonseed (other countries' seeds had been more thoroughly cleaned because of more efficient ginning).

Sometimes governments will intervene to ensure that the local agroindustries have adequate supplies. For example, the Philippine government banned the export of copra in the 1980s to guarantee the local coconut oil mills sufficient raw materials.[36] Through industrial licensing, governments can also regulate the number of firms operating in an industry and their capacity, thereby directly shaping the degree of competition for the available raw material supplies.

Sometimes availability is affected simply by domestic market forces. In one country an exporter ended up short of supplies because local demand was stronger than forecasted and farmers chose to sell to the local market, which was more accessible and had relatively attractive prices. The exporter's error was to assume that local consumption would remain constant while population and incomes grew. The linkages to the international market are severable. If barriers to entry are low, a new agroindustry should expect followers and a consequent increase in competition for raw materials. Business leaders in one country established a new processing firm, assuming that no competitors would emerge because the market and the raw material supply were too small to justify another plant. Nonetheless, a new plant was set up, causing both plants to suffer from raw material shortages and excess capacity. Followers sometimes leap blindly without doing their homework; others believe that they can do it better.

LOSSES. Analysts calculating the net availability of supply must take into account crop losses caused by rodents, insect pests, and poor handling and storage. The last of these losses merits examination because it can, in large part, be prevented. Poor storage facilities can be responsible for a sizeable portion of losses, although reliable statistics are scarce. The Food and Agriculture Organization estimates production losses due to poor storage at 10–30 percent, depending on the crop and region.[37] Other field studies put grain losses at 3–8 percent and tropical root crop losses at around 25 percent.[38] Low-cost storage facilities on the farm or in the village can cut these losses by as much as 80 percent.[39]

Programs to stimulate production sometimes fail to incorporate adequate storage for the increased output. Nicaragua, for example, launched a program to modernize its rice industry. Production rose 146 percent during 1967–69, but the government's grain procurement agency was then overloaded with rice. "We bought more rice than the existing milling, drying, and especially storage capacity could handle. We had to store rough, wet rice wherever we could find space, even in buildings with dirt floors," one government official commented.[40] The inadequate storage facilities caused the paddy rice to lose approximately half of its value. Clearly, an analyst's accurate estimate of the storage needs for new production programs can help to avoid such losses.

## Acceptable Quality of Inputs

A firm should not only have an adequate supply of raw material, but the material should meet the qualitative requirements of the operation. Raw material of poor quality may yield a product of poor quality, which can create consumer resistance and have long-range effects on the firm's market position. Poor-quality raw material can also increase operating costs and decrease efficiency.

### Marketplace Requirements

The analyst must decide on qualitative criteria for the raw material the firm uses. These criteria depend on standards of acceptability in the consumer market. This correlation again shows the interdependencies inherent in agroindustry: to analyze the supply segment, the analyst must examine the marketing segment; to determine the parameters for quality, the analyst must perform the consumer analyses discussed in the marketing chapter. These analyses may indicate that segments within the same market have different standards of quality dependent on variations in consumers' preferences and buying patterns.

Cucumbers produced in Guatemala illustrate this variation. Cucumbers slated for export to the United States would be entering a highly quality-conscious market and would have to meet rigorous criteria for color, size, shape, taste, and general appearance. In addition, the U.S. government imposes sanitary standards on imported produce. If the cucumbers were being grown for the local Guatemalan market, the standards for quality would be lower and, except perhaps in premier restaurants, consumers would refuse to pay the premium price for produce of export quality.

Once the qualitative demands of the market are identified, the analyst must translate them into qualitative requirements for the raw material.

### Determinants of Quality

Several factors affect the quality of raw material, and they must be adjusted to attain the quality required by the marketplace. Three factors in particular deserve the analyst's attention.

INPUTS. The input that affects product characteristics and quality most significantly is the seed (or, for livestock, the breed). Plant and animal genetics can be engineered to achieve desired characteristics. Genetic research, however, has sometimes concentrated on quantity or yield and not given adequate attention to quality. The early IR-8, high-yielding rice variety is a case in point. Introduced in the Philippines because it promised dramatically increased yields, the new seeds did succeed in this respect, but the IR-8 rice also had a shorter grain, higher milling breakage, and poorer cooking qualities than the traditional varieties. IR-8 rice was therefore sold at a discount, thus offsetting much of the revenue gained by its increased yield. Breeding of subsequent IR varieties removed these qualitative deficiencies but retained the high-yield characteristic. Clearly, both quantitative and qualitative dimensions must be considered in any genetic design of inputs. The advances in biotechnology during the 1980s have greatly increased the capability and the desire to create traits that will enhance the quality and value of raw materials.

For agroindustries such as the Guatemalan cucumber-packing operation, seed selection is critical. Varieties have been developed that meet the shape, color, and taste preferences of the U.S. market, but a firm must test these varieties under the agronomic conditions of its growing area (it is advisable to test varieties for at least two crop cycles and in various locations). To attain product quality, firms use additional inputs such as insecticides and fertilizer, but these inputs must be used properly to achieve the desired results. The early cucumbers exported from Guatemala were frequently yellowish rather than the green color preferred by consumers, a deficiency caused by improper application of fertilizer. For both economic and ecological reasons, increasing consideration is being given to natural methods of pest control and to the use of organic fertilizer.

The processing operation can also dictate a need for specific quality characteristics in raw materials. Genetic engineering may address these demands. For example, special varieties of cucumbers and tomatoes have been developed for processing; they are different in size, texture, and fragility from those used for fresh consumption. Finally, the analyst should consider the nutritional quality of the seed because seed variety can significantly influence the final product's protein and micronutrient content.

HANDLING, TRANSPORT, AND STORAGE. The handling and transport of the product—particularly if it is fragile and perishable—can also significantly affect its quality. Cucumbers are fragile and perishable produce: rough handling can bruise them, excessive exposure to sun can burn them, and they can wilt during transport delays. Potatoes, in contrast, can withstand rougher handling.

But more than the aesthetic quality of produce is at risk after harvest. Postproduction procedures can also affect nutritional value. The factors that most affect nutrient retention in harvested fruits and vegetables are injury from mechanical harvesting and temperature and humidity conditions during handling and storage.

Mechanical injury causes structural disorganization of the tissues and allows microorganisms to enter the produce, causing spoilage. Oxidative reactions (chemical and enzymatic) occur when the cellular structure is disrupted and lead to a rapid loss of vitamins A and C. Mechanical injury to produce may occur during harvesting, grading, cleaning, washing, transporting, packing and unpacking, and sale in market. Such damage can often be prevented, however, by using labor rather than machines at appropiate stages of operation. Bruising of produce can be minimized by harvesting in the cool night hours, by quick application of precooling (in water, for example), and by avoiding delays in shipment. In-transit damage can also be minimized: fewer injuries occurred in peaches hauled 100 miles in a truck with air-ride suspension than in peaches hauled the same distance in a truck with leaf suspension.[41]

Temperature and humidity conditions can cause produce to lose moisture, or wilt, with a simultaneous loss of vitamins. Wilting and vitamin loss occur when fresh, leafy vegetables are stored at high temperatures, low humidities, or both. Wilting can be minimized in leafy products by shortening the amount of time between harvest and shipment and by monitoring temperature and humidity in storage. Defective or insufficient storage can also affect the nutritional quality of the product that remains after losses from excessive humidity, heat, or insect damage are taken into account. Certain produce may need refrigeration to reduce perishability. (Storage issues are covered in more detail in chapter 5.)

### Government Standards

Quality requirements are not dictated only by the marketplace. Often governments institute food and fiber quality standards for agricultural raw and processed materials. The lack of accepted standards makes market information more imperfect and hinders price comparisons and trade communication, leading to inefficiencies and unfair practices. In developing countries the first standards to emerge are generally those for export commodities, which must meet international standards to be traded. Governments often play key trade roles in instituting or enforcing these standards through their export marketing boards or export licensing procedures. Governments have an economic interest in export standards because failure to comply can jeopardize the country's trade reputation and foreign exchange earnings. For example, in the mid 1970s investigations revealed quality abuses in U.S. grain exports, which led to closer federal supervision of these exports.

The United States government has a highly developed system to grade the quality of agricultural products. In 1981 the Department of Agriculture graded about 98 percent of turkeys, 77 percent of chickens, 74 percent of butter, 65 percent of frozen fruits and vegetables, 56 percent of beef, 45 percent of fresh fruits and vegetables, and 37 percent of eggs.[42] Grading is mandatory for some products—for example, grains and cotton traded interstate and on the futures exchanges, and exported apples and pears. Standards tend to be based on physical attributes such as size, color, shape, and tenderness. Milk grades are based not only on bacteria count but also on the conditions under which the cows are housed and milked and the milk handled. In this case the sanitary requirements for food safety are incorporated into the grading standards. For other products, such as meat, the processing facilities and the products must meet health standards and pass periodic inspections irrespective of the grading.

Government standards can facilitate agroindustry procurement when they apply to raw materials by creating greater uniformity and facilitating classification of inputs. Similarly, standards for finished goods can guide procurement and processing specifications.

### Quality Control

After examining how product quality is affected by the quality of inputs, transport, handling, storage, and government standards, the next step is to develop quality control measures.

The processor should consider providing the farmer with improved inputs, such as better seed, not only to increase yields but to improve quality. To ensure that the inputs are used properly, the firm may again need to offer technical assistance and training and provide facilities such as warehouses and dryers. The costs of these measures should be weighed against the higher prices the processor can charge for higher quality goods.

One banana company gave its contract growers an "assistance package" that included all inputs and directions for how to use them, harvesting services, and transportation. Because the bananas were branded, these extra quality control measures were essential to ensuring the success of the company's product differentiation strategy.

Another agroindustry, however, stopped giving technical assistance to small farmers when it discovered that competing processors were capturing the benefits of this investment by enticing the farmers to sell to them. This "free rider" risk can be reduced by signing contracts with suppliers or providing the services only to those who agree to sell exclusively to the processor.

At a minimum, the processor should give suppliers a clear idea of the qualitative specifications for the raw material. Some firms offer premium prices and penalty discounts to stimulate farmers' use of inputs and cultivation techniques that improve the quality of raw material. In Kenya the final price the tea processor pays to small teaholders depends on the pooled quality of all the farmers' tea. The tea is inspected and graded in the presence of the farmers, who serve to control the inspectors and errant growers.[43] Other firms inspect crops in the field to detect problems such as insect damage and to minimize loss of quality. Sometimes the processor must produce the raw material itself to ensure adequate quality control. This form of backward vertical integration is discussed below.

## Appropriate Timing

Because of the biological nature of the raw material, time is an important consideration in the agroindustrial procurement system. The raw material's seasonality, perishability, and period of availability are all dependent on time.

### Seasonality

In most industries the raw material flows from suppliers to the plant at an even pace or is adjusted to meet the prevailing pattern of demand. Such flexibility in supply is not possible in agroindustries, where most crops and range-fed cattle are seasonal. The procurement process is bound by the biological dictates of crop and estrous cycles; a farm does not have a nonagricultural firm's advantage of working the "production line" double time. Nonetheless, there is some flexibility. The crop cycle can be lengthened or shortened by planting seed varieties with different maturation periods. Irrigation can allow double or triple cropping, which not only affects the amount of available raw material, but also helps to even out its flow. Intensive feeding can reduce the time it takes to raise livestock and thus increase production, and planting can be staggered somewhat to spread the harvest period and thus lower the processing operation's peak capacity requirements. These adjustments, however, may be costly and difficult for the processor to implement.

Even with such adjustments, storage is the prime regulator between the production and transformation of raw material. Raw material must be held in storage, to be channeled into the processing operation as needed. Although external storage capacity and services may exist, the agroindustrial plant usually needs to provide its own storage. A firm's storage requirements can be calculated from the cumulative flow required during the harvest period to meet the annual raw material needs. As an example, the flow of raw material and the utilization of milling capacity for rice in Thailand are shown in table 4-3. Smaller mills have lower storage capacities and steadier milling rates throughout the season than do larger mills. Differences in the nature of the businesses are responsible for the different storage requirements: the small mills primarily serve farmers who store their paddy rice at home and bring it for milling as they need to consume it, while the large mills buy the rice from farmers at harvest time, mill it, and resell it.

Seasonality also imposes pressures on working capital. It is essential to procure sufficient financing to handle the peak working capital requirements of the harvest period and to carry the inventory during the year. Prompt payment to producers at harvest time is necessary to retain them as loyal suppliers.[44] A shortage of working capital can drain the firm's equity capital, which can cause a permanent and sometimes fatal undercapitalization.

### Perishability

Raw materials are perishable in varying degrees. Some materials must be processed immediately or the product suffers a significant loss in quality and economic value. Nut oil from the African palm, for example, must be processed within a few days of picking or it acidifies and cannot be used. Similarly, if cucumbers are not harvested during the few days they are mature, they rapidly become oversized

**Table 4-3.** *Seasonal Usage of Rice Mills in Thailand, 1975*
(actual daily input in metric tons)

| Quarter | | | | | | Mill capacity (metric tons) | | | | | |
|---|---|---|---|---|---|---|---|---|---|---|---|
| | 0–10 | 11–20 | 21–30 | 31–40 | 41–50 | 51–60 | 61–70 | 71–80 | 81–90 | 91–100 |
| February–April | 0.63 | 6.47 | 11.63 | 18.61 | 25.75 | 35.32 | 48.29 | 38.00 | 40.00 | 58.12 |
| May–July | 0.67 | 3.76 | 7.28 | 14.21 | 14.30 | 32.50 | 31.57 | 35.67 | 30.00 | 50.63 |
| August–October | 0.40 | 2.32 | 5.61 | 8.39 | 11.88 | 25.05 | 23.14 | 29.00 | 30.00 | 40.00 |
| November–January | 0.59 | 2.26 | 5.77 | 5.74 | 7.93 | 20.27 | 24.14 | 24.50 | 30.00 | 28.75 |
| Daily average | 0.57 | 3.70 | 7.57 | 11.74 | 14.96 | 28.28 | 31.78 | 31.79 | 32.50 | 44.38 |

*Source:* Delane Welsch, Sopin Tongpan, Christopher Mock, Eileen Kennedy, and James Austin, "Thailand Case Study," in James E. Austin, ed., *Global Malnutrition and Cereal Grain Fortification* (Cambridge, Mass.: Ballinger Publishing Co., 1979), p. 248.

and unfit for exporting. While post-harvest delays can cause nutrient losses, the time of harvest can also affect nutrient content. For example, vine-ripened tomatoes contain approximately 40 percent more vitamin C than tomatoes picked green for subsequent ripening in storage.[45]

Perishability requires that great care be given to planning the harvest and scheduling farm-to-factory transport, and the analyst must determine whether suppliers have adequate resources for these tasks. Scheduling techniques, such as PERT charts or the Critical Path Method, can be used to manage the production and procurement activities to ensure timely arrival.

Other steps can be taken to lessen the risk that the raw material will deteriorate. For example, mechanical dryers can reduce grain humidity, thereby lowering the chances of stack burn and insect infestation; shaded collection points in the fields can prevent damage to fruits and vegetables from sun and heat. If perishability cannot be reduced, the firm might consider changing the form of the final product. A Central American producer encountered severe delays in transporting okra to the U.S. fresh market, which caused much of the produce to spoil. This producer installed a freezing plant and shifted to the market for frozen okra, which made the operation less sensitive to perishability and seasonality factors.

*Availability*

The time period during which raw material is available to the processing plant—the supply "life span"—can be divided into two parts. The initial phase is the time between the raw material's planting and the beginning of its flow into the factory. For commonly cultivated seasonal crops this first phase lasts only a period of months, but new or unusual crops often require a longer, trial growing period. For beef projects, a lead time is necessary to build up the herd so that a steady supply can flow to the factory. The fruit cannot be harvested from African palms until nearly five years after planting. Other fruit-bearing trees, tea, and coffee have similarly long lead times. Long start-up periods require special considerations for carrying the start-up costs of crops that are not generating any revenue.

The second phase of a raw material's availability concerns the longevity of the supply after the initial start-up period. Unlike minerals, crops are a renewable resource and can be planted again. Tree crops, for example, have an extended but finite life, with an accelerating and then declining productivity pattern (the yield pattern of a Peruvian fruit grower is illustrated in figure 4-3). Sequenced plantings can ensure an even and continued flow for the duration of productivity.

**Figure 4-3.** *Yields of Peach and Apple Orchards, Valle de Majes, Peru*

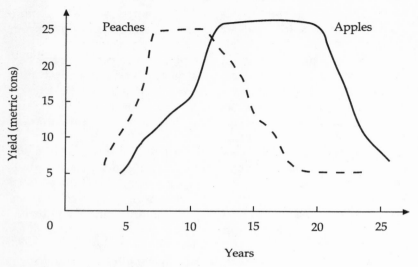

*Source*: Internal World Bank document.

Availability is also affected by improper cultivation techniques, which can exhaust and erode the soil, making the land unproductive. The analyst should consider this longer-term availability and examine the cultivation techniques to ensure continuing supply.

A crop's availability can be jeopardized when suppliers switch to other crops. This risk is especially acute when the raw material is, like cottonseed oil, a by-product of another crop. The supply of cottonseed depends on the demand for cotton; when cotton prices fall, farmers shift to other crops, and seeds are less available. Because cottonseed represents a negligible portion of cotton farmers' revenues, a cottonseed-oil processor's increasing seed prices would not stimulate increased cotton production. This lack of control again suggests the advantages of diversifying a firm's sources of raw material; a cottonseed-oil processor could, for example, explore the use of peanuts, soybeans, or palm kernels as supplementary oil sources. Diversification of this kind frequently requires adaptations in the processing equipment, and the analyst should compare the costs of modifying equipment with the benefits of having multiple sources of raw material, bearing in mind that multiple sources also reduce the risks of crop failure in one raw material or particular geographical area.[46]

## Reasonable Cost

Not surprisingly, raw material costs dominate the economics of most agroindustries. Unlike most other manufacturers, food processing is usually not an additive process but a subtractive one in which the original material is reduced to another form. The main additional inputs in most agroindustries are labor, ingredients, and packaging. The costs of raw material in various agroindustries are listed in table 4-4; they constitute from 40 to 93 percent of the total operating costs. Because of the central importance of raw material costs, the analyst should explore alternative pricing mechanisms and test the sensitivity of profits to cost changes. The effects that government policies have on costs and prices should also be examined.

### Cost Determinants

Several factors—including supply and demand, opportunity costs, system structure, logistical services, and government interventions— affect the cost of the raw material.

SUPPLY AND DEMAND. The major determinant of a raw material's cost is the supply of and demand for the commodity. When supply is scarce, the raw material will go to the firm that bids the highest, so the analyst should assess the economic strength of competing users of the material. But whether the commodity is scarce or abundant, the analyst should estimate the firm's own supply needs and the effect on demand. The project's size is particularly relevant in this respect because the larger the project, the more it will disrupt the equilibrium of supply and demand. Large requirements for a raw material can strain local or regional supplies and push up the price.

If a project is the dominant buyer of a raw material, it may create a semimonopsonistic market position, becoming a price-setter rather than a price-taker. Although that would reduce the project's raw material costs, it might also adversely affect the income of the farmers and their nutritional well-being if they are small, low-income producers.

OPPORTUNITY COSTS. One of the factors limiting the buyer's power and influencing raw material prices is the opportunity cost to the farmer who supplies a particular agroindustrial product. The analyst must determine what other crops the farmer could grow, and what income is foregone by choosing to grow what the agroindustry requires instead. Clearly, the agroindustrial firm must pay a high

**Table 4-4.** *Raw Material Costs in Agroindustry*

| Agroindustry and location | Cost of raw material as a percentage of total operating cost |
|---|---|
| Maize mill, Yugoslavia | 83 |
| Maize mill, Uganda | 53 |
| Wheat mill, Turkey | 93 |
| Wheat mill, Philippines | 54 |
| Oil palm mill, Indonesia | 63 |
| Vegetable oil mill, Kenya | 90 |
| Vegetable oil mill, Thailand | 67 |
| Soybean oil refinery, Mexico | 81 |
| Fruit and vegetable processor, Yugoslavia | 83 |
| Vegetable dehydrator, Ecuador | 92 |
| Vegetable dehydrator, Yugoslavia | 74 |
| Banana processor, Philippines | 48 |
| Fruit juices and jams, Kenya | 40 |
| Winery, Yugoslavia | 82 |
| Sugar refinery, India | 71 |
| Sugar refinery, Ecuador | 63 |
| Sugar refinery, Kenya | 62 |
| Tea processor, Tanzania | 56 |
| Beef processor, Brazil | 92 |
| Dairy, Brazil | 67 |
| Meat processor, Yugoslavia | 76 |
| Poultry processor, Ghana | 60 |

*Sources:* For Philippine wheat mill, Edward Felton, "Republic Flour Mills," Inter-University Program for Graduate Business Education, Manila, 1977. For Mexican soybean oil refinery, Fondo de Garantía (Development for Agriculture, Livestock, and Aviculture), "Planta extractora de aceites" ["Oil Extraction Plant"], Mexico City, 1973. For Ecuadorian vegetable dehydrator and sugar refinery, Yugoslavian winery and meat processor, and Brazilian beef processor and dairy, internal World Bank documents. For Ghanaian poultry processor, Business Promotion Agency Ltd., "Feasibility Report on Integrated Poultry Project," Accra, n.d. For all other data, James G. Brown, "Agroindustry Profiles" working papers, World Bank, Economic Development Institute, Washington, D.C., 1990.

enough price to keep the farmer from switching to another crop. Thus although the firm is not investing in agricultural production, it must understand the farmer's economics.[47]

SYSTEM STRUCTURES. Structural factors in the farm-to-factory chain can also influence raw material costs. The most common of these is the intermediary who buys the product from farmers and then sells it to the factory. There is a tendency to label these intermediaries automatically as exploiters and to consider their presence in the food system as undesirable (governments often use this argument to justify their intervention into agricultural marketing). Much anecdotal evidence exists to support such labeling, and intermediaries certainly have at times exercised oligopolistic control over supply channels. Even the United States in the 1920s passed the Packers and Stockyards Act and the Commodity Exchange Act to prevent marketers from using abusive practices.[48]

But intermediaries usually perform essential functions such as assembly, transport, or financing that someone else would have to perform in their stead if they did not exist. Competition among intermediaries is often high. For example, Thailand's 25,000 rice mills and a widely dispersed network of traders have generally kept marketing margins and farmer prices at reasonable levels.[49] In Ghana rice assemblers' net margins in 1977 were a modest 6.5 percent.[50] Small rubber producers in Malaysia in the 1980s sold their output to local dealers rather than directly to the factory because the dealers pay cash immediately and the factory pays weekly or fortnightly.[51] In one Asian country the small apple growers sold their fruit on the tree to preharvest contractors who were responsible for all harvesting labor operations, including crop security, and for the packing material and transport from the orchard. These assemblers also bore all the risk of damage to the fruit. The analyst should determine the costs of these intermediary services and compare them to the costs, efficiency, and equity of alternative methods—for example, direct procurement at the farm gate by the factory or direct delivery to the factory by farmer cooperatives.

LOGISTICAL SERVICES. Service costs can significantly increase raw material costs. Storage is one example and has already been discussed; transportation is another. Marketing margins in African countries have been found to be double those in Asian nations, with 40 percent of that difference attributable to higher transportation costs in Africa.[52]

Transport is often superficially analyzed or overlooked. Because raw material prices are often calculated to include delivery to the factory door, the transport charges are not apparent. For example, a sugar mill in a Latin American country wanted to reduce the cost of the raw cane it was purchasing from small farmers because world sugar prices had plummeted, putting the mill in a cost-price squeeze. The mill dropped the price it paid farmers from $7 per ton delivered to the factory to $5, a price it considered still profitable for farmers. However, a large number of the farmers began to shift to different crops, threatening the mill's supply of raw material. Examining the farm-to-mill cost structure, the mill found that transport charges had

**Table 4-5.** *Cost Structure of Sugarcane Production and Delivery in a Latin American Country, 1972*

| Item | Farmer's cost/profit at selling price of $7 per metric ton | | Farmer's cost/profit at selling price of $5 per metric ton | |
| --- | --- | --- | --- | --- |
| | *Dollars per metric ton* | *Percentage of total cost* | *Dollars per metric ton* | *Percentage of total cost* |
| Charges paid to transporter | 3.00 | 43 | 3.00 | 60 |
| Wages paid to worker | 1.50 | 21 | 1.50 | 30 |
| Land costs | 1.00 | 15 | 1.00 | 20 |
| Net return to farmer | 1.50 | 21 | −0.50 | 10 |

*Source:* Author's estimates based on unpublished company documents.

absorbed more than 40 percent of the farmers' revenue at the old price and were absorbing 60 percent at the new price, thus making the farmers' operation at the new price unprofitable (see table 4-5). The mill invested in a fleet of trucks that it could operate at one-third the cost of the previous trucking service, thus preserving the farmers' returns and lowering the delivery cost of the cane. Alternatively, the producers could have collectively set up a transport service.

GOVERNMENTAL INVOLVEMENT. Government investments in transportation infrastructure can reduce transport costs. Other government actions such as subsidies, credit, research, and extension services can significantly affect farmer costs and outputs, and therefore the cost of raw materials for agroindustries. Government import and export controls (and exchange rates) affect the quantity and prices of raw materials available to the processors. When governments use state-owned enterprises to purchase and store agricultural crops, the costs often increase. In Kenya the storage and interregional marketing costs were found to be 15–25 percent higher in government-owned enterprises than in those of private traders.[53] In general, state-owned enterprises are at an institutional disadvantage in performing procurement activities, which demand flexibility, transaction speed, and personal relationships.[54]

It is often necessary to trace costs through the farm-to-factory chain to uncover the effects of government programs. For example, analysts in the poultry-processing industry in a South American country had to follow costs back to the feed-grain farmer to find the cause of—and government responsibility for—price increases for raw material. The government had viewed the poultry industry as a source of inexpensive animal protein for the lower-income segments of the population. The high retail prices of broiling chickens thus led the

**Table 4-6.** *Cost Structure for Broiler Chicken Agroindustry in Guyana, 1972*

| Item | Cost per chicken (dollars) | Percentage of retail price |
|---|---|---|
| *Retailing* | | |
| Retail price | 3.24 | 100.0 |
| Markup | 0.25 | 7.6 |
| | | |
| *Processing* | | |
| Dressing | 0.20 | 6.1 |
| Packaging | 0.05 | 1.5 |
| Distribution | 0.10 | 3.0 |
| General and administration | 0.15 | 4.6 |
| Profit margin | 0.15 | 4.6 |
| | | |
| *Growing* | | |
| Incubated chicks | 0.20 | 6.1 |
| Feed | 1.80 | 54.7 |
| Disease control | 0.05 | 1.5 |
| Mortality | 0.05 | 1.5 |
| Maintenance | 0.04 | 1.2 |
| Transport | 0.10 | 3.0 |
| Profit margin | 0.15 | 4.6 |

*Source:* Author's estimates based on data in Edward L. Felton, Jr., and Ray A. Goldberg, "The Broiler Industry of Guyana," Case Study 4-373-015, Harvard University, Graduate School of Business Administration, Boston, 1972.

government to consider putting price controls on poultry meat to eliminate excessive profits to processors. But when the policymakers traced the cost components from retailer to processor to poultry farmer, they found that processors' profit margins were not excessive and that the primary cost factor was poultry feed (see table 4-6).

Taking the analysis further, they found that the feed mills were also operating on thin profit margins and that the real source of the high cost of feed was the high prevailing support price for feed grains, which the government itself maintained. Given the economic dominance of this raw material in the industry, high prices at the end of the chain were inevitable. Yet the support prices were not high enough to stimulate increased grain output.

### Pricing mechanisms

It is clear that many forces influence the cost of a plant's raw material. But there are a number of alternatives available for obtaining raw materials at a reasonable cost. The analyst should examine each of them.

SPOT PRICES. Buying at spot prices means the company pays the prevailing price in the market. This is a reasonable procedure if the competitors also use it because all firms incur similar costs. Prices, however, tend to vary greatly both within and across years. Prices vary seasonally, for example, rising when supplies are scarce and the cost of carrying inventory is high, and falling during harvest time, when supplies are most abundant. Intraseasonal price increases for grains in various Asian and African countries during 1975–80 ranged between 49 and 87 percent.[55] Thus, buying material at spot prices causes uncertainty in financial planning and wide swings in working capital needs. Firms need to make contingency credit arrangements to ensure that they will have enough funds to buy adequate amounts of raw materials in the event of a price increase.

To use spot prices, the firm ideally should have multiple sources of its raw material. This permits the procurement officer to shift the origin of raw materials, thus achieving the best cost and helping to control price variability and the economic risk of depending on one supplier. If the agroindustry can also import, then the spot prices will reflect international prices and exchange rates. Access to imports reduces the financial risk to agroindustries if local crops fail and prices climb.

GOVERNMENT SUPPORT PRICES. Sometimes the firm has to pay the minimum commodity price as fixed by the government. Although this price may deviate from the price that would have prevailed under free-market supply and demand, support prices represent the farmers' opportunity costs and therefore dictate the minimum price to the agroindustry. For example, in India the government sets a support price at the time of planting. Its procurement price at harvest time is usually higher than the support price but lower than the market price, thereby setting a floor on the private trader's prices.

The nature of a government's price as well as its level can affect procurement significantly. Some governments apply their prices uniformly to all farmers regardless of where they are located (pan-territorial), often on the grounds that this practice enhances national unity, is nondiscriminatory, and reduces rural migration. For an agroindustry this means that all suppliers must be paid at the same rate, regardless of differing transport costs from the farms to the factory. Consequently, the private agroindustry will buy from the nearer farmers and leave the farther ones to the government. If the processor can buy from the government, then it will have access to more distant supply sources at a subsidized price. This can cause crop shifts. For example, in Zambia pan-territorial pricing led to shifts from sorghum, cassava, confectionery groundnuts, and cotton to maize—crop switches inconsistent with the comparative advantages of various regions.[56]

Governments sometimes also provide a single support price that holds throughout the season (pan-temporal). This practice discourages private firms from holding inventories after the point at which the carrying costs and margins are no longer covered by the government's price. To the extent that the agroindustry can buy from the government at this price, it receives a de facto storage subsidy. Pan-temporal pricing is aimed at increasing price stability and economic access to staples late in the year. Nutritional vulnerability often increases because of seasonal price rises and declining family food reserves. Pan-temporal prices may provide some protection to consumers, but they can cause farmers to sell their crop rather than retain it, thereby reducing their food security unless they have later access to the subsidized food.[57]

It is also important to ascertain to what extent the support price varies to reflect quality differentials in the raw materials. For example, the Malaysian government set a single price for clean, dry paddy rice with deductions only for excessive humidity, foreign matter, or immature grains. As a result, farmers sold their lower-quality rice to the government and their higher-quality rice to private millers who paid premium prices.[58]

The recipient of the subsidy can also have a bearing on project feasibility. An association of peasants in Mexico planned to set up a plant to make balanced animal feed from their sorghum production. Their pilot project demonstrated that they could produce feed of a quality acceptable to local dairy farmers. However, they could not compete with the prices of existing larger feedmills because the government sold sorghum to them at a subsidized price.[59]

CONTRACTING. One method of ensuring the supply of raw material is to extend purchase contracts to producers. Such contracts often specify delivery quantities, quality standards, delivery dates, and price. Price is the most problematic of these because despite the contract, a firm has pricing options. The spot price upon delivery could be used, but the firm and the supplier would have to agree on what the source of the spot price should be. This approach is used by the Windward Islands Banana Association and the exporting company it contracts with; prices are set based on independently observed prices in the export market.[60] The contract could also fix the price on a cost plus a fixed fee or margin. Another possibility would be to base the price on opportunity costs, thus minimizing crop shifting and stabilizing supply. Yet another alternative would be to pay a base price plus a variable bonus derived from the final prices of the processed products. In examining these various contract alternatives, the analyst should weigh the costs against the certainty of supply obtained under each.

Firms might accompany contract pricing with benefits to suppliers such as technical assistance or advances of working capital. Working capital requirements for purchases of raw material and for storage are an important dimension of procurement operations and should be given special attention in project analysis. Providing credit to suppliers increases the agroindustry's financial exposure and so must be approached with caution. The firm might also check on the availability of government agricultural development funds at preferential interest rates or even get a government agency to lend directly to the suppliers.

Project analysts should also consider the length of the contract. Long-term contracts based on fixed prices may be convenient to producers and processors because they increase economic certainty and facilitate financial planning. But while they avoid the risks of variability under spot pricing, they miss out on the potential benefits as well.

Whether long- or short-term, contracting is effective only as long as external conditions do not significantly alter the underlying economics of the contracts. Such alterations affected the cotton industry of Nicaragua in 1973. In May 1973 many cotton farmers had sold forward contracts to Japanese buyers for approximately $39 per hundredweight of lint cotton. By January 1974, however, world prices had soared to $86 per hundredweight, and farmers refused to honor the contracts because higher agrochemical prices had raised the cost of their inputs and because they wanted a share in the higher world prices. The government finally intervened with a compromise whereby the farmers had to deliver 70 percent of their contracts at the original prices but could receive the world prices for the remaining percentage.[61]

The value of contracts ultimately depends on the goodwill of the parties involved. Legal enforcement is often infeasible because of the costs and delays of adjudication; contracts may need to be flexible enough to adjust the benefits as outside conditions change.

JOINT FARMER-PROCESSOR VENTURES. Another method of achieving reasonable costs for raw material is to invite producers to invest in the industrial plant. The aim is to give them a vested interest in the success of the processing operation, but this may not always be the result. In one dairy plant the suppliers, who were also shareholders, maintained their own interests by demanding higher prices for their raw milk. Because they perceived the processing firm's profitability as unimportant, they drained the dairy of its retained earnings; it was unable to maintain or modernize its equipment and it fell into disrepair and financial difficulty. Successful joint ventures require farmers to expand their viewpoint to see their new business as something more than an outlet for their production.

BACKWARD INTEGRATION. Instead of buying from farmers, the agroindustrial enterprise should consider integrating backward to produce some or all of its raw material, which converts raw material pricing to an internal accounting process. For some products this alternative is highly economical and reduces raw material costs. The example discussed earlier of a sugar mill that organized its own transport fleet illustrates effective backward integration. Cost, however, is not the only consideration in deciding on integration; others will be discussed in the section ''Organization of the Procurement System,'' below.

### Sensitivity Analysis

Raw materials are the biggest production costs for an agroindustry, yet those costs vary depending on market factors. Therefore, the firm should conduct a sensitivity analysis of raw material cost to determine the effect of variations in raw material prices on profits and investment returns.

The analysis should be analogous to the price sensitivity analysis discussed in chapter 3. The example of the spice manufacturer from that chapter (see page 74 and table 3-4) illustrates the financial implications of changes in raw material costs. Total annual costs to that plant were $300,000; of that, 82 percent, or $246,000, was attributable to the raw material. Thus, if raw material prices increase 10 percent, total costs would rise 8.2 percent and profits would drop 12.5 percent. A 20 percent increase in raw material prices would consume one-quarter of the firm's profits. Conversely, if raw material prices drop, profits would increase. The analyst can assess the effect of such variations and calculate an expected cost for raw material. A full sensitivity analysis would integrate the variations in both the sales of finished goods and the cost of raw material. A combined sensitivity analysis of this kind is shown in table 4-7.

## Organization of the Procurement System

Whether the agroindustrial processor obtains an adequate supply of quality raw material at the appropriate time and for a reasonable cost

**Table 4-7.** *Sensitivity Analysis of Sales and Raw Material Costs*
(thousands of dollars)

| | Scenario | | | |
|---|---|---|---|---|
| Item | Historical trend holds | Raw material costs rise 10 percent | Revenues fall 10 percent | Costs rise 10 percent; revenues fall 10 percent |
| Revenues | 500 | 500 | 450 | 450 |
| Costs | 300 | 325 | 300 | 325 |
| Profits | 200 | 175 | 150 | 125 |
| Change in profits (percent) | 0.0 | −12.5 | −25 | −37.5 |

Source: Author's calculations.

ultimately rests on the organization of the procurement system. This organization can be examined through the system's structure, power relationships, vertical integration, and producer organizations.

*Structure*

Earlier, it was suggested that the projected supply of raw material could be computed from production statistics. But there is a difference between statistical and actual supplies. Unless an organizational structure exists linking farm and factory, the potential supply to the factory may never be realized. The experience of a modern, multi-million dollar beef-processing plant constructed in a Southeast Asian nation illustrates the point. The project analysis included national statistics that revealed a large and growing cattle population. Six months after opening, however, the factory was operating at only 8 percent of capacity because it lacked raw material. Contrary to expectations, the statistical cattle did not materialize as beef: the cattle owners were small farmers with transport problems who, unaware of the plant's needs, did not, or could not, alter their custom of selling their cattle to the local abattoir or to intermediaries who in turn sold to the abattoirs.

The structure and relationships in the production chain must be analyzed to determine where and how the new project's procurement system will fit in. Several dimensions of this structure should be examined.

NUMBER OF PRODUCERS, TRANSPORTERS, BUYERS. Knowing the number of operators in the system will help the firm to evaluate methods of reaching potential suppliers. If the structure is fragmented, containing many small producers, the organizational burden of assembling sufficient produce may be great. Analysis of the operators in the system will also help the firm to identify possible bottlenecks in crop assembly or transport and will suggest the competition in buying. It is also important to identify the extent of direct government involvement in the chain through state-owned enterprises or marketing boards, because these organizations can wield great influence.

SUPPLIER SIZE. When farms are large, the plant needs fewer suppliers. Large farms can also use a variety of production techniques, such as irrigation or mechanized harvesting, that can improve supply certainty and the processing plant's scheduling. Nevertheless, firms should be careful to avoid a bias against smaller farm suppliers, who can be excellent sources of raw material and whose involvement is important for economic and social development. The issue is that suppliers of different size have different resources and production techniques that may require different services from the factory or government. Small farms may require transport services, whereas larger ones may have their own vehicles. With the appropriate technology, small farmers can make desired output gains.

Seeds and fertilizer can equally benefit large and small farms if the project can ensure that financial and technical assistance are also available. In Pakistan, for instance, small farmers adopted low-cost tubewell systems, suggesting that irrigation needs can be addressed at both the small- and large-scale levels.[62] Small farms are generally family-based operations that can best be understood with an integrated perspective on their household economics and farming system.[63] In particular, it is important to identify the relative roles of men, women, and children in the household's farming and social activities. Although the relative efficiency of large versus smaller farms is still debated, there is sufficient evidence to conclude that smaller farms can be acceptably efficient producers for agro-industries.[64]

SUPPLY LOCATION AND CROP MIX. The firm must know where its producers are located to determine transport costs, optimal plant location, logistical control problems, and the vulnerability of supply to disease or drought, which may be geographically concentrated. The analysis should identify growers of specific crops and the relative market importance of these growers and crops to anticipate shifts by suppliers from one crop to another. Patterns of crop specialization will also be revealed by the analysis. In other words, the firm needs to identify who is producing what, where, and when.

OWNERSHIP PATTERNS. The analysis should distinguish between land that is owned, rented, sharecropped, or squatted. Owners may be more willing than renters to adopt new cultivation techniques because of the fixed investments but, again, the project planners should consciously avoid favoring land-owning farmers over renters and instead encourage a diverse agricultural structure. The project may need to include financial incentives and land-reform programs to maintain this evenhandedness. Inequitable land tenure is a fundamental constraint on the ability of agroindustries to help foster a country's social and economic development.

FLOW. The analyst should also determine the quantity and sequence of produce flows through each operator in the procurement system. These distribution channels should be analyzed to determine if the project can gain entry to the existing flow system.

## Analysis of Power Relationships

The production structure is only one aspect in the organization of the procurement system; its inner operations, including the power structure, must also be considered. In the systems approach, analyzing relationships is essential. To understand the procurement channels, one must know who holds power and what the source of that power is. Indicators of power are the size of profit margins, the volume of produce handled (as a percentage of total marketed crop), and the number of participants involved in each intermediate step (transporters, storage operators, industrial buyers, and the like). These data can be gathered by examining the procurement system's structure or by interviewing participants in the system.

Clearly, all participants in the system have some power. Farmers derive power from possessing the product buyers desire. Transporters' power comes from the service they offer. Financiers' power is based on their critical input of capital. An agroindustry is powerful because, as a market outlet, it is a buyer. Sometimes power derives from noneconomic factors such as personal or family ties.

The analysis should focus not only on the system's relative distribution of power but also on its imbalances, because these can create inequities, disruptions, and inefficiencies in a factory's procurement activities. The challenge facing an agroindustry's procurement operation is to achieve a "positive sum game," by which the new factory benefits, rather than exploits, the participants in the system. If the new factory threatens to exploit the participants, they will resist the firm's entrance to the market. If small farmers are the injured participants, the project's social desirability is questionable and it may elicit negative repercussions from government. Agroindustries should also be cautious if the number of suppliers is small. This concentration increases the power of the suppliers. A monopsony facing a monopoly may create a stalemate or, alternatively, a powerful strategic alliance. The outcome is uncertain and the risk high.

Mexican breweries illustrate how agroindustries can gain bargaining power in the procurement system.[65] First, they created a joint procurement organization (IASA) to buy barley from the farmers, thereby reducing competition for the raw material supply and creating an effective monopony. Their buying organization provided to producers, on credit, the seed of the specified characteristics the breweries needed, and the seeds were grown according to IASA technicians' specification. Thus the buyers exercised financial and technical control over the suppliers. The rain-fed highland farmers organized into a seller's organization to obtain higher prices, but the breweries had additional power because they had other supply sources: they could wait for the subsequent winter crop from the irrigated farms in another area or they could get licenses from the government to import barley from the United States. The government was predisposed to avert barley shortages because of tax revenues it received from beer sales.

The farmers were in a relatively weak bargaining position. However, their mobilization efforts attracted enough media and political attention that Mexico's president instructed the secretary of agriculture to urge the breweries to negotiate with the organized barley farmers. The breweries complied. In effect, the farmers used political leverage as a source of bargaining power. Still, the negotiations yielded a relatively small price increase, so the farmers used their ultimate weapon: they switched to another crop, and the breweries lost this supply source.

A government itself sometimes exercises monopolistic power through marketing boards or through price supports and procurement programs operated by state-owned enterprises. In such instances the government may become the agroindustry's potential supplier or it could be a rival competing for the farmers' output. In the 1980s governments tended to withdraw from these direct marketing activities, but vested interests, fears about intermediaries' exploitation, and the desire to control politically sensitive food supplies and prices have limited these moves toward market liberalization.[66]

Even without state-owned enterprises, governments have considerable power to affect both the structure and behavior of procurement activities. Venezuela's state food-marketing enterprise was quite ineffective and so was closed down.[67] The government subsequently used its import and exchange rate controls to stimulate development of the agricultural sector. To reduce the need to import vegetable oil, for example, the government allocated oil import quotas, at preferential exchange rates, among the vegetable oil processors, partially in accordance with how much credit each gave farmers and what share of the local production each was able to procure. This created an enormous incentive for the processors to forge close links and positive relationships with the suppliers. Consequently, they mounted extensive credit programs, provided various production inputs and technical assistance, and helped with other services such as transport. One producer even launched a major biotechnology research effort to develop oilseeds of superior quality. Profits from the quota of cheaper imported oil more than paid for these supplier support activities, which the agroindustries carried out far more efficiently and effectively than the government had previously done, and they successfully stimulated more local production of oilseed.

### Backward Vertical Integration

A major issue in designing the procurement system is whether the agroindustry should use the existing suppliers or assume some production, assembly, or transport functions. The advantages to this latter option, known as backward vertical integration, depend on the needs of each project. The analyst should, however, be aware of the following possible effects of integration.

CONTROL. If the agroindustry has employees qualified to perform the new functions, its control will increase with integration. Increased control improves the likelihood that the firm can obtain the desired quantity and quality of raw material. Centralizing the decisionmaking should also improve product coordination and increase the dependability of supply. Sometimes the characteristics of the raw materials increase the importance of control. For example, the quality of palm oil nuts deteriorates significantly if they are not processed rapidly; that is not the case with rubber. Accordingly, palm oil production and processing mills in Malaysia are integrated while the rubber operations need not be.

By having at least some of its production coming from its own farms, the agroindustry also can conduct agronomic research aimed at enhancing quality or productivity; such knowledge gains can be disseminated to the contract growers, thereby improving their performance and linking them to the processor. Additionally, being engaged in farming will increase the processor's understanding of the farmers' problems and perspectives and contribute to greater empathy and mutual problem solving.

CAPITAL REQUIREMENTS. Integration can significantly increase the fixed and working capital requirements of the agroindustrial project, which in turn increase the project's costs and capital exposure. Two agroindustries attempted unsuccessfully to enter the crop assembly and purchasing area but they were financially and administratively unequipped to advance credit to the farmers. The farmers therefore chose to sell to the traditional intermediaries, who were willing and able to provide working capital financing to tie up the supply.

FLEXIBILITY. Backward integration tends to lock the agroindustry into fixed investments and costs and a predetermined structure. This limitation reduces multiple source options, which could be important if adverse disease or weather conditions strike the integrated operations. More of the eggs are going into the proverbial basket. Similarly, if demand plummets, the integrated operation is stuck with the fixed costs of the farm, while the unintegrated operation simply reduces its purchases from suppliers.

COSTS. An integrated system can permit efficiencies and economies of scale that are otherwise unattainable, thereby lowering the firm's variable costs. This is one of the anticipated benefits that compensates for the increased risks that accompany the assumption of production activities and their fixed costs. In determining costs, however, one should not underestimate the larger managerial requirements, in both time and talent, of running an integrated operation; the complexity of the activities is greatly magnified and the time to mount the system often significantly lengthened.

Although definitive guidelines for backward vertical integration are impossible, the strategy is more appropriate than operating solely through existing channels when a firm is introducing a new crop or opening new production areas. This opening of new ground is what led Central American banana firms to develop from the start totally integrated structures for cultivation, packing, and export. There were no existing supply systems. A more common method for organizing sources, currently used by the banana industry, is to obtain a portion of the raw material from the factory's own farms and a portion from outside producers. This dual sourcing pattern has the advantages of retaining significant sourcing flexibility while reducing the risk of supply shortages and control problems. When the Mexican government began privatizing its sugar mills in 1988, the major soft drink companies and bakeries were among the groups that created alliances to buy and operate the mills. Their rationale for this backward vertical integration was to ensure their supply source. If your competitor is integrating backwards, you may have little choice but to follow.

Backward vertical integration may not be feasible because others in the chain may resist the concentration of power or because the possible labor displacement from integration may not be deemed socially desirable. Alternatively, the firm can use producer organizations, a strategy that has its own advantages.

## Producer Organizations

Agroindustries have sometimes served as catalysts for the collective organization of farmers. Producers often fail to organize because they lack a strong focal point around which to mobilize community interest and participation. By providing a new market outlet, agroindustries create a necessary economic incentive for farmers to organize.

Producers' organizations can be advantageous to the agroindustrial plant, especially when procurement depends on numerous small suppliers. If suppliers organize, the plant has a conduit for communication and negotiation with farmers, a channel that can save the plant considerable effort, time, and money. Organizing producers, however, is a difficult and time-consuming task, and analysts should identify the barriers to organizing and the potential inducements to surmount them.

Farmers sometimes organize without the plant's encouragement, especially if the plant has created a power imbalance in the farm-to-factory system, as the case of the Mexican barley producers showed. In another country, a new tomato-processing plant began purchasing the bulk of the local farmers' output. Dissatisfied with the prices, the farmers formed a cooperative; by consolidating their power, they were able to negotiate supply contracts with the factory at improved prices. The agroindustry can encourage producers to organize by incorporating incentives in its procurement strategy. One effective method is to identify the multiple constraints surrounding the small farmers' efforts in marketing their produce and then to suggest a solution. The most common marketing barriers include infrastructure (for example, roads and storage), services (for example, transport and shelling), inputs (for example, bags and credit), and information (for example, prices and market standards). Because the marketing system is also a social system, barriers from social obligations and behavioral patterns can also be expected.[68]

When the barriers are attitudinal, economic incentives are not sufficient. For example, one government launched a major program to increase its cattle supply. The farmers affected by the program were primarily rice producers, each of whom owned an average of eight cattle, which grazed freely on common land and the farmer's plot. Each farmer raised and sold the cattle as he chose. The government intended to form cooperatives, fence the common land, pool the farmers' cattle in large herds, and provide veterinary services and financing for tractors and inputs for new pastures. These components of the program were expected to decrease cattle mortality and morbidity rates, shorten the growth cycle, and raise the slaughter weight. When the program started, farmers refused to enter the cooperatives and pool their cattle because both concepts were dramatic departures from traditional patterns of individual ownership and production. Even though the program was economically sound, it required too great a change in the producers' attitudes toward trust relationships and collective action, and its potential remained unrealized.

Frequently, several barriers must be confronted simultaneously before farmers see the benefits of organization. This was the conclusion of Compañía Nacional de Subsistencias Populares (CONASUPO), the Mexican government's agricultural produce-marketing organization.[69] Although CONASUPO's support prices were higher than those of intermediaries, few farmers sold to the organization and, consequently, its warehouses had tremendous excess capacity. A survey revealed that farmers lacked transport for their grain to the CONASUPO warehouses, adequate price information, bags, and shelling equipment. Furthermore, the farmers had promised their crops to buyers who had lent them preharvest money. In response to these findings, CONASUPO mounted a program to (a) reimburse farmers for the cost of farm-to-warehouse transport, with the farmers assembling their grains and locating the means of transport, (b) provide shelling services at cost, (c) lend bags to the farmers, and (d) provide consumer credit that would free the farmers from store owners and other intermediaries. The net result was a significant increase in supplies sold to the organization.

In this case it was the government that developed a marketing system for the small farmers, but the processing plant could have done it. Several multinational agribusiness companies have mounted extensive programs to assist and help organize producers.[70] The Anand Cooperative, a producer-owned milk-processing plant in India, successfully organized hundreds of small farmers and landless rural dwellers as suppliers. By providing technical production inputs, a guaranteed market outlet, and fair prices paid upon delivery, the cooperative doubled the income of the landless laborers who comprised one-third of its members.[71]

These examples introduce a final aspect of procurement organization that merits consideration: a producer's forward vertical integration. Just as a processor may integrate backward to take on production functions, so may farmers integrate vertically forward to the processing stage, becoming the owners and operators of an agroindustry. Larger, wealthier, and more managerially sophisticated producers are more likely than small farmers to integrate vertically forward. Yet small farmers are not excluded from entering the processing stage; combining their efforts to form a cooperative or corporation can lead to this integration.

Producer cooperatives in the process of integrating vertically forward, however, frequently encounter managerial problems. An agroindustrial operation is different from farming, and the analyst advising such cooperatives should ensure that the producers have had adequate training, receive technical assistance, or obtain contracted, external management. A poorly managed agroindustry can become an economic burden to farmers if their production profits are consumed by processing losses. Successful producers' cooperatives exist, but they generally have developed over time. The effective fruit-marketing cooperatives of Taiwan, China, for example, took thirty years to evolve.[72] In Maharashtra, India, cooperatives produce

**Table 4-8.** *Degree of Vertical Integration for Selected Products in the United States, 1980*
(percent)

| Product | Integration mechanism | | Total integrated |
| | Contractual | Ownership | |
| --- | --- | --- | --- |
| Sugar beets | 98 | 2 | 100 |
| Sugar cane | 40 | 60 | 100 |
| Processing vegetables | 85 | 15 | 100 |
| Citrus fruits | 65 | 35 | 100 |
| Broiler chickens | 89 | 10 | 99 |
| Fluid milk | 95 | 3 | 98 |
| Potatoes | 60 | 35 | 95 |
| Seed crops | 80 | 10 | 90 |
| Turkeys | 62 | 28 | 90 |
| Eggs | 52 | 37 | 89 |
| Fresh vegetables | 18 | 35 | 53 |
| Manufactured milk products | 23 | 7 | 30 |
| Cotton | 17 | 1 | 18 |
| Feed cattle | 10 | 6 | 16 |
| Sheep, lambs | 7 | 3 | 10 |
| Oil-bearing crops | 10 | 0 | 10 |
| Food grains | 8 | 1 | 9 |
| Feed grains | 7 | 1 | 8 |
| Tobacco | 2 | 2 | 4 |
| Hogs | 2 | 2 | 4 |
| All farm products | 23 | 7 | 30 |

*Source:* Adapted from Richard L. Kohls and Joseph N. Uhl, *Marketing of Agricultural Products*, 6th ed. (New York: Macmillan, 1985), p. 253, using data from the U.S. Department of Agriculture.

and process about 90 percent of the white sugar, outcompeting private mills because of their better access to the raw material.[73] In the United States, some integrated cooperatives, such as the dairy-based Land O' Lakes with 1989 sales of $2,377 million, are among the nation's top 500 firms in terms of revenue.[74]

In practice, forward and backward vertical integration take place through ownership and contracts. Through either mechanism the strategic thrust of integration is to capture advantage by establishing tighter linkages in the production chain. Circumstances, which differ by product and country setting, will determine the desirability of integration for each project. In the United States, the trend has been toward increased integration, with contractual mechanisms being the dominant mode (see table 4-8).

## Summary

Because of the transformative nature of agroindustries, procurement of raw material is critical to the processing plant's success. Defects in procurement and supply are carried through, and sometimes magnified in, the processing and marketing activities. Raw material costs are generally the major cost of the agroindustry. Moreover, the organization of the project's procurement system can significantly determine its socioeconomic benefits.

An effective procurement system attempts to obtain a quantity of raw material that will satisfy both market demand and a plant's processing capacity. Defining that quantity requires an examination of the raw material's historical, current, and projected planting area, yields, and alternative uses. The raw material must also meet the quality standards of each market segment. It is essential for an agroindustry to determine what characteristics of the raw material will produce the desired end product and then set quality requirements for suppliers. Farm inputs, cultural practices, and storage and transport services all affect the quality of raw material. The plant will need quality-control mechanisms to monitor and upgrade its raw material.

In addition to obtaining the desired quantity and quality of raw material, the procurement system must also ensure that the raw material is delivered to the plant at the appropriate time. Timing is complicated by several factors. The seasonality of production, inherent in the biological nature of the raw material, causes an uneven flow to the factory. This cyclical pattern creates a peak flow, which requires extra processing or storage capacity. The agroindustrial firm should consider methods to spread the flow of raw material more evenly.

The perishability of raw material similarly emphasizes the importance of timing in moving produce from the farm to the factory.

Storage and processing techniques can reduce losses because of deterioration. Availability—determined by the raw material's growth cycle and the expected duration of supply—also affects procurement timing. Before going ahead with its project, a firm should measure the certainty of supply and the relative permanence of the crop.

Although the quantity and quality of the raw material and the timing of its procurement may all be acceptable, the procurement system is not economically viable unless the raw material is reasonably priced. The cost must be low enough to allow the processing plant to generate a profit that yields an acceptable return on investment. The analyst must examine the main factors affecting costs: supply and demand, opportunity costs, structural factors, logistical services, and governmental interventions. The mechanisms and alternatives for establishing raw material prices should also be evaluated: spot prices, governmental price supports, contracting, joint ventures, and backward vertical integration. In addition, the analyst should calculate the sensitivity of profits and investment returns to changes in raw material prices.

The procurement system's overall effectiveness ultimately rests on its organization. To achieve a sound organization, the firm should study the farm-to-factory structure, which is built upon the number, size, and location of farmers, intermediaries, transporters, storage operators, and other industrial buyers. The analyst should also examine the pattern of farmland ownership, existing degrees of vertical integration, and the volume and channels of commodity flow. This structural analysis leads to an examination of power within the supply channels, the basis of that power, and the implications for the project's raw material supply. The plant's major alternative to using the existing structure is backward vertical integration, and the desirability of this alternative should be assessed in relation to control, capital requirements, flexibility, costs, social effects, and political feasibility. Project analysts should also determine whether producers are, or could be, grouped into cooperative organizations and how such organizations would affect the agroindustry's procurement system. One last option to explore in examining procurement activities for a project is the possibility of farmers' integrating vertically forward into processing.

The analysis of the procurement system must also carefully consider the system's links with government policies and actions. These can affect all of the five elements in procurement: quantity, quality, timing, cost, and organization. Government impact on procurement comes through (a) its control over access to production inputs, raw material sources, and markets; (b) its influence on input and output prices; (c) its effect on industry structure; and (d) its regulatory standards. The following are all ways that governments can influence the procurement system: providing public lands and research to farmers; developing irrigation, transportation, and storage infrastructure; subsidizing production inputs and marketing services; imposing duties and quotas on imports of inputs and raw materials; imposing export controls and taxes; fixing exchange rates; supporting the price of raw materials; setting up state-owned enterprises to act as buyers, storers, and suppliers of raw materials; licensing agroindustries; supporting producer organizations; and setting quality standards and food safety requirements. The mega-force of government is pervasive in agroindustry.

## The Procurement Factor: Salient Points for Project Analysis

The project analyst should consider the following questions when reviewing the procurement dimensions of an agroindustrial project.

### Adequate Quantity

*What was the total production pattern?*
- Production levels in the past?
- Degree of variability?
- Causes of variability?

*What is the usage pattern of the area planted?*
- Variation in area?
- Area economically arable but uncultivated?
- New trends in opening land?
- Government policies affecting land expansion?
- Irrigation usage and double cropping possibilities?
- Extent and role of farm mechanization?
- Extent and feasibility of crop shifting?
- Nutritional consequences of crop shifting?
- Effects of urbanization, industrialization, land reform?

*What is the crop yield (or livestock procreation rate)?*
- Levels and variability in yield?
- Causes?
- Quality of land?
- Irrigation effects on yield?
- Extent of usage of agrochemicals and improved seed (or improved breed)?
- Barriers to increased usage of inputs?
- Deficiencies in the distribution system?
- Input costs?

- Government policies affecting costs?
- Lack of knowledge?

*How profitable is the crop (or animal production)?*
- Profitability relative to alternative crops (or animal production)?
- Cost structure relative to alternative crops (or animal production)?
- Perceived risk?

*What is the possible effect of biotechnology on supply?*
- State of biotechnology research, facilities, personnel, and companies?
- Roles of molecular, cellular, and whole plant biology?
- Possible effects on yield, insect prevention, disease detection and resistance?
- Cost effects?
- Opportunities for differentiation via special traits?
- Government policies toward biotechnology?
- Who does technology affect and how?

*How sensitive is supply to production changes?*
- Effect on output of changes in area planted?
- Incentives needed to increase acreage?
- Cost and probability of increasing yields?

*Is the raw material a by-product of another agroindustry?*
- Supply and market demand of primary product?
- Availability of import supply?
- Availability of substitute raw material?

*What is the on-farm consumption?*
- Portion of crop consumed before marketing?
- Effect of higher output or prices on commercial marketing?
- Nutritional effects of increased commercialization?

*How is the product consumed?*
- Fresh, processed, or both?
- Proportions and trends of consumption?
- Complementary or competitive uses?

*What is the animal versus human usage?*
- Animal, human, or mixed usage?
- Proportions and trends of usage?
- Governmental priorities?

*What are the industrial uses of the raw material?*
- Number of end products?
- Relative demand and price differentials?

*Are similar agroindustries competing for the same raw materials?*
- Number of competitors?
- Domestic or foreign?
- Size of their raw material needs?
- Their procurement methods?
- Government policies affecting procurement competition?

*What are the probable crop (or animal) losses?*
- From rodents, insects, disease, handling, storage?
- Measures to reduce losses?
- Adequacy of on- and off-farm services and storage facilities?

### Acceptable Quality

*What are the market's quality requirements?*
- Different segments' standards?
- Price premiums for quality?

*What is the quality of the inputs for farm supply?*
- Effects of seed varieties (or breeds)?
- Effects of agrochemicals?
- Possible contribution of biotechnology?
- Farmers' knowledge of input usage?

*How do handling, transport, and storage affect quality?*
- Personnel adequately trained?
- Availability and quality of transport?
- Type and quality of storage facilities?
- Nutritional deterioration?
- Adverse changes in appearance?

*What government grading and health standards exist?*
- Requirements for raw materials?
- Requirements for processed products?
- Implications for procurement and processing specifications?

*What services can increase quality control?*
- Inputs provided by processor?
- Cost?
- Increased quality control?
- Economic benefits?

*What quality specifications and inspection procedures should be instituted?*
- Standardized specifications for raw material?
- Communicated to farmer?
- Inspection procedures?

*What quality control would result from backward vertical integration?*
- Additional control?
- Cost versus benefits?

## Appropriate Timing

*What is the seasonal harvesting pattern?*
- Period of harvest (or time of slaughter)?
- Effect of seed (or livestock breed) on timing?
- Effect of planting (or feeding) on timing?
- Costs and benefits of changing the harvesting (or slaughter) pattern?

*What facilities does the seasonal pattern require?*
- Drying (or corral) capacity?
- Storage capacity for peak inventory?
- Availability of rentable storage space?

*How perishable is the raw material?*
- Timing of harvest (or slaughter)?
- Period after harvest (or slaughter)?

*What facilities are required to prevent the raw material from deteriorating?*
- Harvesting (or slaughter), transport, and storage?
- Scheduling?
- Special treatments to reduce perishability?

*When and for how long will the raw material be available?*
- Crop (or breed) new to area?
- Agronomic testing period?
- Planting-to-harvest period (or breeding cycle)?
- Farmer financing during start-up period?
- Ecological viability of agricultural practices?
- Pattern of life-cycle yield of perennial crops (or breeding stock)?
- Effect of raw material flow on continuity?
- Switching among land uses expected?
- Effect of multiple sources?

## Reasonable Cost

*How do supply and demand affect the cost of raw material?*
- Strength of demand from competing users?
- Effect of project on demand and prices?
- Availability of supply at different prices?

*What are the farmers' opportunity costs?*
- Alternative uses of land?
- Relative profitability of alternative uses?

*How do structural factors affect costs?*
- Margins of intermediaries?
- Cost and feasibility of factory's performing these functions?

*How do logistical services affect raw material costs?*
- Existing transport charges?
- Storage and handling services?

*How does governmental involvement affect raw material costs?*
- Infrastructure investments in roads, storage, wholesaling facilities?
- Production input subsidies?
- Import and export controls and exchange rates?
- State-owned enterprise marketing activities?

*Should spot prices be used?*
- Prevailing spot prices?
- Variability during and across years?
- Competitors' buying practices?
- Possibility of multiple sources—domestic and imports?
- Feasibility of shifting geographical sources of raw materials?
- Relative price levels and variability?
- Lowest cost combination?
- Organizational or technical problems?

*How do government support prices affect pricing?*
- Existence of support prices?
- Portion of crop (or herd) affected?
- Comparability with spot prices?
- Pan-temporal? Effect on storage pattern?
- Pan-territorial? Effect on geographical sourcing pattern?
- Quality differentials?
- Access to support prices?

*Is contracting a potential pricing mechanism?*
- Current use of production contracts?
- Duration of price agreements?
- Expected contract compliance?

*Are joint ventures feasible and desirable?*
- Farmers interested in investment?
- Effects on raw material costs?

*Would backward integration lower raw material costs?*
- Feasibility of integration?
- Effect on costs?

*What does the sensitivity analysis of raw material costs reveal?*
- Effect of raw material cost changes on profits and return?
- Probability of such changes?

## Organization

*Who are the operators in the production system?*
- Number of producers, transporters, buyers?
- Government's position in structure?
- Implications for organization and control of system?
- Percentage of crop (or herd) handled by each?
- Size of supplier and its interaction with plant?

*What is the supplier's location and crop mix?*
- Implications of supplier's location for plant's location, logistical control, and vulnerability to agronomic supply?
- Current crops (or livestock)?
- Extent of specialization?
- Degree of crop (or livestock) shifting?

*What are the patterns of land ownership?*
- Land ownership, renting, sharecropping, or squatting?
- Farmer mobility?
- Effects on plant's procurement relations?

*What are the routes, timing, and accessibility of the raw material's flow?*
- Channels?
- Size of flow?
- Timing of flow?
- Availability to plant?

*What does the analysis of power relationships reveal?*
- Who holds power in system?
- Extent of power?
- Basis of power?
- Government's power?
- Basis and strength of projected agroindustry's power?

*Should producers integrate vertically backward?*
- Added control over quantity, quality, and timing?
- Extent of integration?
- Additional requirements for fixed investment and working capital?

- Reduction of flexibility in obtaining sources of raw material?
- Effect on variable and fixed costs and break-even point?
- Political feasibility?
- Social feasibility?

*Are there producers' organizations?*
- Degree of organization?
- Purposes and activities?
- Barriers to organization?
- Possible incentives for producers to organize?
- Use of organizations to communicate, control quality, transmit services?

*Should farmers integrate forward?*
- Financial and managerial resources available for, and economic and social benefits from, forward vertical integration?
- Integration via ownership or contracting?

# 5 *The Processing Factor*

HAVING EXAMINED AGROINDUSTRIAL OUTPUT (marketing) and input (procurement) activities, let us now assess processing, the transformative activity of an agroindustry. Processing is the central operation in an agroindustrial enterprise and the point at which project analysts must make crucial investment decisions.

## Primary Elements

To analyze the processing component, it is important to understand its functions, which are both technical and strategic. From a technical standpoint the purposes are to make plant or animal materials portable, palatable, and preservable—the "3 P's" of food processing. Most processing involves reducing the bulkiness of the raw materials or converting them into a more easily or economically transportable and tradable form; for example, whole animals are converted to portion cuts, sugarcane to sugar, palm nuts to oil. Processing also achieves palatability—creating a product that is edible (or industrially usable), digestible, nontoxic, and pleasurable to the senses in taste, sight, smell, and texture. Additionally, the processing operation aims to reduce the natural processes of deterioration inherent in all biological material, thereby preserving the product's quality until consumed.

Processing functions should also be understood as strategic activities that add value in the production chain and create competitive advantage. These goals are achieved by designing and operating processing activities in ways that attain cost economies or product differentiation. The technical functions of processing should be viewed from this strategic perspective.

Although food and fiber processing varies widely in form and complexity, depending on the type of process and kind of raw material, the processing operations themselves share several common factors. The transformation of the raw materials occurs through physical, chemical, or biological processes, and the processing operations generally involve all or some of the following: receiving, conditioning, storing, separating, concentrating, mixing, forming, stabilizing, and packaging (see table 5-1).[1] These common features suggest six primary elements that should be considered when examining an agroindustry's processing stage:

- *Processing technology.* Before choosing appropriate processing technology, the analyst reviews the market requirements; technical processing requirements; costs and availability of labor, capital, energy, materials; capacity utilization; skill capabilities; and nutritional consequences.
- *Plant location.* The analyst examines considerations of raw material, market, transport, labor, infrastructure, land, and how the plant is likely to affect development in the area.
- *Inventory management.* The analyst assesses storage capacity, physical facilities, and financial aspects.
- *Packaging and other materials.* The analyst evaluates the functions of and options for product packaging and identifies needs for other input required in the processing operations.
- *Programming and control.* The analyst considers the design of production, product quality, and environmental control systems.
- *By-products.* The analyst examines the economic possibilities of secondary outputs of production.

## Processing Technology

Technology selection is often the most important decision in designing the project's processing operation. A note of warning: Although the discussion here focuses on the factors to be considered in selecting processing technology, once the choice is made, it is critically important to do adequate pilot testing of the chosen technology, particularly if the technology or materials are new to the country or the company. Appropriate performance guarantees and ongoing technical and engineering backup need to be obtained from the technology suppliers at least through the start-up and initial operation stages. Technical and operational glitches are inevitable in plant start-ups, and the uncertainties surrounding technological newness magnify these problems. Rushing into full-scale production without adequate pilot testing has led many agroindustries into costly, or even fatal, operating problems.

### Market Requirements

The processing technology should be tailored to meet the market's requirements for product quality (as determined by the marketing analysis). Because consumers' preferences for quality vary, there are a variety of technological options that will yield varying levels of

**Table 5-1. Agroindustry Processing Operations**

| Receiving | Conditioning | Storing | Separating | Concentrating | Mixing | Forming | Stabilizing | Packaging |
|---|---|---|---|---|---|---|---|---|
| Unloading | Cleaning | Handling | Cutting | Heating: | Agitation | Molding | Curing | Canning: |
| Weighing | Sorting | Control: | Crushing | Air | Aeration | Extruding | Fermentation | Aluminum |
| Inspection | Grading | Temperature | Rolling | Water | Measuring | | Drying | Tin |
| | Drying | Humidity | Shearing | Pressure | Blending | | Aggregation | Steel |
| | Cutting | Ventilation | Milling | Vacuum | Pelletizing | | Cooling | Glass |
| | | Pest | Screening | Distillation | | | Freezing | Paper |
| | | Insect | Vibrating | Centrifugal: | | | Freeze drying | Plastic |
| | | | Centrifuge | Acceleration | | | Heat | Aseptic |
| | | | Flotation | | | | sterilization | Controlled |
| | | | Aspiration | | | | Irradiation | atmosphere |
| | | | Enzyme | | | | | |
| | | | treatment | | | | | |
| | | | Chemical | | | | | |
| | | | extraction | | | | | |

*Note:* Not all agroindustry products undergo all of these operations or subprocesses.

142

desired quality in the agroindustrial end products. The firm can avoid unnecessary investments and maximize revenue by modulating its processing technology to the requirements of its selected market segments. For example, a major quality factor governing the price of rice is wholeness of the grain. A primary objective in rice milling is to obtain the maximum yield of unbroken grain, and thus a higher price. The export prices of Thai rice in 1975 reflect this factor:

| Quality (percent broken grains) | Price (dollars per metric ton) | Quality discount (percent) |
|---|---|---|
| 0 | 345 | 0 |
| 5 | 303 | −12 |
| 15 | 287 | −17 |

In milling operations, breakage is determined by seed variety and the kind of drying and milling equipment. Changes in texture and structure during drying significantly affect breakage rates during milling.[2] Technological options for milling range from pounding by hand to almost completely automated milling. The higher capital investments for more sophisticated technology must be compared with the higher revenues from the larger total milling yield and the premium prices that the increased yield of whole grain will obtain. The quality demands of the market and the price spread between whole and broken grain are two criteria for deciding on more or less sophisticated technology.

Choosing a technology that will produce a quality superior to that already in the market might fulfill unmet preferences and thus be a good way to increase market share. A business group in Pakistan set up a milk-processing plant to produce sterilized milk in special packages that allowed the milk to be stored unrefrigerated for several weeks, in contrast to the raw and pasteurized milk currently on the market.[3] The firm was successful in introducing a differentiated product aimed at fulfilling unmet preferences. In the United States the NutraSweet company has used food technology to create new foods to meet consumers' desires to avoid excess calories and fats. It recently developed a process for treating a premix (milk and egg proteins, vegetable gum, lecithin, sugar, acid, and water) with deaeration and heating and then intense agitation (microparticulation) to create uniform microparticles that appear as fluid. This new ingredient (Simplesse), used to make frozen desserts, salad dressing, mayonnaise, and other products, has the nutritional advantages of being almost fat-free, low in cholesterol and calories, and high in protein.

The NutraSweet example illustrates a second point: Consumers' quality demands are dynamic. The analyst should, therefore, assess the risk that changing quality preferences will make a particular technology obsolete; the analyst should also ascertain ways to improve quality to meet consumer needs.

The quality requirements of the export market frequently exceed those of the domestic market. A production shift to exporting may require corresponding technological adjustments. Alternatively, servicing both markets may permit a broader use of raw material because products unacceptable for the export market can be sold domestically. Similarly, it may be desirable to operate both fresh and processed fruit and vegetable operations simultaneously. Produce that is unacceptable in the fresh market because it blemishes easily or matures too quickly can be processed. A marketing project for fresh apples in India, for example, significantly increased farmers' income when it added a processing component to use the culled apples, which represented 20 percent of its gross production.[4] However, basing a processing operation on a by-product entails several additional considerations, which are examined in the final section of this chapter.

### Process Requirements

Certain kinds of processing can be carried out only by a narrow range of technology because of the nature of the transformative process. Consequently, little choice exists regarding the type of equipment to be used. These technical constraints can also have economic implications. A capital-intensive process, for example, will have a minimum economic scale of operations, below which the agroindustry will not be financially viable. These possible requirements of scale must be assessed against the market forecasts to see if the project should proceed (see table 5-2).

Other technical requirements may limit the range of choice. If the operation is a continuous flow rather than a batch process, then the technology may dictate automatic measuring devices for adding ingredients because precision and timing are critical. Sometimes the government imposes requirements to ensure food safety or grading standards. Compliance is compulsory and may require a specific technology, for example, pasteurization, irradiation, or effluent treatment.

### Costs

Within the constraints imposed by the market and process requirements, the project must attempt to select the technology that will minimize costs. In calculating costs, however, the analyst should consider public as well as private costs, which can differ significantly. Different technologies can also make varying uses of the factors of

**Table 5-2.** *Minimum Shipments for Efficient Scale of Operation in U.S. Food Manufacturing Plants, 1972*
(percentage of total industry shipments)

| | |
|---|---|
| Bakery products | 1.1 |
| Bread, cake, and related products | 0.1 |
| Cookies and crackers | 2.0 |
| Beverages | 2.0 |
| Distilled liquor | 2.6 |
| Flavorings | 1.2 |
| Malt | 4.3 |
| Malt beverages | 1.4 |
| Soft drinks | 0.1 |
| Wines and brandy | 2.1 |
| Canned and frozen foods | 1.4 |
| Canned fruits and vegetables | 0.2 |
| Canned specialties | 2.6 |
| Dried fruits and vegetables | 2.3 |
| Frozen foods | 0.9 |
| Pickles, sauces, and dressings | 0.8 |
| Dairy products | 0.7 |
| Condensed and evaporated milk | 1.5 |
| Creamery butter | 1.1 |
| Fluid milk products | 0.1 |
| Ice cream and ices | 0.4 |
| Natural and processed cheese | 0.4 |
| Fats and oils | 2.3 |
| Animal and marine fats and oils | 0.4 |
| Cottonseed oil | 1.5 |
| Shortening and cooking oils | 1.8 |
| Soybean oil | 1.0 |
| Vegetable oil | 6.7 |
| Grain mill products | 5.1 |
| Animal feeds | 0.1 |
| Blended and prepared flour | 5.0 |
| Cereal breakfast foods | 9.5 |
| Flour | 0.7 |
| Milled rice | 9.9 |
| Pet food | 3.0 |
| Wet-milled corn | 7.5 |
| Meat products | 0.6 |
| Dressed poultry | 0.3 |
| Packaged meats | 0.3 |
| Prepared meats | 0.3 |
| Processed poultry and eggs | 1.6 |
| Sugar and confectionery products | 7.8 |
| Chewing gum | 19.8 |

*(Table continues on the following page.)*

**Table 5-2** *(continued)*

| | |
|---|---|
| Chocolate and cocoa | 9.6 |
| Confectionery products | 0.6 |
| Raw cane sugar | 2.6 |
| Refined beet sugar | 1.9 |
| Refined cane sugar | 12.0 |
| Miscellaneous food products | 1.6 |
| Canned and cured seafood | 0.9 |
| Food preparations | 0.3 |
| Fresh and frozen packaged fish | 0.6 |
| Macaroni and spaghetti | 1.8 |
| Manufactured ice | 0.2 |
| Roasted coffee | 5.8 |

*Source:* Derived from John M. Connor, Richard T. Rogers, Bruce W. Marion, and Willard F. Mueller, *The Food Manufacturing Industries: Structure, Strategies, Performance, and Policies* (Lexington, Mass.: Lexington Books, 1985), pp. 154–55.

production. Thus, the analyst should examine the relative scarcity and costs of these factors. The principal production factors to be considered are labor, capital, energy, raw materials, and the management input that organizes these other inputs. Appendix C at the end of the book gives illustrative operating and investment costs of three common food-processing technologies: drying, freezing, and canning.

It is important to recognize that the technological options range widely because food processing is an ancient activity with a long history of technological evolution. Cassava, for example, is an old food crop with roots that, upon hydrolysis, produce highly toxic hydrocyanic acid. A process to remove the toxicity is therefore required. About 4,000 years ago the Amerindians invented a woven wicker press to squeeze the cyanide-containing juice out of the mashed cassava, which was then heated to produce a dry, stable flour.[5] Today Brazil is among the biggest producers of processed cassava and does it on an industrial scale using hydraulic presses. Both the traditional and the modern technology accomplish the transformation through physical and chemical processes and use the same operations of separation, concentration, and stabilization. But the mix of factors of production and the corresponding costs of the two technologies are quite different.

LABOR VERSUS CAPITAL. Labor versus capital is the most discussed tradeoff in the debate over "appropriate technology." Labor is viewed as abundant and capital as scarce; therefore, logic dictates that labor- rather than capital-intensive technology should be used.

Pools of surplus labor that have few employment alternatives result in low opportunity costs and low wages. It makes business and social sense to choose the labor-intensive technological option, especially when increased employment is a political priority.

But government policies sometimes change the equation. Minimum wage laws, social benefits, or other factors may require the factory to pay a wage higher than the workers' opportunity cost. Furthermore, artificially low interest rates, tax credits for depreciation on equipment, or overvalued exchange rates may make the import and use of capital equipment more financially attractive to the owner of the factory than intensive use of labor. (These "prices" could be adjusted in the analysis of the social costs and benefits.) In this case the public and private interests would diverge, and means of reconciling these differences through policy adjustments or the redesign of the project would be in order.[6]

Sometimes the analysis leads to the choice of intermediate levels of technology. One study of Indonesian rice milling techniques concluded that a small plant that milled four tons an hour with two machines for hulling and whitening was economically superior both to hand-pounding operations and to larger mills with mechanized drying and storage facilities.[7] In Bangladesh a study found that the traditional rice husking and polishing method obtained a higher milling yield than either a small, Engleberg-type mechanical rice huller or the larger modern rubber roll mill, but it produced a higher percent of broken grains.[8] Furthermore, the Engleberg huller increased labor productivity 86 percent and required relatively small capital investment, which resulted in lower processing costs than the traditional method.

In both of these examples, the intermediate technology yielded lower costs but displaced labor; whether the technological change is socially desirable thus requires analysis of the alternative work opportunities for the displaced labor. In Bangladesh traditional rice husking is reportedly done mostly by women. If they are working as hired labor and are displaced by the new technology, they may have limited access to other employment opportunities.[9]

One way a project can increase its use of low-cost labor is to disaggregate the technology. This requires the plant to identify each step in the production process and to assess the use of manual labor for each activity. Frequently, workers can handle and sort materials more cheaply than it can be done mechanically. In textile production, for example, six alternative machine-labor combinations exist to open and clean cotton bales. These range from $250,000 in equipment with four workers to $430,000 and two workers.[10] Some packaging activities can also use labor rather than automation. Even when the operation is already manual, new techniques to increase productivity may be developed. For example, workers in a Kenyan fruit-processing plant used to fill the cans one by one. Now they fill twelve cans at once by covering them with a metal sheet with twelve holes and shoving the fruit across the sheet, letting it drop into the cans.[11]

Activities that require high precision or chemical transformation, however, can often only be done mechanically (that is, the process requirements limit factor substitution). Economies of scale must also be considered before the technological process is disaggregated.

Achieving the lowest-cost production possible for the total set of agroindustrial processes within an industry does not, however, necessarily exclude small-scale industries. The firm should examine the agroindustrial system to identify the functions that are better performed by small-scale production units than by larger, capital-intensive units. For example, the leather and footwear industry in India comprises the processes of skinning, curing, tanning, finishing, and fabrication.[12] Skinning and curing are small-scale functions because hides can only be procured from animals that have died naturally (religious beliefs forbid the slaughter of cows). The tanning and finishing processes require large equipment and, therefore, high volume. The shoe- and leather-goods-fabrication stage of the process, however, can be efficiently conducted on a small scale with a modest amount of equipment. The successful Italian shoe export industry and Brazil's expanding shoe industry rely heavily on small-scale fabricators. In Italy more than 95 percent of the footwear firms employ twenty or fewer workers. (Italy is the design leader, while Brazil has an advantage over India because cattle are slaughtered for meat and the hides are of superior quality.)

A project can often save significant capital—without sacrificing product quality or jobs—by purchasing used machinery. High labor costs in more industrialized nations put a premium on labor-saving innovations; hence, manufacturers purchase new machinery to compete. Although the equipment displaced by this practice is not economically viable in the industrialized market where it originated, it can be viable in the less industrialized nations. These nations have lower labor costs and are willing to install the labor-intensive equipment for both financial and social reasons. The used equipment does not alter the quality of the end product but simply takes advantage of the cost differentials between factors; what has become inappropriate technology for one environment can be quite appropriate for another.

For example, a Colombian textile manufacturer purchased a large equipment complex from a U.S. textile firm that was shifting to a newer, labor-saving technology. The capital savings to the Colombian firm from purchasing used, rather than new, equipment were sufficient to cover not only the costs of training workers to operate the equipment but also of disassembling the whole equipment complex in the United States, shipping it, and reassembling and installing it in Colombia. Similarly, a Venezuelan textile producer integrating backward into cotton ginning was able to obtain a rebuilt gin at half the cost of a new one but with almost equivalent performance parameters.

There are several reasons why secondhand equipment is not purchased more frequently. Information on the kind and quality of available equipment is scarce, and the purchaser from a developing country may have to travel to the industrialized country to inspect the machinery. The supply of replacement parts for older machinery may be difficult to obtain.[13] Policymakers or plant engineers may psychologically view used equipment as "low status" or "unprogressive."[14] In this case, the analyst should remind these parties that in socioeconomic terms, new is not necessarily better. The value of used equipment is also difficult to appraise and, therefore, its purchase complicates the government's task of fiscal assessment. An alternative to buying secondhand equipment is to acquire technology by licensing, subcontracting, or direct foreign investment.[15]

ENERGY. Another production factor to be considered in selecting technology, and one that is of increasing economic concern to both developed and developing nations, is the amount of energy the technology requires. Agroindustries use significant amounts of energy. In the United States, for example, food processors use about 4–5 percent of all energy (farm production alone uses about 3 percent[16]) and is the fourth largest user of energy.[17] Before committing itself to one technology and energy source, the agroindustrial firm should assess the supply and price of alternative fuels and the energy usage of various technologies. Rice, for example, can be dried by the sun or by machine. Solar energy is, of course, free, but the energy savings of this source would have to be weighed against other factors, such as the quality of the end product. Rice dried in the open air is subject to damage by insects or weather. If the alternative sources are coal, fuel oil, or wood, the product would have to be indirectly heated to avoid contamination by soot or smoke. (The use of wood might also accelerate deforestation.) If the alternative is natural gas, the cost might be greater but the processor could use direct combustion heaters, which have lower capital and operating costs and greater efficiency. Sometimes the government subsidizes energy. Subsidized energy in Saudi Arabia has led certain private entrepreneurs to set up vegetable dehydration plants there. If the energy had been shadow priced at its opportunity cost to society, these projects would have shown a negative economic cost-benefit ratio. Thus, the need to assess the social as well as the financial costs is as important for determining energy costs as it is for analyzing the labor and capital factors.

Procedures for "energy accounting" of food-processing operations have been developed. R. Paul Singh[18] has proposed that the analyst:

- Decide on an objective (for example, to improve the efficiency of thermal energy used in a process);
- Choose a system boundary (for example, a piece of processing equipment or a series of processing operations);
- Draw a flow diagram of the process (using standard symbols);[19]
- Identify and quantify all mass and energy inputs (for example, steam, heated air, or electrical energy that crosses the system boundary);
- Identify and quantify all mass and energy outputs (including any increase in energy incorporated in the product itself).

This accounting can generate alternative energy costs per unit of product for different technologies and fuel sources. It can also reveal points in the process where alternative energy sources might be used—for example, using solar energy to heat water required in processing, or using by-products such as rice husks or sugarcane bagasse as fuel. Counterflows and other processing techniques can optimize the use of heat generated for one step in the process by reusing it in another. Food technologists or industrial engineers can provide the requisite calculations for the estimates in energy accounting.

An emerging source of energy for some countries is the agroindustrial production of ethanol from biomass, the basic technology of which is well known.[20] Biomass-based ethanol can be produced from sugar-bearing materials, starches, or cellulose. Brazil has used sugar-based ethanol on a large scale to produce gasohol. The economics of this energy source depend significantly on the cost of the raw material. When sugar prices were extremely low and petroleum prices high, this agro-derived fuel was attractive; under the reverse price conditions, the economics are less attractive. One study indicated that bioprocessed ethanol would be competitive with gasoline when oil prices were at least $20 a barrel.[21] Advances in biomass technology will continue, making this an energy source to be considered.

RAW MATERIAL.  For some agroindustries the scarcest resource may not be capital or energy but raw material. Consequently, priority must be given to that technology which makes most efficient use of the raw material. Because raw material costs are the greatest expense for most agroindustries, any technology that can produce savings here can yield a significant economic benefit and potentially important cost advantage. Some technologies might also allow the processor to utilize alternative types of raw materials, such as different kinds of vegetable oil. Such equipment configuration might represent a higher fixed investment but enable the processor to obtain substantial raw material savings by switching among sources depending on their relative price shifts, which can be sizable.

GOVERNMENT POLICIES. Because government policies can affect the costs of materials, capital, labor, and energy, they also affect the economics of technology selection. For example, in one country a biotechnology processing operation was set up to produce high fructose syrup from a local grain. A primary economic rationale for this project was the relatively high price of sugar and the relatively low price of the surplus grain. However, the analyst must carefully examine the basis for the relative price differentials in the raw materials. In this case the high sugar price was attributable to a shortfall in local production and unusually high international prices; the grain price was low due to soft demand in the animal feed sector. The government raised its support price for sugarcane growers and provided investment tax incentives to sugar mills. As a result, sugar production and milling capacity rose significantly; the government released its stocks, which combined with a drop in world sugar prices to cause local sugar prices to fall. The local demand for the feed grain increased and the government-owned food marketing enterprise also began exporting it to earn foreign exchange, thereby causing a rise in the price of this raw material. The new factory found its original economic assumptions about relative prices shattered by government actions and international market linkages.

Government wage and worker benefit regulations can alter the relative costs of labor, tax policies related to equipment depreciation allowances and import duties can change the cost of capital, price regulations and subsidies can affect the price of energy, and environmental protection and food safety regulations can change technical requirements.

## Use of Capacity

One common problem facing agroindustries is the underuse of capacity because of the seasonality of raw material and market demand for the product (for example, ice cream, chocolates, or certain beverages). To some extent, the kind of technology selected can reduce idle time caused by seasonal factors. Many processing steps are the same for different products requiring the same kind of transformation. Consequently, a plant constructed to process beans, for example, can readily process certain other vegetables or fruits with modest additional equipment and changes in labor procedures. Similarly, dairies equipped for heat processing or canning could also process tomatoes and pineapples.[22] By adjusting the technology to handle a broader range of products, agroindustries can take advantage of the harvesting cycles of different crops.

Other ways to reduce the effects of seasonality are available; these include planting multiple crops through use of irrigation or new seed varieties; attaining shorter breeding cycles through animal genetics; substituting stored, semiprocessed raw material, such as powdered milk, in the production process; and directing special advertising to consumers during the off season. This latter point is illustrated by the example of the U.S. walnut and raisin producers, who successfully promoted year-round, rather than just holiday, use of their products. Finding ways to increase full use of project capacity is important not only for increasing the revenue-generating period of the investment but also for reducing the adverse socioeconomic consequences of seasonal unemployment.

Although variability during the year is hard to reduce because of seasonality, stability from year to year is attainable due to the relatively steady demand for food products. In the United States, for example, capacity utilization for food manufacturing averaged 77 percent between 1974 and 1980, with annual variations of only 1 percent. That stability is in striking contrast to many other industries, such as automobile manufacturing, which suffer wide swings in capacity utilization.[23]

### Skill Capabilities

Another criterion for technology selection is whether the technology fits with the enterprise's managerial and technical skill resources. Managerial talent is often scarce in developing countries, particularly at the supervisory level. Technology selection can minimize the supervisory burden, perhaps by substituting machines for those parts of a process that require the most intensive supervision. (The qualifications regarding tradeoffs between capital and labor made earlier, however, would then apply.) Skilled technicians are also scarce, and so the maintenance and repair requirements of equipment must be carefully assessed. Highly sophisticated agroindustrial equipment has often ended up idle because of a plant's deficient maintenance capacity.

## Nutritional Effects

A commonly overlooked criterion in technology selection is the processing method's effect on the nutritional value of food products. Yet technology can have a significant effect on the nutritional value of foods, and the agroindustrial analyst should give explicit attention to this facet of technology selection.

Until the late 1970s food processors in industrialized countries showed relatively little interest in the nutritional content of their products, except from a health safety perspective, because they did not think nutritional value was a major consideration in consumers' purchasing decisions.[24] Food processors in developing countries have continued to lag behind. In developing countries nutrient deficiencies are a serious problem; in more industrialized nations overnutrition and imbalances characterize the nutritional problems. Consumer awareness and concern about nutrition and health aspect of foods have increased significantly during the last fifteen years. Nutritional attributes and enhancements have increasingly become a means of creating product differentiation.

Food technologists and nutritionists can provide technical information for the analysis of a product's nutritional value, but because the nutritional aspect of project analysis has been largely neglected, it will be addressed here in some detail. Food nutrients can be roughly divided into two categories, macronutrients (proteins, carbohydrates, fats) and micronutrients (vitamins, minerals). The constituents of these two categories, as well as the nutritional effects of various kinds of food processing, are discussed below.

PROTEINS. Processing can increase or decrease the digestibility of proteins. For example, heat-induced denaturation can enhance the general digestibility of foods, but heat can also reduce protein quality by degrading, or blocking metabolism of, the $\epsilon$-amino group of lysine (especially in the presence of reducing sugars such as glucose, fructose, and lactose).

CARBOHYDRATES. These energy-yielding nutrients contain starches and sugars. Under normal processing conditions starch is stable, but reducing sugars may degenerate and simultaneously brown in the presence of catalysts and heat.

FATS. During processing and storage, isomerization and oxidation of fats may decrease the biological value of unsaturated fatty acids. The deterioration of fats—which is increased by heat, light, and the presence of trace metals—may cause losses in the organoleptic values of foods (taste, color, odor, and texture). Such deterioration may be retarded by the action of antioxidants that are naturally present in fats or that can be added to fats during processing.

VITAMINS. Some water-soluble vitamins—among them, thiamine (vitamin B-1), riboflavin (vitamin B-2), niacin, pyridoxine (vitamin B-6), and ascorbic acid (vitamin C)—are lost during processing; the extent of the loss depends on the degree of solubility and stability, the kind of food, and the processing conditions. Ascorbic acid is readily oxidized during processing, especially in the presence of copper or iron at neutral pH. Thiamine readily degrades in neutral and alkaline solutions even at moderate temperatures and is also sensitive to heat, copper, iron, and sulfites. Riboflavin is stable except in the presence of light at neutral or alkaline pH. Niacin, probably the most stable vitamin, has excellent stability under heat and light. Pantothenic acid is stable at mildly acidic or neutral pH but is heat sensitive at more acidic pH. The stability of folic acid depends partly on its chemical form: the monoglutamate form is moderately stable under heat at acidic or neutral pH, but the tri- and heptaglutamate conjugates are unstable under heat. Folic acid is also sensitive to copper and iron. Cobalamin is stable at mildly acidic pH, but it is rapidly destroyed by heat at alkaline pH, by light, or in the presence of trace metals (copper and iron, for example). Pyridoxine is stable under heat in acidic and alkaline solution, but it is light-sensitive at neutral or alkaline pH. Pyridoxal, a major form of pyridoxine in milk and other foods, is unstable in heat.

In addition to the losses from chemical degradations, all the water-soluble vitamins are susceptible to losses from leaching. The degree of loss depends on the solubility of the specific vitamin. Thus, thiamine, folic acid, ascorbic acid, pyridoxine, and niacin—which are all highly soluble in water—are easily lost through leaching, whereas riboflavin is more resistant because it is less soluble. Unlike water-soluble vitamins, fat-soluble vitamins (vitamin A; the carotenes, or provitamin A; vitamin D; vitamin E; and vitamin K) are stable against leaching losses but are susceptible to oxidative degradation, especially in the presence of light, metals, and other catalysts. Vitamin A and the carotenes are also unstable under heat, which changes them into less active forms.

MINERALS. In general, processing has minor effects on minerals in foods, such as calcium, phosphorus, iron, and magnesium, except that losses from leaching can occur. Losses of trace minerals may also occur, but the nutritional effects of this are less known.

EFFECTS OF RICE MILLING. Rice is the basic food for more than half the world's population, and it supplies 70–80 percent of dietary caloric intake in the Orient. Consequently, milled rice is a good example to illustrate how alternative technologies can alter nutrient value. Rice in its hull is called rough or paddy rice. White rice is the polished endosperm that remains when other parts of the grain have been removed.

In rice milling a series of mechanical operations remove the hull, the embryo, and the outer layers of the rice kernel. When hulled brown rice is again passed through hullers or pearling cones, the pericarp, most of the embryo, and the outer aleurone layers are removed as a powder called "bran." The inner alenrone layers and the remainder of the embryo are subsequently rubbed off by brushes, forming a powder called "polish." Bran is not used for human consumption and polish has limited uses because it tends to turn rancid quickly.[25] In the United States, for example, 8.5 percent of the whole grain weight of rice is removed as bran, and 1.8 percent is removed as polish.

The approximate nutritional composition of selected rice products is contained in table 5-3; vitamin content is shown in table 5-4. The percentages given in the tables indicate that those parts of the rice grain that are removed by milling—namely, the bran and the polish—are richer in nutrients than the endosperm. (The same, incidentally, is true of wheat.) Although whole rice is a good source of vitamins and minerals, these micronutrients are largely removed during milling. Although protein losses through milling are relatively small, protein fractions—which are rich in lysine, the amino acid present in the smallest amount of rice protein—are removed with the bran and polish. Thus, proteins in polished rice contain approximately 3.3 percent lysine,[26] whereas proteins in brown rice contain 4.5 percent lysine.[27] Estimates of nutrient retention in rice products, calculated from the data in tables 5-3 and 5-4, are given in table 5-5.

Although the degree of rice milling may be varied to increase nutrient retention, programs for promoting consumption of undermilled rice in undernourished populations are generally unsuccessful because of consumer prejudice against nonwhite rice. Because of its high fat content, undermilled rice is more apt to become rancid than white rice; it is also susceptible to microbial damage because of its protein-rich outer layers. In some countries, rice is coated with glucose to 0.2 percent of its weight and with talc to 0.08 percent of its weight to increase the shininess of the grain.[28] This practice is nutritionally unsound because the asbestos in talc may be carcinogenic and because the rice has to be washed before it can be cooked, which causes further nutritional losses.

**Table 5-3.** *Approximate Composition of Selected Rice Products*
(percent)

| | | Product | | | |
|---|---|---|---|---|---|
| Biological profile | Brown rice | Polished rice | Parboiled rice | Bran | Polish |
| Protein | 10.1 | 7.2–9.0 | 7.4 | 10.6–14.0 | 12.1–14.2 |
| Carbohydrate | 86.6 | 90.8 | 81.3 | n.a. | 59.9 |
| Fat | 2.4 | 0.3 | 0.3 | 11.7 | 12.7 |
| Fiber | 0.9 | 0.1 | 0.2 | 11.1 | n.a. |
| Ash (minerals) | 1.2 | 0.5 | 0.7 | 13.1 | 12.3 |

n.a.  Not applicable.

*Note:* Percentages are calculated to a moisture-free basis.

*Source:* A. M. Altschul and R. W. Planck, "Effects of Commercial Processing of Cereals on Nutrient Content: Rice and Rice Products," in Robert S. Harris and H. W. von Boesecke, eds., *Nutritional Evaluation of Food Processing*, 1st ed. (New York: John Wiley and Sons, 1960), p. 204.

It is clear from tables 5-4 and 5-5 that parboiled rice, which is widely consumed in South Asia, retains most of the nutrients originally present in whole rice grain. Parboiled rice is rough rice steeped in water, steamed, and dried before milling. During this process, water-soluble nutrients in the germ and alenrone layers are forced into the starchy endosperm of the grain. The brief steaming gelatinizes the starch in the outer layer of the endosperm and helps the polished rice retain the water-soluble nutrients. Because of these effects, the parboiling process enhances a rice product's nutritional value.

**Table 5-4.** *Vitamin Content of Selected Rice Products*
(milligrams in 100 grams)

| | | Product | | | |
|---|---|---|---|---|---|
| Vitamin | Brown rice | Polished rice | Parboiled rice | Bran | Polish |
| Biotin | 0.12 | .. | 0.1 | 0.6 | 0.6 |
| Folic acid | — | 0.2 | 0.2 | 1.5 | 1.9 |
| Niacin | 46.2–47.2 | 10.0–25.0 | 30.0–48.0 | 336.0 | 330.0 |
| Pantothenic acid | 10.3–17.0 | 6.4–8.0 | 13.7 | 22.0–27.7 | 33.3 |
| Riboflavin | 0.6 | 0.2–0.3 | 0.3–0.6 | 2.0 | 2.2 |
| Thiamine | 2.0–4.8 | 0.4–0.8 | 1.9–3.1 | 24.0 | 22.0 |
| Vitamin B-6 | 6.9–10.3 | 3.3–4.5 | — | 25.0 | 20.0 |

.. Negligible.

— Not available.

*Source:* Delane Welsch, Sopin Tongpan, Christopher Mock, Eileen Kennedy, and James Austin, "Thailand Case Study," in James E. Austin, ed., *Global Malnutrition and Cereal Grain Fortification* (Cambridge, Mass.: Ballinger Publishing Co., 1979), p. 248.

**Table 5-5.** *Estimated Nutrient Retention in Selected Rice Products*
(percent)

| Nutrient | Polished rice | Parboiled rice | Bran | Polish |
|---|---|---|---|---|
| | *Product* | | | |
| Protein | 72 | 76 | 10 | 2 |
| Carbohydrate | 94 | 95 | n.a. | 1 |
| Fat | 13 | 13 | 42 | 10 |
| Fiber | 10 | 20 | 90 | n.a. |
| Vitamins | | | | |
|   Biotin | 37 | 75 | 32 | 9 |
|   Niacin | 34 | 75 | 61 | 10 |
|   Pantothenic acid | 48 | 91 | 16 | 5 |
|   Riboflavin | 34 | 67 | 28 | 7 |
|   Thiamine | 16 | 66 | 60 | 12 |
|   Vitamin B-6 | 41 | — | 25 | 4 |
| Ash (minerals) | 37 | 52 | 60 | n.a. |

— Not available.

n.a. Not applicable.

*Note:* Estimates are based on the data given in tables 5-3 and 5-4 and are derived by the following formulas:

$$(1)\ \text{percentage nutrient loss} = \frac{\left[\text{Percentage nutrient in brown rice} - \text{percentage nutrient in product}\right] \times \dfrac{\text{percentage yield of product}}{100\ \text{percent}}}{\text{percentage nutrient in brown rice}} ;$$

(2) percentage nutrient retention = 100 percent − percentage nutrient loss.

Percentage yield of product is assumed to be 8.5 percent for bran, 1.8 percent for polish, 89.7 percent for polished rice, and 90 percent for parboiled rice. Percentage nutrient retention in polished rice, bran, and polish does not always add up to 100 percent because the data in tables 5-3 and 5-4 were originally compiled by Altschul and Planck using data from various sources. When a lower and an upper figure were given for nutrient content, the average of the two numbers was used for calculations.

*Source:* Adapted from Altschul and Planck, ''Effects of Commercial Processing of Cereals,'' p. 204.

EFFECTS OF WHEAT MILLING. Milling can similarly affect grains other than rice. The vitamin and mineral content of wheat products decreases markedly with milling (see table 5-6). These data indicate that most vitamins and minerals are concentrated not in the wheat endosperm but in the germ and bran, which are lost during milling. The decrease in the mineral content of wheat through milling is also important for quality control in the flour-milling industry, because high mineral content in flour is generally an indication of contamination by bran particles. The milling process makes calcium more biologically available in flour than in whole wheat.

**Table 5-6.** *Estimated Nutrient Retention in Wheat Flour for Different Degrees of Whole Wheat Extraction*
(percent)

| Nutrient | High extraction (85 percent) | Standard extraction (70 percent) | Patent extraction (44 percent) |
|---|---|---|---|
| Protein | 83 | 63 | 39 |
| Carbohydrate | 91 | 77 | 51 |
| Fat | 58 | 35 | 15 |
| Fiber | 47 | 3 | ... |
| Vitamins | | | |
| Niacin | 19 | 10 | 5 |
| Riboflavin | 54 | 24 | 13 |
| Thiamine | 70 | 17 | 5 |
| Vitamin B-6 | n.d. | 10 | 4 |
| Vitamin E | n.d. | 8 | 2 |
| Ash (minerals) | 41 | 18 | 10 |

... Retained in trace amounts.
n.d. Not detected.
*Note:* Estimates are derived by the following formulas:

$$(1)\ \begin{array}{c}\text{percentage}\\\text{nutrient}\\\text{loss}\end{array} = \frac{\left[\begin{array}{c}\text{percentage}\\\text{nutrient in}\\\text{whole wheat}\end{array} - \begin{array}{c}\text{percentage}\\\text{nutrient}\\\text{in product}\end{array}\right] \times \dfrac{\text{percentage}\\\text{extraction}}{100\ \text{percent}} \times \dfrac{\begin{array}{c}\text{percentage}\\\text{relative nutrient}\\\text{concentration}\end{array}}{100\ \text{percent}}}{\text{percentage nutrient in whole wheat}} ;$$

(2) percentage nutrient retention = 100 percent − percentage nutrient loss.

*Source:* Adapted from Altschul and Planck, "Effects of Commercial Processing of Cereals," p. 204.

Although only a small fraction of protein is removed with the wheat germ and bran, milling decreases lysine and tryptophan content because they are concentrated in bran protein. (Even before the bran and germ are removed, wheat protein is low in lysine and tryptophan relative to other grains.) Milling also decreases the fat content of wheat products; such decrease reduces the caloric value per unit of the wheat product, but it also reduces the chance that the products will turn rancid, thus enhancing their storage stability. British firms have used higher whole wheat extraction rates (80–85 percent) with minimal change in the color of the flour and the baking quality.[29]

EFFECTS OF FRUIT AND VEGETABLE PROCESSING. Fruits and vegetables can also suffer significant losses of micronutrients during processing. The losses vary with crop, nutrient, and process. For example, blanching peas with steam causes a 12.3 percent loss of their vitamin C content, while blanching them with water causes a 25.8 percent loss.[30] Some nutrients can be almost totally lost during canning; canned corn, for instance, loses 80 percent of its thiamine.[31]

PRODUCT FORTIFICATION AND MODIFICATION. When the processing firm's choice of technology significantly affects the nutritional quality of its product, the government or industrial associations may intervene to set nutritional standards. The agroindustrial analyst should try to minimize nutrition losses and other negative effects of processing by adjusting the technology or by restoring nutrients through fortification. Food technology in this regard is not necessarily a nutritional liability; it can enhance nutritional value by fortifying the product against nutrient losses unavoidable in processing and by retarding spoilage or transforming poor nutrient resources into foods of higher value.[32]

The work of the Institute of Food Product Research and Development in Thailand illustrates the virtues of food technology.[33] Working with the protein residue of the mung bean, which Thai starch factories had extracted and discarded, the institute used food technology to create a protein isolate that it then transformed into a nutrient-dense weaning food for preschoolers. Thus, technology was employed to recapture a wasted by-product and transform it into a form suited for use by a nutritionally vulnerable group.[34] Other food processors have differentiated their products by fortifying them or enhancing them in other ways, such as lowering cholesterol or increasing fiber content.

## Plant Location

Where to locate the processing plant is another critical decision in project design. The first consideration is where the plant should be relative to its raw material suppliers and its markets; transport is an essential component of this decision. Other considerations are labor supply, the availability of infrastructure, land costs, and developmental effect.

### Raw Materials, Markets, and Transport

The plant must decide whether to locate near the raw material or near the market for finished goods. The decision depends on the characteristics of the raw material and its transformative process, as well as on the costs and availability of transport services. Following are the kinds of conditions of raw materials and transport that favor locating near raw material suppliers.

- Highly perishable produce that requires immediate processing, such as cucumbers and palm oil.
- Fragile products, such as eggs and tomatoes, that can withstand only minimal handling.
- Products, such as lumber, grain, cotton, grapes, sugarcane, and livestock, that are considerably reduced in weight or volume by processing, thus facilitating transport.

The following conditions of raw materials and transport favor locating near the market for finished goods.

- Produce that is not very perishable or fragile, such as potatoes, or processed products such as flour that are more perishable than the raw material, in this case wheat.
- Products whose weight or volume is increased by processing; bottled or canned beverages are examples.
- Processing that requires supplies from different sources; pencil manufacturing is an example.

The decision on location requires the ranking of one factor, such as transport costs, against another.[35] As transport technologies change, costs shift and the economics of the plant's location can alter. In the United States, for example, declining costs for grain transport made it economical for flour mills to move from distant grain collection points to urban centers, thus providing better service to nearby consumers. In contrast, meat packers in the United States, thanks in part to the emergence of refrigerated trucking, moved from cities to animal-producing areas, thereby saving on transport and processing costs.

Transport costs are also central to decisions regarding the number and size of the plants an agroindustry should construct. If raw material suppliers or markets are scattered and transport costs are high, multiple plants, rather than one large plant, might be advisable. The savings on transport may offset the economies of scale from a single-plant operation. In effect, transport costs become determinants of market boundaries.

The economic importance of transport is also related to the value of the product. For example, a high-value produce for export, such as cut flowers, would have a relatively lower elasticity of demand for transport because transport costs are a small percentage of total costs. A firm processing such a product would be more concerned with locating near the supplier—to lessen the risk of perishability—and with the quality of the transport service (for example, speed and refrigeration) than with its cost. Inadequate transport services may eliminate some desirable locations. When this occurs, the firm should consider operating its own transport services. Such a decision would require an analysis of the incremental capital investment and the potential savings in increased reliability.

## Labor Supply

Because agroindustries seldom directly employ many workers, they usually are not sensitive to the supply of unskilled labor. Skilled labor and managerial talent is more difficult to find, a constraint especially acute if the plant is in a rural area. If this is the case, the firm may have to offer special financial incentives or social amenities to attract and retain qualified personnel. A large-scale integrated operation requiring agricultural and processing labor, such as a sugarcane plantation and mill, can have a major impact on the local labor market, so availability needs to be assessed carefully.

## Availability of Infrastructure

Because defective infrastructure can increase costs and reduce quality, the agroindustrial firm should consider the facilities and services available at alternative locations. Two experts in this field have recommended that a firm examine a location for the following infrastructural aspects of electricity and water supply.[36]

### Electricity
- Demand by the plant and community (both actual and projected, to identify possible bottlenecks)
- Source and availability
- Reliability
- Record of interruptions during the past year (some utility companies do not regard momentary outage as an "interruption," so verify the record)
- Availability of desired demand on year-round basis
- Tie-ins with state power grid
  - Effect of grid outages on power for plant site
  - Willingness of electricians to repair "hot" or live lines
- Cost of purchased power
  - Terms of contract
  - Documentation

### Potable water
- Demand, load and pressures, temperatures
- Source and availability

- Boiler feed-water treatment required
- Cost
- Kind of boiler fuel, its source, and its availability

*Cooling water*
- Maximum wet bulb design
- Cooling tower: river water or seawater?
- Intake works
- Discharge
- Corrosion protection
- Pollution problem
- Distance to intake
- Right of way for supply and discharge
- Permits required
    - Officials: names, titles, addresses
    - Obtained by whom? When?
    - Present status
    - Documentation
- Cost

*Process water*
- Demand (both actual and projected) and load at full capacity
- Source and availability
- Treatment requirements including land site
- Cost

In addition, the analyst should also assess the transport infrastructure, including roads, railroad sidings, and storage terminals. In one East African country, a corned-beef processing plant experienced raw material shortages at the same time that cattle growers in a neighboring province were unable to bring their animals to the plant because the roads and climate were not suitable for transporting live animals. Consequently, the government helped the cattlemen put up a slaughterhouse and freezing plant in the cattle-raising areas. The frozen beef blocks were then transported to the corned-beef plant for further processing.

If the infrastructure is deficient, the project should compare the investment cost of providing its own infrastructure with the advantages of the location. Similarly, the plant should install an emergency generator to ensure against costly power outages.

The analyst should also inventory the social infrastructure—including housing, schools, and health and recreational facilities—because these components may affect the project's ability to recruit the necessary personnel.

Social infrastructure should generally be established with the cooperation of the government and should incorporate community ownership of facilities. This sharing of responsibilities minimizes the managerial and social problems associated with "company towns."

Some governments have promoted agroindustries by creating industrial estates or parks. These developments provide the production infrastructure for a complex of agroindustries, encourage complementary industries to locate in the same complex, and permit greater efficiency by enabling the firms to share services (buying or marketing) and facilities. In rural areas, however, these developments have sometimes become "islands" of developmental activity that are not integrated into and do not affect the adjoining rural areas.

### Land Costs

Land costs usually represent a relatively small percentage of total capital outlay because processing plants do not need much land. Nonetheless, land costs vary, and comparative shopping for a site is necessary. If the owner of the project's potential land is also a project promoter, the land cost should be compared with other land costs to verify its fair market value. Urban land is usually more expensive than rural land, but the price depends on the site's alternative uses. The firm should purchase enough land to accommodate future expansion. Expanding suburbs increase outlying land values and the cost of future land acquisitions. Locating in cities experiencing rapid urbanization may result in subsequent traffic congestion and higher transport costs. A Peruvian business group, which operated a successful corn starch factory, established a similar operation in Ecuador by acquiring an existing plant in the capital city of Quito on land valued at 530,000 sucres. Urbanization increased the congestion around the factory, but it also raised the value of the land 700 percent, to 3,710,000 sucres, creating a potential capital gain that could be used to finance relocation.[37]

### Developmental Effects

One final consideration concerns the different developmental effects of alternative locations. The analyst should consider the increased employment and income redistribution the project will generate. Developing relatively backward regions may be a governmental priority, and locating a processing plant in a backward region might provide the necessary market outlet to stimulate agricultural production, furnish a use for marginal lands, or stem rural-to-urban migration. One researcher, for example, found rural prosperity and rural emigration to be inversely related.[38] A site may be selected because it fulfills a country's sociopolitical objectives, even though other considerations do not make it an ideal location.[39] But to induce private firms to make such decisions, governments may have to provide fiscal incentives to compensate firms for the added costs of locating in underdeveloped regions in support of its development policies. These benefits may make a project's financial return to the private investors compatible with its economic return to the country, thus ensuring the project's implementation.

## Inventory Management

Inventory management for agroindustries is complicated by the biological nature and the seasonality of the raw material. In recommending an inventory management system, the analyst should be sure to examine the capacity factors, physical facilities, and financial aspects of the project.

### Storage Capacity

The purpose of managing raw material inventory is to minimize any imbalances between supply and processing capacity. Seasonal raw materials may require the plant to store its entire annual or semi-annual supply of raw material until it can all be processed; for example, a factory may receive its annual supply of wheat all at once but process it into flour over the course of a year. Some raw materials, such as tomatoes, must be processed quickly because of their high perishability. Raw materials that perish quickly reduce the need for storage capacity but increase the capacity needed for processing and storing finished goods.

Processing reduces some products' ability to be stored, a factor that can pose significant problems for inventory management. Under proper conditions, for example, wheat can be stored for years, but after processing, it is much more perishable. A wheat flour processor in the Philippines constructed minimal wheat storage but built and rented considerable space for storing finished flour.[40] When demand fell, the company possessed large inventories of perishable flour that, even with chemical treatment, had a shelf life of only four months. The problem was exacerbated by the arrival of a large grain shipment, which had to be processed because there were not enough silos to store it.

One inventory management alternative is intermediate storage. The raw material can be semiprocessed—into forms such as tomato paste, orange juice concentrate, or powdered milk, for example—to reduce its perishability; the semiprocessed form can then be stored for later processing into the finished product. For example, semiprocessing tomato solids into paste permits enormous cost savings in cans, transportation, warehousing, and handling. Even greater savings are possible by eliminating small containers and shipping the heat-stabilized concentrate in bulk, if the marketing strategy makes that desirable.[41] Semiprocessing offers the advantage of reducing the plant's investment in finishing equipment.

The analyst should consider the tradeoff between the cost of raw material and the cost of inventory facilities for finished goods. If the size of the raw material is significantly reduced in processing—for example, oranges converted into frozen juice—the space requirements for storing the finished goods are substantially lower. The quality and cost of the storage facilities for raw and finished products may differ, however; in the example of frozen orange juice, the difference is between unrefrigerated and refrigerated storage. In any event, the perishability and seasonality of agroindustrial raw materials require that standard inventory management procedures, such as economic order quantity systems, be altered.[42] The plant should also ensure that there is adequate inventory capacity for supplies and processing inputs other than raw material, including parts for equipment repair. These inventories generally require minimal cost and space, but without them, an entire processing operation can come to a sudden halt.

### Physical Facilities

The major causes of post-harvest losses are pest and insect infestation and microbial infiltration.[43] Proper storage can partially eliminate these problems. Inventory facilities should include preparation facilities, such as drying houses, as well as storage structures. Biological materials naturally deteriorate. Bacteria, yeasts, molds, enzymes, temperature, moisture, air, oxygen, and time all contribute to deterioration. Water activity in foods is a significant factor in deterioration. At high levels bacteria cause the most deterioration; at lower levels yeast and mold growth become the prime spoilage organisms.[44] If microbiological problems are eliminated by controlling the water activity, chemical reactions, such as nonenzymatic browning (reaction of sugars and proteins) or lipid oxidation may limit storage life. The storage requirements for, cereals, legumes, animal products, fruits, and vegetables are discussed below.

CEREALS.  Grains contain more than 20 percent moisture at harvest and are highly susceptible to deterioration from microbial growth and pest and insect damage. Cereal grains (seeds consisting of a seed coat and an embryo of reserve nutrients) are resistant to deterioration when they are dried to a moisture content below 14–15 percent. At moisture levels above this, microbial growth may create "hot spots" (localized areas of temperature increase) that can char the stored grains. Grains that are improperly dried in a field can develop mold and musty odors. Even in the United States, with its highly developed agroindustrial technology, as much as 9 percent of the total crop may be lost because of insects, pests and microorganisms that attack stored grain.[45] In developing countries, with more labor-intensive harvesting, reported losses have actually been lower. If a processing plant stores its unmilled cereal grain in bins, storage huts, and bags, it can minimize adverse changes in the grain's nutritional value and taste by ventilating the supply to prevent the moisture from condensing and by protecting the supply from insects and rodents. At moisture levels below 14–15 percent, there is very little change in the proteins, carbohydrates, fats, vitamins, and minerals in cereal grains.

In addition to causing losses in the nutrients and organoleptic (taste, smell, sight, texture) qualities of grains, microbial growth can also produce toxic metabolites that, if consumed, may be hazardous to a person's health. Grain that has been damaged during storage by fermentation, insect and pest infestation, microbial respiration ("hot spots"), or sprouting is often mixed with sound grain to produce a mixture that is organoleptically acceptable for human consumption. This is, however, a dangerous practice because of the microbial toxins that storage-damaged grains may contain, toxins that are not easily destroyed by processing. Damaged grain of this kind is also less nutritional and sanitary.

Feeding damaged grains to livestock is similarly dangerous because the animals may die of the microbial toxins or the toxins may affect certain tissues that are later consumed by humans. Damaged grain can be used to produce commercial alcohol. The process involves a distillation step that removes the toxins, and the ethanol yield from damaged grain is comparable to that of sound grain (unless there has been extensive carbohydrate degradation).[46] However, overheated maize may cause difficulties in brewing or distillation because the hardened matrix of the starch granules blocks the enzymatic process.[47] Some nations have mixed grain alcohol with gasoline to make "gasohol," an alternative fuel.

Milled grain products are more vulnerable to insect and pest infestation, microbial growth, and chemical degradation than unmilled whole grains because milling removes the grain's protective seed coat. Nevertheless, storage in dry and cool conditions will result in minimal nutrient changes and good palatability in milled products.

One danger is that the fat in milled products may chemically oxidize and become rancid. Whole wheat flour, brown rice, and whole corn have shelf lives of only a few weeks or months because they quickly become rancid.[48]

LEGUMES. Storage of oil-rich seeds also requires that they be dried to avoid deterioration; legumes are best dried to a moisture level of approximately 7 percent.[49] Because the moisture level in stored seeds depends primarily on atmospheric moisture, leguminous seeds stored in humid, tropical, or subtropical regions may deteriorate from mold growth and the release of free fatty acids. Crude oil from oil-seeds contains 70–85 percent unsaturated fatty acids, which are especially sensitive to oxidative deterioration.[50] When the seed accumulates free fatty acids, it has a lower yield of edible oil and a lower "smoke point" (the smoke point is the temperature at which the seed's crude oil becomes smoky). For instance, the free fatty acid content of cottonseeds increases from 4.3 percent to 30 percent when cottonseed containing 11.9 percent moisture is stored in bins for ten days.[51]

Stored leguminous seeds with a high moisture level deteriorate more quickly when a large percentage of already damaged seeds are present.[52] Mold causes a loss of organoleptic quality (for example, off-flavor in cooked beans) and aids the formation of toxic compounds (mycotoxins). Peanuts, for example, may grow moldy and generate aflatoxin if not properly stored.

MEAT PRODUCTS. Fresh meat products are susceptible to rapid spoilage from both microbial growth and enzyme action. The organoleptic quality of fresh meat is so perishable that spoilage may make the product unacceptable for consumption even before there are significant nutrient losses. Meat must be refrigerated to prevent deterioration. Stored processed meats, however, do not lose significant nutrients even when unrefrigerated, unless they are stored in a hot, humid environment. Packaging can also prevent deterioration; for example, vacuum-packaged cured meats can have a refrigerated shelf life of several weeks (see section on packaging, below).[53]

FRUITS AND VEGETABLES. Although fruits and vegetables contain few proteins, they constitute the principal source of vitamin C. Several fruits and vegetables—among them, apricots, peaches, melons, cherries, carrots, leafy green vegetables, and sweet potatoes—also are sources of provitamin-A carotenes.[54] Even after their harvest, fruits and vegetables are living entities that continue to carry out life processes. Significant changes in color, flavor, texture, and nutritional

**Table 5-7.** *Losses of Vitamins C and A in Selected Vegetables under Various Storage Conditions*

| Vegetable | Storage condition | Loss (percent) |
|---|---|---|
| | *Vitamin C* | |
| Asparagus | 24 hours at 19–25°C | 20–40 |
| | 24 hours at 2°C | 3 |
| | 1 week at 0°C | 50 |
| | 1 week at 21°C | 70 |
| Broccoli | 24 hours at 21°C | 50 |
| | 24 hours at 8–10°C | 10–30 |
| | 96 hours at 21°C | 80 |
| | 96 hours at 8–10°C | 25–40 |
| Green beans | 24 hours at 21°C | 20 |
| | 24 hours at 8–10°C | 10 |
| | 96 hours at 21°C | 30 |
| Kale | 3 weeks at 0°C | 40 |
| | 2 days at 21°C | 40 |
| | 9 days at 0°C[a] | 40 |
| | 1 day at 21°C[a] | 40 |
| Snap beans | 10 days at 0°C | 40 |
| | 6 days at 10°C | 40 |
| Spinach | 24 hours at 21°C | 34–48 |
| | 48 hours at 21°C | 78 |
| | 192 hours at 21°C | 95 |
| | 72 hours at 1–3°C | 0 |
| Swiss chard | 24 hours at 21°C | 35 |
| | 96 hours at 21°C | 85 |
| | 24 hours at 8–10°C | 30 |
| | 96 hours at 8–10°C | 70 |
| | *Vitamin A* | |
| Carrots | 1 month at 21°C | Slight |
| Collards | 4 days at 0°C | 2 |
| | 4 days at 21°C[a] | 82 |
| Kale | 4 days at 0°C | 0 |
| | 4 days at 21°C[a] | 76 |
| Peas | 48 hours at 21°C | 15–27 |
| Spinach | 37 hours at 21°C | Slight |
| Swiss chard | 24 hours at 21°C | 0 |

°C, degrees Celsius.

a. Wilting occurs under these conditions.

*Sources:* J. M. Krochta and B. Feinberg, "Effects of Harvesting and Handling on the Composition of Fruits and Vegetables," in Robert S. Harris and Endel Karmas, eds., *Nutritional Evaluation of Food Processing*, 2d ed. (New York: John Wiley and Sons, 1975), p. 98; H. W. von Boesecke, "Effects of Harvesting and Handling Practices on Composition of Unprocessed Foods: Foods of Plant Origin," in Harris and von Boesecke, *Nutritional Evaluation of Food Processing*, 1st ed., p. 58.

quality occur during storage. The sizable losses of vitamins A and C through storage—and their significant preservation through adequate refrigerated storage—are shown in table 5-7. Controlled-atmosphere packaging has also been used to improve shelf life of fresh fruits and vegetables. In assessing the inventory facilities' requirements, the analyst should compare the potential physical and quality losses of the fruits and vegetables with the investment outlay needed to minimize them.

The final aspect of the physical facilities analysis is their location. As noted in the chapters on marketing and procurement, it may be desirable to locate the warehouses near producers to facilitate assembling economical lots of raw materials, or near distributors to provide rapid delivery service. The firm may decide to have separate warehouses to reduce the risk of fire losses (an important consideration, for example, in baled cotton warehousing) and thereby reduce insurance premiums. Another example is apples: the field heat of apples must be reduced within twenty-four hours of picking to extend their shelf life and nutritional qualities. Therefore, apple firms should locate their storage centers near the production areas. Such location also allows the firm to transport the apples to the processing centers in unrefrigerated trucks, thereby saving on this added investment cost.

## Financial Aspects

The seasonal nature of agroindustrial products raises the peak working capital requirements of agroindustries to levels proportionately higher than those in other industries. Many processors have encountered problems of undercapitalization because they have inaccurately estimated needs for working capital. If the processing plant runs out of funds during the height of the harvest period, farmers will sell to other processors and leave the plant short of raw materials, which means that the plant will not run at full capacity and will suffer adverse financial consequences. Thus, the analyst should determine when the plant's working capital needs will be highest and verify that credit lines correspond to these peaks.

If such bank credit or additional equity capital is not available, the agroindustry may have to convince the farmers or assembler intermediaries to carry the raw material inventory financially until the plant is able to regenerate liquidity through sales. Farmers with few alternative buyers may be willing to supply such credit, but they will generally charge higher prices for the raw materials to compensate for their credit. Another financial determinant is the price level of the raw material, which will only be known at harvest time unless a fixed price, long-term contract exists. Consequently, credit lines must be flexible enough to cover price variations.

Large inventories also increase the processor's price risk. The price of the processed product can fall during the inventory period, thus leaving the processor with fixed raw material costs and a lower profit margin. Many U.S. processors use the futures markets in grains, orange juice, livestock, potatoes, and other commodities to hedge against the inventory price risk.[55] Although some developing countries have budding futures markets, most lack the conditions such as standardized product grades, ability to deliver, highly developed information systems, and large pools of speculative capital, necessary to support successful futures markets. Commodity exporters in the developing nations can, however, use the futures markets of the industrialized nations to obtain some price protection for their exports.

There are alternative approaches to price management. If the processor buys from wholesalers and the product does not have to be processed as soon as it is harvested, the processor can buy the product as it is needed and minimize inventories. The tradeoff is that the processor may have to pay the distributor premium prices for carrying the costs of the inventory, its storage, and the price risk. If the harvest period is short, a processor who cannot stock up because of inadequate storage facilities may face supply shortages, high wholesale prices, or a production stoppage. If the processor does carry the inventory, it may use forward contracts as a surrogate for the futures market: the factory's expected output would be sold in advance at a fixed price expected to cover costs and preserve a margin. Retailers or further processors may favor a fixed price because it is stable. Both seller and buyer reduce their uncertainty, although the buyer still carries the end-market price risks.

## Packaging and Other Inputs

To analyze the agroindustry's packaging and other input needs the analyst needs to understand the functions of packaging; select the optimum packaging, taking into consideration market requirements, the nature of the product, and the attributes and cost of the packaging technology; and consider the availability of packaging supplies and other inputs.

### Packaging Functions

Although the agricultural raw material is the most important input for the processing operation, packaging performs several vital functions that often make it the next most critical input. Packaging protects the product's quality in several ways. It keeps the product clean and prevents physical damage, including tampering and adulteration. It gives odor resistance, helps retain flavor and aroma retention, and controls or reduces spoilage. Packaging creates consumer convenience through ease of opening, resealing, storing, and cooking. It transmits product image through its appearance and user information through its labeling. Packaging also facilitates transport with its form, size, and protection, and enhances trade through its standard unit of measure. Clearly, packaging contributes to each of processing's three P's: portability, palatability, and preservability.

Packaging adds value to the processed product and is therefore an important source for creating competitive advantage through differentiation, which is particularly important for those food products whose intrinsic characteristics make them difficult to differentiate. But such differentiation comes at a cost. In the United States, packaging accounts for about 8 percent of total food manufacturing costs or about 11 percent of the total excluding that paid to farmers.[56] Packaging plays an increasingly significant role economically and competitively as countries' marketing systems develop and consumers become more demanding.

### Packaging Selection

To determine which type of packaging to use, the analyst must weigh market requirements, the characteristics of the processed product, the condition of the infrastructure, and the attributes and costs of alternative packaging technologies.

MARKET REQUIREMENTS. In choosing the type of packaging to use, the analyst must identify the mix of quality and cost that creates the greatest value. Quality is in the eyes of the user. As with product design, packaging selection should be rooted in the consumer analysis discussed in chapter 3. One does not want to "overpackage," providing more than the consumer demands or is willing to pay for; this can put a company at a cost disadvantage.

PRODUCT CHARACTERISTICS. The nature of the food or fiber product is a fundamental determinant of the packaging parameters.[57] For dry foods, such as powdered milk, the packaging should block insects, odors, and water vapor and prohibit oxygen filtration in varying degrees. For foods high in fat, such as chocolates, packaging should be grease- and odor-proof and somewhat resistant to water vapor. Packaging for fresh fish and meats should block water vapor, odor, and gases; should be leak- and drip-proof; and should not stick to the meat. For frozen foods, such as vegetables, packaging should be pliable and not stick to the food and should resist water vapor. Packaging for fresh vegetables depends on the produce's degree of respiratory activity, which is high for leafy vegetables and low for tubers.

Each particular food has specific packaging requirements driven by its distinctive biological characteristics. The government is likely to impose some packaging requirements or restrictions to ensure product safety. Relatively nonperishable fiber products may need special packaging to protect them from dirt or handling damage or to achieve greater packaging or handling efficiencies.

INFRASTRUCTURAL CONDITIONS. The transportation and storage infrastructure can also affect packaging requirements. Where markets are distant, roads rough, or transport services unreliable, the demands placed on the packaging's durability and its ability to preserve the product are intensified. Testing the packaging's suitability to the operating conditions is essential. One firm tested a new type of packaging for fifteen months, but the tests were done only in the nearby city. When full-scale operations started, the new packaging materials did not stand up under the additional stresses of rougher transport to the more distant market, forcing the company to revert to its traditional, more expensive packaging material.

TECHNOLOGY ATTRIBUTES. In meeting these product requirements and meshing them with the consumers' preferences (and the needs of the distributors regarding shelf life and handling), the analyst often has a choice of packaging technology options. The costs of these options tend to be closely related to the barrier properties of the packaging (its ability to withstand permeation of liquids or gases); stability (its resistance to change in properties due to water, heat, or light); and mechanical strength (its resistance to tearing).

Worldwide trends in packaging materials, reported at the 1988 World Packaging Congress, forecast steady tinplate consumption but with reductions in thickness that will lower tonnage.[58] Because of price differentials, aluminum will not displace tin, but its use in trays and single-portion packs will increase. Glass usage will remain stable, primarily because its image conveys quality and cleanliness. Cardboard consumption will remain stable, with greater emphasis on wraparound cartons to economize material and labor. Plastic usage will rise, largely because of its ability to create new package looks and resolve packaging problems at reasonable costs. Films and laminates will be used in increasing amounts as more single-portion packs are produced and as companies switch from cans to soft packs. Metalized film will displace aluminum foil because of cost advantages.

Some of the emerging packing technologies in the United States illustrate their ability to achieve both cost and quality advantages.[59] Various plastics, films, and laminates (sometimes coextruded) that are highly resistant to gas permeability are being increasingly used to package foods such as ketchup, salad dressing, peanut butter, and soft drinks. These new packagings have almost entirely replaced the two-liter glass containers for soft drinks and are beginning to be used for beer.

These new materials offer several advantages. Because they are resistent to high temperatures, they can withstand hot fillings. They are lighter in weight, shatterproof, clear, and readily tailored into different shapes to help differentiate a product or provide greater consumer convenience. Heat-tolerant plastic packaging and other materials such as fiberboard are being increasingly used in packaging that can be used in conventional and microwave ovens.

These materials are increasingly being used for beverages with high acid content. In this aseptic packaging technique, the food and the package are sterilized separately, and the container is then filled and sealed in a sterile environment. This packaging technique uses 30–50 percent less material than metal and glass and has higher thermal efficiency than canning. The packaged product is cheaper to distribute, has a longer shelf life, retains quality without refrigeration, and is lighter and more portable.

Two other technologies create within the package specific atmospheres aimed at reducing and managing the oxygen level in the package and thereby delaying the onset of spoilage.[60] Modified atmosphere packaging (MAP) is a one-time introduction of an atmosphere; controlled atmosphere packaging (CAP) regulates and maintains a specific atmosphere in the container. Each product has its own unique atmosphere requirements. A well-designed MAP or CAP should be able to compensate for temperature-induced respiration change by adjusting its oxygen/carbon dioxide permeability over a ten- to fifteen-degree temperature range.[61] The major benefit of this packaging is that shelf life is extended 30–100 percent. The packaging is being used for products such as meats, fruits, vegetables, baked goods, salads, sandwiches, and snacks. It reduces waste, increases freshness, and creates opportunities for new presentations of existing products. It is still a relatively demanding and costly packaging approach, so it tends to be used with higher-value products.

In considering costs, the analyst should identify not just the costs of the packages or packaging materials, but also the variable operating costs of the packaging options and the level of investment in fixed assets that each will require. The analyst should also consider the ecological consequences of each packaging choice. Plastic is of particular concern because of its rising use (the United States uses more plastic than it does steel). Worldwide, 27 percent of all plastic is used for packaging, and plastic constitutes 7.2 percent of the total packaging waste in municipal solid-waste sites.[62] Incineration is an alternative disposal technique and is being used more frequently because of the energy recovery; plastics provide a rich energy source. Recycling is the other major method for disposing of plastic packaging, especially soft-drink containers. Agroindustries that opt for plastic packaging should carefully think through the recycling possibilities, for both ecological and economic reasons.

### Availability of Ancillary Supplies

The major ancillary agroindustrial supplies in addition to packaging materials are added ingredients (for example, flavorings and preservatives), processing chemicals, and maintenance supplies. It is preferable—but frequently infeasible—to buy these products locally. Their manufacture is a secondary industry that operates on derived demand. Consequently, producers of these ancillary supplies usually develop more slowly than suppliers for the primary industry. If local manufacturers of ancillary supplies exist, the quality of their inputs may not meet the processor's requirements for export, or even domestic, markets. That is particularly true for packaging supplies because product preservation and appearance can be important variables in the consumer's purchasing decision. Maintenance supplies, such as spare parts, may not be produced locally because of low demand.

The processor may be forced to rely on imported ancillary supplies until these local industries are established or improved. The disadvantages of relying on imports are the foreign exchange requirements, delivery delays, high transport costs, and import duties. The processor can stimulate the development of local input suppliers through contracts, technical assistance, inspection, and incentives. Alternatively, the processor can integrate and begin producing these inputs. Integration is more feasible when the processor's input needs are large. Some wineries and breweries, for example, have obtained economies of scale and cost advantages by taking over the bottle-producing operations. Even if input requirements are small, integration still might be feasible if the production technology for the input is adaptable to small-scale production. A sawmill might be able to produce packing crates, for example (although one project's demand for wooden crates exacerbated the existing deforestation problem in the region).

## Programming and Control

Three aspects of programming and control merit the particular attention of the agroindustrial project analyst: production design, quality control, and environmental control.

### Production Design

The analyst should review at least the following items of the project's production design: its implementation plans, engineering, and production scheduling.[63]

IMPLEMENTATION PLANS. The focus of this book has been on the analysis and design aspects of agroindustry projects, but even in this context, it is important for the analyst to ensure that the investment, if approved, can be successfully implemented. Consequently, a preliminary implementation plan should exist that delineates the steps to be taken after the investment decision and before production begins. This plan should include adequate pilot testing of the technology and operating systems before full-scale operations are launched.

In drawing up its implementation plans, the project can make use of such management techniques as Gantt charts, which divide the implementation process into distinct activities with time periods attached to each. For more complex projects, other network diagramming techniques—such as the Critical Path Method (CPM) or Project Evaluation and Review Technique (PERT)—might be used.[64] In formulating or reviewing the implementation schedule, the analyst should keep in mind the seasonal nature of the agroindustry's raw material. The timing of this availability sets basic temporal parameters for the start of production.

This implementation programming should also encompass a plan for preventive maintenance. Too often this aspect is neglected in planning and handled in an ad hoc way. The result can be serious erosion of the physical plant, leading to unexpected and highly costly breakdowns. Preventive maintenance is an investment vital to operational sustainability.

PROJECT ENGINEERING. The project's investments, production design, and organization should be based on detailed engineering, the degree and sophistication of which will depend on the size and nature of the undertaking. The United Nations Industrial Development Organization has suggested that preparing the following charts and layouts is often useful:[65]

- *General functional layouts.* These show the relations among equipment, buildings, and civil works.
- *Materials flow diagrams.* Such charts show the direction and quantities of all inputs (materials, supplies, and energy) and outputs (intermediate and final products, by-products, and emissions) throughout the plant. Agroindustries will find it is useful to extend these diagrams back through raw material procurement, especially if the product is highly perishable and likely to require special preprocessing treatment.
- *Production-line diagrams.* These show the location, equipment specifications, space requirements, water, power, and electricity requirements, and mounting device sizes for each processing stage.
- *Transport layouts.* These diagrams show the distances to, within, and from the production line and the modes of transportation used at each stage.
- *Utility consumption layouts.* These show where utility lines are to be located and the amount of water, power, and electricity required for the purpose of guiding installation and calculating costs.
- *Communications layouts.* These diagrams show the location and kind of communications devices needed throughout the facility.
- *Personnel layouts.* These indicate the number of personnel and the skill level needed at each stage of the production process; these layouts are useful in identifying areas in which labor intensity can be increased.
- *Physical layouts.* These charts fit the functional layouts to the actual conditions at the site and are thus based on geodetic, geological, hydrological, soil, mechanical, and other surveys.[66]

PRODUCTION SCHEDULING. The raw material's seasonality complicates production scheduling. The processor should design a master schedule that programs dates and quantities of raw material procurement, processing volume and duration, and inventory levels. From this the analyst can explore the possibilities of reducing investment in equipment capacity by operating multiple shifts, extending the processing period by multiple crop inputs or semiprocessing raw materials, minimizing fluctuations in product flow, and obtaining adequate supplies of labor and material. For example, the production schedule of a milk processing plant might show a strong seasonal variation in capacity use because milk production drops during the dry season when cattle forage is scarce. This variation might stimulate the processor to use soy for protein feed in the off-season and to produce soy-based milk as another of its products to maintain output.

In effect, the production schedule becomes the working document for analyzing many of the issues examined in the previous sections.

### Quality Control

Agroindustries in developing countries frequently lack systematic quality-control procedures. As a result, their product quality is erratic, can cause consumer dissatisfaction, and, sometimes, can be hazardous to consume.

Product quality is influenced by many factors, beginning with the genetic material (seed or breed) used on the farm and the farmer's agricultural practices. It is at this stage that quality control must begin. At the processing stage, quality control should be applied to the raw material inventory, work in process, and finished goods. The quality of the raw material stock can be preserved by adequate storage facilities, but periodic sampling of the inventory to test for pest or insect damage or microbial growth is advisable. These measures can spot problems while they can still be corrected. Spoilage can begin inconspicuously and accelerate rapidly, causing massive inventory losses and production stoppages. By contrast, monitoring is relatively inexpensive and, usually, cost-effective. Some of this quality control will be necessary to comply with government food safety standards and regulations.

Most food and fiber processing is relatively quick, but in-process monitoring is feasible to check for contamination levels, packaging integrity, temperature, and chemical composition. Some measurements can be made by automated instrumentation systems to ensure accuracy. Quality control charts can be maintained to monitor processing variables.[67] Finished goods can be inspected by variable (that is, a particular characteristic) or by attribute (level of quality). Quality-control mechanisms include visual inspection, mechanical measuring devices, and laboratory analyses.

Sampling techniques are relatively reliable and efficient, but the processor must first set an acceptable level of quality. After that has been defined (sometimes by government regulations), sampling can take place within limits of probability for committing either a "Type I" error (accepting a lot that should be rejected) or a "Type II" error (rejecting a lot that should be accepted). Nutritional quality of finished goods should be monitored by biochemical analysis to measure nutrient retention and any microbial contamination.

In the United States the National Food Processors Association recommended recently the "Hazard Analysis and Critical Control Point" system as a strategy to overcome deficiencies in existing inspection and quality control programs for the new generation of refrigerated foods and some traditional refrigerated products. The system includes the following five main components:[68]

1. Describe the product and how the consumer will use it.
2. Prepare a flow diagram for intended manufacturing and distribution of the product.
3. Conduct risk analyses for ingredients, product, and packaging; reduce risks by making changes in the design; and incorporate these changes into the processing and packaging schemes.
4. Select critical control points, describe them, and designate their location on the flow diagram; establish monitoring procedures at these points.
5. Implement this system in routine activities.

The level of sophistication of food safety and quality control systems in developing countries must be adapted to the prevailing market and regulatory demands and the capabilities of personnel and technology. Nonetheless, such systems should be viewed as integral and strategically important parts of the processing operation. Poor quality control can have disastrous consequences for product acceptability. Problems tend to arise more frequently in export operations where the agroindustry's knowledge or appreciation of the foreign market's quality requirements are more limited. One East European country's exports of salami were found wanting because the packaging was coming unwrapped and the products were moldy. Although demand was strong for this product category, this particular product did not pass the U.S. Department of Agriculture's inspection and so was not allowed into the market. The same country lost its market for chocolate-covered cherries when consumers complained that some of the cherries still contained their pits. All of these problems were avoidable through better quality control systems.

### Environmental Protection

Another area to be considered in project design is pollution control. The first environment that must be protected is that of the plant itself; employees should not be endangered by contaminants arising from the processes or other aspects of the operations. The entire production process should be reviewed to see if the air quality, materials contact, and procedures contain any sources of endangerment, and, if so, measures should be taken to guarantee worker safety.

The other protection is of the external environment. Agroindustries, like most other industrial operations, produce gaseous and liquid emissions and solid waste. These can contribute significantly to pollution of rivers, land, and air. For example, one study in Canada examined the pollution effects of discharges into a river from five fruit and vegetable canneries, a potato processing plant, a meat packing plant, two poultry processing plants, and seven municipal sewage treatment plants.[69] The bacteria count in the river was found to be comparable to that found in raw sewage, and salmonellae were found in the poultry and meat plant discharges and those from five of the sewage treatment plants. The fecal coliform counts in the river exceeded the safe limits for bathing and shellfishing.

Agroindustries are often particularly heavy users of water in their processes, making wastewater effluents a primary focus of environmental controls. In the United States, for example, 1,600 fruit and vegetable plants produce 30 million tons of product each year and discharge about 430,000 million liters of wastewater. About 46 percent of these effluents go into public treatment systems, 28 percent into surface waters, and 26 percent to land irrigation.[70]

The processor's water effluent control system should focus on measures within and after the processing operations. To the maximum extent safely feasible, water should be reused within the operations. In some instances it can be treated (particulate matter can be filtered out, for example, and the water chlorinated) and recycled to its original use. In other instances it can be put to a different use requiring lower water purity (spent cooling water, for example, might be used to clean the plant). Such practices reduce total effluent output.

The project design must include adequate equipment and facilities, including extra land area, to treat discharges. Considerable progress is being made in developing biological treatment systems that reclaim processing effluent for reuse in the processing operations. The organic content of the effluents are reduced by biological processes, such as aerated lagoon treatment or activated sludge; excess suspended solids are removed; and microbiological organisms are eliminated through disinfection. One U.S. fruit processing cooperative was able to use reclaimed water for half of the cannery's water needs.[71] Effective use of anaerobic treatment of wastewater from fruit and vegetable and meat processing plants in Brazil has also been reported.[72]

The experience of the palm industry in Malaysia is informative.[73] The industry was the country's largest polluter, contributing 83 percent of the industrial organic pollution load. Every ton of palm oil produced generated five cubic meters of effluent with an average biological oxygen demand (BOD) concentration of 25,000 milligrams per liter. (BOD is the oxygen used in meeting the metabolic needs of aerobic organisms in water containing organic compounds.) The government issued regulations to control the effluent problem and instituted effluent fees based on the pollution load discharged (measured by concentrations of BOD). The higher the pollution level, the higher the fee; for the palm oil industry, the charges exceeded the capital costs of anaerobic lagoon treatment technology, thereby creating an economic incentive to adopt the technology. The government worked closely with the industry and the country's research institutions to develop and implement appropriate technologies and procedures. The program dramatically reduced the industry's effluent discharge even while palm oil production increased significantly: although the effluent load increased from 690 tons a day in 1979 to 1,640 in 1984, the BOD pollutants discharged were reduced to 4 tons a day. The processing plants are instituting in-process measures to reduce effluent levels, and the entrapped wastes are being converted to by-products such as animal feed, biogas, and fertilizer, which is being applied to the land on the palm oil estates.

The Malaysian example reveals not only that government is likely to become more heavily involved in environmental regulation, but also that government-business cooperation can lead to constructive and economical ways to handle the environmental challenges confronting agroindustries.

## By-products

One final aspect of processing is the role of by-products. Unlike other manufacturing operations, agroindustrial processing generally disaggregates one raw material, rather than aggregating various materials. The biological nature of the raw material endows it with many useful parts, and the product often has multiple derivatives. Because by-products can be important in the economics of agroindustries, they warrant close inspection.

The analyst should identify all the outputs of the processing flow. Pure wastage should be minimized, but economic opportunities from possible by-products are often overlooked, especially in an agroindustry's early development. The analyst should look for recoverable but economically unexploited by-products. Such an example was the discarded mung bean protein that was eventually used as weaning food or animal feed. An example of a neglected by-product occurred in Guyana, where broiler chicken processors initially failed to retain the discarded chicken blood for use as a protein source in animal feed.[74]

To forecast total revenues accurately, the processor must project the prices of its by-products. Even though this is sometimes difficult because it requires an analysis of supply and demand conditions in another commodity system, these projections should take into account price levels and variability. If the realizable revenue and profit margin are small relative to the main product, then extensive price projections are not warranted. Nevertheless, estimates of a by-product's market are important—in some cases the by-product might become more valuable than the main product. For example, a sugar manufacturer in a South American country developed a process for converting bagasse (sugarcane residue after extraction) into pulp for the production of paper. Initially, this process gave economic value to a previously unused by-product (before, it had a negative value because the processor had to pay to dispose of the bagasse as waste). Changes in the international sugar market subsequently caused a drastic decline in sugar prices, while at the same time prices for paper products in the domestic market continued to increase. The shifts in the paper industry were so dramatic that the sugar refinery's profits from its bagasse sales exceeded its profits from processed sugar: in effect, bagasse became its primary product and sugar its by-product. The analyst must realize that, in keeping with agroindustry's inter-sectoral nature, the agroindustrial firm is in many businesses simultaneously and that a project's operating strategies must be adjusted according to the overall price dynamics.

Another aspect worth considering is the extent to which the variability in by-product price provides countercyclical or seasonal balancing to the variations in the primary products' prices. A further consideration is whether the by-products can be used as energy sources. A vegetable-oil processor in a Central American country uses cottonseed husks as boiler fuel (in sugar refining, bagasse can be similarly used). Some feedlots in the United States recycle and convert their animal wastes into fuel, thereby simultaneously solving problems of waste disposal and environmental pollution. Similarly, small-scale biogas plants are operating at the village level in India. The energy created from by-product processing might be salable to outsiders.

## Summary

Analysis of a project's processing operations derives from analyses of its procurement and marketing. Processing, however, links the stages of the project together and is the focal point of the investment. Physical, chemical, and biological processes transform raw materials into products that are more preservable, portable, and palatable, thereby adding value and creating opportunities for competitive advantage.

A primary element in processing is technology; it must be tailored to fit the market's requirements, and as such, it is a potential source of product differentiation. Various factors, such as the need for a minimum size that is still economical, or to attain a specific degree of precision, or comply with government food safety standards, will impose certain limits on choice of technology. Another critical selection criterion is cost, and here the analyst should examine the possibilities for substituting labor for capital as well as the relations between energy and raw material usage. Other criteria for technology selection include the degree to which the technology minimizes the plant's downtime because of seasonality, and the skill capabilities required to meet the supervisory and technical demands of the technology. The processor should also consider the technology's potential effects, both those that might adversely affect nutrient quality and those that might nutritionally enhance the product and provide a basis for product differentiation.

Another decision the processor must make is plant location. Whether it is better for the plant to locate near the markets or near the suppliers of raw material depends on the nature of the raw materials, the transformative process of the agroindustry, and the cost and reliability of the needed transport services. Labor supply, the availability of infrastructure, land costs, and the developmental effects of the project are additional considerations for plant location.

Inventory management also requires special attention because of the constraints of seasonality. The processor must determine the correct mix of raw and semiprocessed material and finished goods to reach optimal processing capacity. Adequate physical facilities are essential to prevent losses in product quantity and quality from pest and insect infestation or microbial growth. The raw material's seasonality accentuates both the processor's needs for working capital and the inventory's exposure to price risks. The processor should explore the methods available for handling both.

Packaging plays a vital role in agroindustries. It provides quality protection and meets various consumer needs. It is a vehicle for achieving product differentiation and is a major cost element. The type of packaging used will be determined by the interplay of consumer needs, the products' characteristics, and the attributes and costs of the packaging technology. The sources of the packaging and other production inputs need to be carefully assessed for availability and delivery dependability.

Programming and control procedures should also be reviewed to ensure that production design and quality control will be adequately carried out. An implementation plan, project engineering, and a master production schedule should be drawn up before starting production. Careful planning is required to ensure that adequate environmental protection and work safety measures have been considered. Finally, almost all agroindustries generate by-products. Because these can be important to the project's economics, the processor should estimate their financial contribution.

## The Processing Factor: Salient Points for Project Analysis

The project analyst should consider the following questions when reviewing the processing dimensions of an agroindustrial project.

### Technology Selection

*Is the processing technology consistent with the quality requirements of the marketplace?*
- Match with quality standards of market segments?
- Incremental revenue from added quality versus added technological investment?
- Technology appropriate for local and export markets?

*What constraints do process requirements impose?*
- Nature of requirements?
- Number of technological options?
- Scale requirements?
- Demand adequate for scale?

*Which technology configuration has the greatest cost advantage?*
- Mixes of labor and capital?
- Desirability of using secondhand equipment?
- Energy requirements?
- Biomass-based energy sources?
- Raw material savings?
- Possibility of multiple raw material sources?
- Government policies affecting labor, capital, raw material, and energy costs?

*How will the technology affect use of project capacity?*
- Adjustments to diversify products processed and lengthen operating cycle?
- Costs and benefits of adjustments?

*How well does the technology fit with the firm's managerial and technical capabilities?*
- Supervisory skills adequate?
- Technical skills adequate?
- Adjust technology to reduce skill requirements?

*What are the technology's nutritional consequences?*
- Effects on quality and quantity of nutrients?
- Methods of minimizing nutrient loss?
- Opportunities for increasing nutritional quality and product differentiation through adjusting technology?

## Plant Location

*Do raw material, market, and transport factors support the proposed location?*
- Perishability of the raw material?
- Weight added or reduced by processing?
- Cost and quality of transport services?
- Multiple plants versus single plant?
- Should plant provide own transport?

*Is labor supply adequate?*
- Unskilled, skilled, managerial supply adequate?
- Special personnel incentives required?

*Is the infrastructure of the location acceptable?*
- Energy and water supply, their ecological effects, reliability, and cost?
- Fire protection facilities?
- Transport?
- Social infrastructure?

*What will the plant's land cost?*
- Comparative prices for a square meter?
- Adequate for future needs?
- Urbanization trends?

*What are the likely developmental effects of the location?*
- On employment and income distribution?
- On regional development?
- Fiscal incentives for plant to support development?

## Inventory Management

*What are the best storage facilities for raw materials and finished goods?*
- Product perishability?
- Effect of processing on storability?
- Raw versus semiprocessed material to reduce storage needed for finished goods?
- Storage for processing supplies and repair parts?

*Are the facilities adequate?*
- Costs and benefits of reducing inventory deterioration?
- Location relative to producers and distributors?

*Have the requirements for working capital and the inventory price risks been adequately analyzed?*
- Peak needs for working capital?

- Feasible to hedge price risks through futures markets?
- Continued buying versus stockpiling?
- Advance contracting?

## Packaging and Other Inputs

*What functions will the packaging perform?*
- Quality protection?
- User convenience?
- Image conveyance?
- Information transmittal?
- Processing or distribution cost savings?
- Product differentiation?

*Which packaging should be used?*
- Requirements of the consumer and the distribution channels?
- Unmet needs?
- Requirements due to nature of the product?
- Transportation, storage, and handling demands?
- Government regulations?
- Technology attributes?
- Quality enhancements?
- Materials, operating, and investment costs?
- Ecological considerations?

*Where should the plant procure its ancillary supplies (packaging, ingredients, and chemicals)?*
- Locally or abroad?
- Foreign exchange requirements if purchased abroad?
- Development of local suppliers?
- Horizontal integration?

## Programming and Control

*Is there a clear and systematic implementation plan?*
- Postinvestment and preproduction steps delineated?
- Pilot testing of technology and operating processes?
- Programming techniques such as Gantt charts, CPM, or PERT used?
- Preventive maintenance program formulated?

*Has project engineering been diagrammed?*
- General functional layouts made?
- Flow diagrams of materials designed?
- Production-line diagrams specified?

- Transport, utility, communications, and manpower layouts set forth?

*Does a master schedule for procurement and processing exist?*
- Seasonal availability of raw material considered?
- Possibility of working multiple shifts?
- Alternative uses of production capacity?

*Are there systematic quality-control procedures for raw materials, work in process, and finished goods?*
- Inspection system for raw material as it is grown?
- Controls for contamination levels, packaging integrity, temperature, and chemical composition?
- Sampling procedures? Laboratory testing facilities?
- Nutritional quality verifiable?
- Export market standards fulfilled?
- Corrective procedures specified?

*Have adequate environmental protection measures been planned for?*
- Safety risks to employees from contaminants, materials, processes?
- Pollution effects to air, land, or water?
- Design measures to maximize in-process reuse and minimize effluent load?
- Biological treatment to enable effluent reuse?
- Conversion of wastes to other uses?
- Compliance with government regulations?

## By-products

*What do by-products contribute to revenue?*
- Outputs?
- Unsold by-products with economic or nutritional value?
- Levels and variations in price of by-products?
- Any countercyclical or seasonal balancing to product's price variation from by-product sales?

*Can by-products be used as energy sources for the processing operations?*
- Additional investment required to convert by-product to energy source?
- How can such energy be used for the agroindustry's fuel needs?
- Can energy from by-products be sold outside the agroindustry?

# Notes

## Chapter 1

1. Not all agroindustries share these characteristics equally; for example, timber, unlike tomatoes, does not have a marked, seasonal production pattern, nor is it very perishable.

2. James E. Austin, ed., *Global Malnutrition and Cereal Fortification* (Cambridge, Mass.: Ballinger Publishing Co., 1979), p. 244.

3. Austin, *Global Malnutrition and Cereal Fortification*, p. 162.

4. For an economic gender analysis methodology, see Catherine Overholt, Mary Anderson, Kathleen Cloud, and James Austin, eds., *Gender Roles in Development Projects: A Casebook* (West Hartford, Conn.: Kumarian Press, 1985).

5. John C. Abbott, "Alternative Agricultural Marketing Institutions," in Dieter Elz, ed., *Agricultural Marketing Strategy and Pricing Policy* (Washington, D.C.: World Bank, 1987), p. 17.

6. UNIDO (United Nations Industrial Development Organization), *Industrialization and Rural Development* (New York, 1978), p. 8; also see Bejsin Behari, *Rural Industrialization in India* (New Delhi: Vikas Publishing House, 1976).

7. IDB (Inter-American Development Bank), Division of Agriculture, "Guide to Preparation of Agroindustrial Projects" (Washington, D.C., April 1974), p. 1.

8. Fernando Caldas, "Consideraciones sobre las agroindustrias en Costa Rica" ["Considerations Regarding Agroindustries in Costa Rica"] (New York: United Nations Industrial Development Organization, August 1976).

9. World Bank, *World Development Report 1990* (New York: Oxford University Press, 1990), p. 188.

10. The historical description of the U.S. food industry is taken from John M. Connor, Richard T. Rogers, Bruce W. Marion, and Willard F. Mueller, *The Food Manufacturing Industries: Structure, Strategies, Performance, and Policies* (Lexington, Mass.: Lexington Books, 1985), p. 45.

11. International Federation of Cotton and Allied Textile Industries, *International Cotton Industry Statistics* 17 (1974), pp. 13, 19.

12. World Bank, *World Development Report 1990*, pp. 188–89.

13. Hollis B. Chenery, "Patterns of Industrial Growth," *American Economic Review* 50 (September 1960), pp. 624–54; Walter D. Hoffman, *The Growth of Industrial Economies* (Manchester, U.K.: University of Manchester Press, 1958).

14. World Bank, *Sub-Saharan Africa: From Crisis to Sustainable Growth* (Washington, D.C., 1989), derived from table 9, p. 236; data for 1986 or 1980 depending on availability.

15. Data for 1988 from World Bank, *World Development Report 1990*, calculated from pp. 178, 238; projection for year 2000 from James E. Austin, *Confronting Urban Malnutrition: The Design of Nutrition Programs*, World Bank Staff Occasional Paper 28 (Baltimore, Md.: Johns Hopkins University Press, 1980), p. 4.

16. United Nations Centre on Transnational Corporations, *Transnational Corporations in Food and Beverage Processing* (New York, 1981), p. 4.

17. United Nations Centre on Transnational Corporations, *Transnational Corporations in Food and Beverage Processing*, p. 7.

18. Comisión de la Estrategia Agroalimentaria Nacional, *La Estrategia Agroalimentaria Nacional* [*National Agricultural Food Strategy*] (Caracas: CAVIDEA, 1989), p. 9.

19. Donald R. Snodgrass, "Small-scale Manufacturing Industries: Patterns, Trends, and Possible Policies," Development Discussion Paper 54 (Cambridge, Mass.: Harvard University, Institute for International Development, March 1979), pp. 12–13. Within the small-scale industries sector, forestry-based activities are an important employment generator in many countries, accounting, for example, for 20–30 percent of the total nonfarm small-scale enterprise employment in Sierra Leone and Jamaica. See Hans Gregersen, Sydney Draper, and Dieter Elz, eds., *People and Trees: The Role of Social Forestry in Sustainable Development* (Washington, D.C.: World Bank, 1989), p. 78.

20. UNIDO, *Industrialization and Rural Development*, pp. 39–44.

21. The term "agribusiness" was coined by John H. Davis and Ray A. Goldberg, who subsequently elaborated their concept in the book *A Concept of Agribusiness* (Boston: Harvard University, Graduate School of Business Administration, Division of Research, 1967).

22. A project's economic desirability for a country should be assessed through the application of economic cost-benefit analysis methodology. This might reveal, for example, that generating foreign exchange by exporting or saving foreign exchange by replacing imports with domestic goods is more beneficial to a country than the nominal valuation would suggest, due to the use of a shadow exchange rate in economic cost-benefit analysis to reflect the true value of foreign exchange. For a discussion of cost-benefit methodology, see the citations in note 1 of chapter 2.

23. Increased transformation will not necessarily improve price stability. Some intermediate products, such as palm oil, may face markets as unstable as those for less-processed commodities, whereas the investment—and hence the capital exposure—in intermediate products has increased. Value added . has increased, but the price risk has not necessarily decreased.

24. IMF (International Monetary Fund), *World Economic Outlook: May 1990* (Washington, D.C., 1990), p. 153.

25. For data on export profiles for 1984–86, see IMF, *World Economic Outlook*, pp. 118–19.

26. Central Bank of Nicaragua, *Informe Anual—1970* [*Annual Report*] (Managua, 1971).

27. All dollar figures in this book are in U.S. dollars unless otherwise stated.

28. United States Department of Agriculture, Economic Research Service, *High-Value Agricultural Exports: U.S. Opportunities in the 1980s,* USDA Foreign Agricultural Report 188 (Washington, D.C., 1983), p. 2.

29. James E. Austin and Gustavo Esteva, eds., *Food Policy in Mexico: The Search for Self-Sufficiency* (Ithaca, N.Y.: Cornell University Press, 1987).

30. The World Food Council, "The Global State of Hunger and Malnutrition: 1990 Report," paper presented at the Sixteenth Ministerial Session, Bangkok, Thailand, May 21–24, 1990, p. 4.

31. Comisión de la Estrategia Agroalimentaria Nacional, *La Estrategia Agroalimentaria Nacional,* p. 19.

32. Joseph C. Wheeler, ed., *Development Co-operation in the 1990s* (Paris: Organization for Economic Cooperation and Development, 1990), pp. 228, 233.

33. Derived from World Bank lending data bank.

34. Uma Lele, "Growth of Foreign Assistance and Its Impact on Agriculture," in John W. Mellor, Christopher L. Delgado, and Malcolm J. Blackie, eds., *Accelerating Food Production in Sub-Saharan Africa* (Baltimore, Md.: Johns Hopkins University Press, 1987), p. 329.

35. John W. Lowe, "The IFC and the Agribusiness Sector," *Finance and Development* 14, no. 1 (March 1977), p. 25; IFC (International Finance Corporation), *Annual Report 1989,* (Washington, D.C., 1989), p. 18.

36. James G. Brown with Deloitte & Touche, *Agroindustrial Investment and Operations,* EDI Development Study (Washington, D.C.: World Bank, forthcoming).

37. For a more detailed analysis of issues involved in the design of nutrition programs, see Austin, *Confronting Urban Malnutrition,* and James E. Austin and Marian Zeitlin, eds., *Nutrition Intervention in Developing Countries: An Overview of Nutrition Programs* (Cambridge, Mass.: Oelgeschlager, Gunn, and Hain, 1980).

## Chapter 2

1. For a clear presentation of both financial and economic analysis for agricultural projects, see J. Price Gittinger, *Economic Analysis of Agricultural Projects,* 2d ed. (Baltimore, Md.: Johns Hopkins University Press, 1982) and William A. Ward and Barry J. Deren with Emmanuel H. D'Silva, *The Economics of Project Analysis: A Practitioner's Guide,* EDI Technical Materials (Washington, D.C.: World Bank, 1991). For the general methodology for economic cost-benefit analysis, see Michael Roemer and Joseph J. Stern, *The Appraisal of Development Projects: A Practical Guide to Project Analysis with Case Studies and Solutions* (New York: Praeger, 1975) and Lyn Squire and Herman G. vander Tak, *Economic Analysis of Projects* (Baltimore, Md.: Johns Hopkins University Press, 1988). For a managerial perspective, see James E. Austin, *Managing in*

*Developing Countries: Strategic Analysis and Operating Techniques* (New York: The Free Press, 1990), pp. 156–65.

2. James G. Brown with Deloitte & Touche, *Agroindustrial Investment and Operations*, EDI Development Study (Washington, D.C.: World Bank, forthcoming).

3. John M. Connor, Richard T. Rogers, Bruce W. Marion, and Willard F. Mueller, *The Food Manufacturing Industries: Structure, Strategies, Performance, and Policies* (Lexington, Mass.: Lexington Books, 1985), p. 25.

4. Information about this situation comes from personal communication between the author and an official of the government.

5. Edward L. Felton, Jr., "The Influence of New Technology on the Marketing of Production Inputs in a Developing Economy: The High Yielding Rice Varieties in the Philippines," D.B.A. diss., Harvard University, Graduate School of Business Administration, Boston, 1971, p. 228.

6. J. N. Efferson, "Observations on Current Development in Rice Marketing in West Pakistan," paper prepared for the Government of West Pakistan, Agricultural Department, Planning Cell, Lahore, January 20, 1969, p. 4.

7. James E. Austin, *Marketing Adjustments to Production Modernization: The Case of the Nicaraguan Rice Industry* (Managua: Instituto Centroamericano de Administración de Empresas, 1972).

8. Henry B. Arthur, James P. Houck, and George L. Beckford, *Tropical Agribusiness Structures and Adjustments—Bananas* (Boston: Harvard University, Graduate School of Business Administration, 1968), chapter IX.

9. Michael E. Porter, *Competitive Advantage: Creating and Sustaining Superior Performance* (New York: The Free Press, 1985).

10. For an elaboration of the concept of the government as a mega-force, see Austin, *Managing in Developing Countries*, chapters 4 and 5.

11. Austin, *Managing in Developing Countries*, p. 77.

12. For a thorough treatment of the issues and an analytical approach to food policy, including the macro-micro dimensions, see C. Peter Timmer, Walter P. Falcon, and Scott R. Pearson, *Food Policy Analysis* (Baltimore, Md.: Johns Hopkins University Press, 1983). Timmer produced a concise and lucid sequel work focusing more specifically on agricultural price policy: *Getting Prices Right: The Scope and Limits of Agricultural Price Policy* (Ithaca, N.Y.: Cornell University Press, 1986). For a very useful methodology for understanding the effects of macropolicies on agricultural systems, see Scott R. Pearson and Eric A. Monke, *The Policy Analysis Matrix for Agricultural Development* (Ithaca, N.Y.: Cornell University Press, 1989).

13. Michael E. Porter calls rivalry, barriers to entry, substitution pressures, and supplier and buyer bargaining power the five forces driving industry competition; see Porter, *Competitive Strategy: Techniques for Analyzing Industries and Competitors* (New York: The Free Press, 1980).

14. Chip Hance and Ray A. Goldberg, "American Rice: A Farmers Cooperative Goes Public," Case Study 589-044, Harvard University, Graduate School of Business Administration, Boston, 1988, p. 2.

15. Instituto Nacional de Fomento Cooperativo, *Datos Basicos del Sector Cooperativo Costaricense* [*Basic Data on the Costa Rican Cooperative Sector*] (San José, Costa Rica, 1986).

16. D. M. Atwood and B. S. Baviskar, "Why Do Some Co-operatives Work but Not Others?" *Economic and Political Weekly* 22, no. 26 (June 27, 1987), p. A-40.

17. John C. Abbott, "Alternative Agricultural Marketing Institutions," in Dieter Elz, ed., *Agricultural Marketing Strategy and Pricing Policy* (Washington, D.C.: World Bank, 1987), p. 17.

18. Odin Knudsen and John Nash, with contributions by James Bovard, Bruce Gardner, and L. Alan Winters, *Redefining the Role of Government in Agriculture for the 1990s*, World Bank Discussion Paper 105, Washington, D.C., 1990, p. 52.

19. United Nations Centre on Transnational Corporations, *Transnational Corporations in Food and Beverage Processing* (New York, 1981), p. 18.

20. United Nations Centre on Transnational Corporations, *Transnational Corporations in Food and Beverage Processing*, p. 99.

21. Anthony J. F. O'Reilly, "Establishing Successful Joint Ventures in Developing Nations: A CEO's Perspective," *Columbia Journal of World Business* 23, no. 1 (spring 1988), p. 65.

22. For an approach to sociological analysis, see Michael M. Cernea, ed., *Putting People First: Sociological Variables in Rural Development*, 2d ed. (New York: Oxford University Press, 1991).

## Chapter 3

1. Benjamin Higgins, *Economic Development* (New York: W. W. Norton, 1968), p. 68.

2. A community-run small-scale industry in Mexico became very successful only after it reviewed consumers' needs and eliminated several products that had been made simply because the production skills existed; see UNIDO (United Nations Industrial Development Organization), "Case Study on the People's Collective Industries of Jalisco," in *Industrialization and Rural Development* (New York, 1978), p. 28.

3. Small-scale industries based in rural areas should first assess local needs and ascertain whether the rural market might be large enough to support the industry without tying into urban markets. Meeting local needs might increase the agroindustry's effect on regional development.

4. Richard L. Kohls and Joseph N. Uhl, *Marketing of Agricultural Products*, 6th ed. (New York: Macmillan, 1985), p. 84.

5. Francisco L. Roman, Jr., "Barriers to Agricultural Exports and the High-Value Product: Problems and Opportunities for the Philippine Mango Industry," D.B.A. diss., Harvard University, Graduate School of Business Administration, Boston, 1989, p. 111.

6. Kenneth Hoadley and James E. Austin, "Sabritas," in James E. Austin with Tomás Kohn, *Strategic Management in Developing Countries: Case Studies* (New York: The Free Press, 1990), pp. 337–58.

7. For further discussion of marketing research, see Erdener Kaynak, "Marketing Research Techniques and Approaches for LDCS," in G. S. Kindra, ed., *Marketing in Developing Countries* (New York: St. Martin's Press, 1984); Subhash C. Jain, *International Marketing Management*, 2d ed. (Boston:

Kent Publishing, 1987); Thomas Kinnear and James Taylor, *Marketing Research: An Applied Approach* (New York: McGraw-Hill, 1983).

8. Governments must also define the "market" and the "consumer" before undertaking social interventions such as programs to serve malnourished children. For the information requirements relevant to such undertakings, see James E. Austin, *Confronting Urban Malnutrition: The Design of Nutrition Programs*, World Bank Staff Occasional Paper 28 (Baltimore, Md.: Johns Hopkins University Press, 1980), pp. 18–51.

9. For additional discussion of information sources, especially for agroindustrial export projects, see James G. Brown with Deloitte & Touche, *Agroindustrial Investment and Operations*, EDI Development Study (Washington, D.C.: World Bank, forthcoming).

10. See James E. Austin, *Managing in Developing Countries: Strategic Analysis and Operating Techniques* (New York: The Free Press, 1990), pp. 54, 295–99.

11. Michael E. Porter, *Competitive Strategy: Techniques for Analyzing Industries and Competitors* (New York: The Free Press, 1980).

12. See Brown with Deloitte & Touche, *Agroindustrial Investment and Operations*, for a detailed description of investment costs in a wide range of agroindustries.

13. Austin with Kohn, *Strategic Management in Developing Countries*, pp. 107–28.

14. Michael E. Porter, *Competitive Advantage: Creating and Sustaining Superior Performance* (New York: The Free Press, 1985).

15. Roman, "Barriers to Agricultural Exports," p. 78.

16. Juan Enriquez and Ray A. Goldberg, "Bernard Matthews: Entrepreneurship in Agribusiness," Case Study 9-587-112, Harvard University, Graduate School of Business Administration, Boston, 1986.

17. Felicia Morrow, "Flowers: Global Subsector Study," World Bank, Industry and Energy Department, Industry Series Paper 17, Washington, D.C., December 1989, pp. 1, 45.

18. The product life cycle model has been used to explain domestic and international trade flows and competitive patterns. For an excellent overview of the international application of the model, see Louis T. Wells, Jr., ed., *The Product Life Cycle and International Trade* (Boston: Harvard University, Graduate School of Business Administration, Division of Research, 1972).

19. Malcolm D. Bale, "Government Intervention in Agricultural Markets and Pricing," in Dieter Elz, ed., *Agricultural Marketing Strategy and Pricing Policy* (Washington, D.C.: World Bank, 1987), p. 101.

20. J. S. Sarma, "Determining Administered Prices for Foodgrains in India," in Elz, *Agricultural Marketing Strategy and Pricing Policy*, p. 94.

21. Theodore Panayotou, "Thailand: The Experience of a Food Exporter," in Terry Sicular, ed., *Food Price Policy in Asia: A Comparative Study* (Ithaca, N.Y.: Cornell University Press, 1989), pp. 65–108.

22. Roman, "Barriers to Agricultural Exports," appendix C.

23. For fiber, leather, or wood agroindustrial products, factors such as durability, malleability, washability, and fashion should be considered.

24. Unless the product is a relatively undifferentiated commodity, small-scale industries may need governmental assistance to design the initial product.

25. Porter, *Competitive Advantage*, pp. 150–53.

26. This procedure was used, for example, by one of the leading Japanese trading firms in contracting for corn from Thailand. See "C. Itoh and Co., Ltd.," Case Study 4-576-041, Harvard University, Graduate School of Business Administration, Boston, September 1975.

27. The markup on a cost basis may be derived from the markup on the price basis as follows: price-basis markup ÷ (100 percent − price-basis markup).

28. Per Pinstrup-Andersen, "The Social and Economic Effects of Consumer-Oriented Food Subsidies: A Summary of Current Evidence," in Per Pinstrup-Andersen, ed., *Food Subsidies in Developing Countries: Costs, Benefits and Policy Options* (Baltimore, Md.: Johns Hopkins University Press, 1988), p. 5.

29. Pinstrup-Andersen, "The Social and Economic Effects of Consumer-Oriented Food Subsidies," p. 5.

30. Pinstrup-Andersen, "The Social and Economic Effects of Consumer-Oriented Food Subsidies," p. 13.

31. Sarma, "Determining Administered Prices for Foodgrains in India," p. 92.

32. Grant M. Scobie, "Macroeconomic and Trade Implications of Consumer-Oriented Food Subsidies," in Pinstrup-Andersen, *Food Subsidies in Developing Countries*, pp. 60–61.

33. Panayotou, "Thailand: The Experience of a Food Exporter," p. 95.

34. Ravi Gulhati, *Impasse in Zambia: The Economics and Politics of Reform*, EDI Analytical Case Study 2 (Washington, D.C.: World Bank, 1989), pp. 44–45.

35. For a discussion of approaches to business-government relations, see Austin, *Managing in Developing Countries*, chapter 6.

36. Kohls and Uhl, *Marketing of Agricultural Products*, p. 100.

37. Porter, *Competitive Advantage*, p. 153.

38. Philip Kotler and Eduardo L. Roberto, *Social Marketing: Strategies for Changing Public Behavior* (New York: The Free Press, 1989).

39. Alan Berg, *The Nutrition Factor* (Washington, D.C.: The Brookings Institution, 1973), pp. 89–106. The author estimates that the lost economic value of reduced breastfeeding in developing countries ranges in the hundreds of millions of dollars.

40. Neil Harrison and Claudine B. Malone, "Nestlé Alimentana S.A.-Infant Formula," in Austin with Kohn, *Strategic Management in Developing Countries*, pp. 377–97.

41. Kathryn Sikkink, "Codes of Conduct for Transnational Corporations: The Case of the WHO/UNICEF Code," *International Organization* 40, no. 4 (1986), pp. 815–40.

42. Morrow, "Flowers: Global Subsector Study," p. 45.

43. Austin, *Managing in Developing Countries*, p. 54.

44. Porter, *Competitive Advantage*, p. 153.

45. Kohls and Uhl, *Marketing of Agricultural Products*, p. 214.

46. C. Peter Timmer, Walter P. Falcon, and Scott R. Pearson, *Food Policy Analysis* (Baltimore, Md.: Johns Hopkins University Press, 1983), p. 169.

47. Kelly Harrison, "Improving Food Marketing and Delivery Systems," in Elz, *Agricultural Marketing Strategy and Pricing Policy*, p. 32.

48. C. Peter Timmer, *Getting Prices Right: The Scope and Limits of Agricultural Price Policy* (Ithaca, N.Y.: Cornell University Press, 1986), p. 63.

49. For further discussion of marketing boards, see Sidney Hoos, ed., *Agricultural Marketing Boards* (Cambridge, Mass: Ballinger Publishing Co., 1979); John C. Abbott, "Alternative Agricultural Marketing Institutions," in Elz, *Agricultural Marketing Strategy and Pricing Policy*, pp. 14–21; Elliot Berg, "Obstacles to Liberalizing Agricultural Markets in Developing Countries," in Elz, *Agricultural Marketing Strategy and Pricing Policy*, pp. 22–27.

50. See Philip Kotler, *Marketing Decision Making: A Model-building Approach* (New York: Holt, Rinehart & Winston, 1971); Philip Kotler, *Marketing Management: Analysis, Planning and Control*, 3d ed. (Englewood Cliffs, N.J.: Prentice-Hall, 1976).

51. Definitions are drawn from a literature review by Vithala R. Rao and James E. Cox, Jr., *Sales Forecasting Methods: A Survey of Recent Developments* (Cambridge, Mass.: Marketing Science Institute, 1978), appendix A, pp. 88–94. See also Kinnear and Taylor, *Marketing Research*, chapter 2; and Vincent P. Barabba, "The Marketing Research Encyclopedia," *Harvard Business Review* 68, no. 1 (Jan.–Feb. 1990), pp. 105–17 (can be ordered as reprint 90103 from HBS Publishing, Boston, Mass. 02163).

52. Rao and Cox, *Sales Forecasting Methods*.

53. Timmer, Falcon, and Pearson, *Food Policy Analysis*, p. 53.

54. Cross-price and substitution effects as well as income-level food-type differences make the choice of commodity particularly important to the effectiveness of consumer subsidy programs aimed at assisting the poor. See Per Pinstrup-Andersen and Harold Alderman, "The Effectiveness of Consumer-Oriented Food Subsidies in Reaching Rationing and Income Transfer Goals," in Pinstrup-Andersen, *Food Subsidies in Developing Countries*, p. 27.

55. Rao and Cox, *Sales Forecasting Methods*, pp. 88–94. For econometric modeling for food policy analysis, see Timmer, Falcon, and Pearson, *Food Policy Analysis*.

56. S. Makridakis and S. Wheelwright, "Forecasting: Issues and Challenges for Marketing Management," *Journal of Marketing* 41, no. 4 (October 1977), pp. 24–38.

57. For a further exposition of this need, see John Chambers, Salinder Mullick, and Don Smith, "How to Choose the Right Forecasting Technique," *Harvard Business Review* 49, no. 4 (July–August 1971), pp. 45–74.

## Chapter 4

1. John H. Sanders and Frederick L. Bein, "Agricultural Development on the Brazilian Frontier: Southern Mato Grosso," *Economic Development and Cultural Change* 24, no. 3 (April 1976), pp. 593–610.

2. Theodore Panayotou, "Thailand: The Experience of a Food Exporter," in Terry Sicular, *Food Price Policy in Asia: A Comparative Study* (Ithaca, N.Y.: Cornell University Press, 1989), p. 89.

3. Glenn P. Jenkins and Andrew Lai, *Trade, Exchange Rate, and Agricultural Pricing Policies in Malaysia* (Washington, D.C.: World Bank, 1989), p. 45.

4. Yujiro Hayami and Vernon W. Ruttan, *Agricultural Development: An International Perspective* (Baltimore, Md.: Johns Hopkins University Press, 1985), pp. 73–115.

5. Prabhu Pingali, Yves Bigot, and Hans P. Binswanger, *Agricultural Mechanization and the Evolution of Farming Systems in Sub-Saharan Africa* (Baltimore, Md.: Johns Hopkins University Press, 1987); Hans P. Binswanger, *The Economics of Tractors in South Asia: An Analytical Review* (New York: Agricultural Development Council; Hyderabad, India: International Crops Research Institute for the Semi-arid Tropics, 1978).

6. Felipe Encinales and James E. Austin, "Cut Flower Industry in Colombia," in James E. Austin with Tomás Kohn, *Strategic Management in Developing Countries: Case Studies* (New York: The Free Press, 1990), pp. 625–48.

7. Hayami and Ruttan, *Agricultural Development*, pp. 73–115.

8. Gerald O'Mara, "Pricing and Marketing Policies to Intensify Rice Agriculture: The Example of Thailand," in Dieter Elz, ed., *Agricultural Marketing Strategy and Pricing Policy* (Washington, D.C.: World Bank, 1987), pp. 76–91.

9. Jenkins and Lai, *Trade, Exchange Rate, and Agricultural Pricing Policies in Malaysia*, pp. 46–47.

10. Hans J. Mittendorf, "Input Marketing Systems," in Elz, *Agricultural Marketing Strategy and Pricing Policy*, p. 41.

11. C. Peter Timmer, "Indonesia: Transition from Importer to Exporter," in Sicular, *Food Price Policy in Asia*, pp. 39–40.

12. Malcolm D. Bale, "Government Intervention in Agricultural Markets and Pricing," in Elz, *Agricultural Marketing Strategy and Pricing Policy*, p. 101.

13. Bale, "Government Intervention," pp. 99–100.

14. U.S. Congress, Office of Technology Assessment, *Commercial Biotechnology: An International Analysis* (Washington, D.C.: U.S. Government Printing Office, 1984), p. 3.

15. For a discussion of biotechnology techniques and applications oriented toward the general reader, see the International Council of Scientific Unions' *A Revolution in Biotechnology*, Jean L. Marx, ed., (New York: Cambridge University Press, 1989).

16. National Research Council Board on Agriculture, *Genetic Engineering of Plants: Agricultural Research Opportunities and Policy Concerns* (Washington, D.C.: National Academy Press, 1984).

17. Jack Ralph Kloppenburg, Jr., *First the Seed: The Political Economy of Plant Biotechnology, 1492–2000* (Cambridge, U.K.: Cambridge University Press, 1988), p. 204.

18. Roger N. Beachy, "Genetic Transformation for Virus Resistance: Needs and Opportunities in Developing Countries," in Joel I. Cohen, *Strengthening Collaboration in Biotechnology: International Agricultural Research and the Private Sector* (Washington, D.C.: Agency for International Development, Bureau for Science and Technology, Office of Agriculture, 1989), pp. 157–64.

19. Peter S. Carlson, "One Company's Attempt to Commercialize an Agricultural Biotechnology Technology," in Cohen, *Strengthening Collaboration in Biotechnology*, pp. 413–22.

20. Edward C. Cocking, "Plant Cell and Tissue Culture," in Marx, *A Revolution in Biotechnology*, pp. 117–29.

21. Ronald Meeusen, "Genetically Engineered Insect Resistance in Crops," in Cohen, *Strengthening Collaboration in Biotechnology*, pp. 165–73.

22. Richard K. Lankow, "Crop Disease Detection Through Biotechnology—Worldwide Applications," in Cohen, *Strengthening Collaboration in Biotechnology*, pp. 369–81; Jean L. Marx, "Monoclonal Antibodies and Their Applications," in Marx, *A Revolution in Biotechnology*, pp. 145–58.

23. Bill Freiberg, "Wilson Gets Jump on Industry with High Protein Corn Breakthrough," *Seed Industry* 41, no. 2 (February 1990), p. 10.

24. Kloppenburg, *First the Seed*, pp. 274–75.

25. Cocking, "Plant Cell and Tissue Culture," p. 126.

26. For a thoughtful analysis of the possible effects of biotechnology on the poor, see Michael Lipton with Richard Longhurst, *New Seeds and Poor People* (Baltimore, Md.: Johns Hopkins University Press, 1989), especially pp. 364–83.

27. Jock R. Anderson and Peter B. R. Hazell, *Variability in Grain Yields: Implications for Agricultural Research and Policy in Developing Countries* (Baltimore, Md.: Johns Hopkins University Press, 1989).

28. One ounce avoirdupois = 28.350 grams; 1 pound = 0.453 0.454 kilograms.

29. One acre = 0.405 hectares.

30. Inderjit Singh, *Small Farmers in South Asia: Their Characteristics, Productivity, and Efficiency*, World Bank Discussion Paper 31, Washington, D.C., 1989, p. 2.

31. See Richard Goldman and Catherine Overholt, *Nutrition Intervention in Developing Countries: Agricultural Production, Technological Change, and Nutrition Goals*, U.S. Agency for International Development, Special Study 6 (Cambridge, Mass.: Oelgeschlager, Gunn, and Hain, 1980).

32. OECD (Organization for Economic Cooperation and Development), *Tomatoes: Present Situation and 1970 Prospects* (Paris, 1968), pp. 11, 79.

33. About four pounds of grain are needed to produce a pound of beef; the meat is a higher-quality protein, but generally costlier and less available to the nutritionally needy segments of society. Furthermore, unless the caloric deficits are met, the relatively expensive meat protein will be metabolized for energy rather than growth requirements.

34. Gordon Bond, "Scollay Square Associates (A)," Case Study ICH-13G238, Harvard University, Graduate School of Business Administration, Boston, 1968.

35. One hundredweight = 45.359 kilograms.

36. Cristina C. David, "Philippines: Price Policy in Transition," in Sicular, *Food Price Policy in Asia*, pp. 158–59.

37. E. A. Asselbergs, "FAO Action Program for the Prevention of Food Losses," speech delivered to the Agribusiness Management for the Developed and Developing World Food System Seminar, Harvard University, Graduate School of Business Administration, Boston, May 31, 1978.

38. Michael Lipton, "Post-harvest Technology and the Reduction of Hunger," *IDS Sussex Bulletin* 13, no. 3 (June 1982) pp. 4–11; D. G. Coursey, "Tradi-

tional Tropical Root Crop Technology: Some Interactions with Modern Science," *IDS Sussex Bulletin* 13, no. 3 (June 1982), pp. 12–20.

39. David Dichter and Associates, personal interview (September 20, 1977). For low-cost storage techniques, see South and East African Management Institute, *Workbook for East African Workshop/Training Course on Improved Farm and Village-Level Grain Storage Methods* (Arusha, Tanzania, February 1977).

40. James E. Austin, "Marketing Adjustments to Production Modernization" (Managua: Instituto Centroamericano de Administración de Empresas, 1972), pp. IV-1–IV-2.

41. M. O'Brien and R. F. Kasmire, "Engineering Developments and Problems at Production Source of Fresh Produce," *ASAE Transactions* 15 (1972), p. 566.

42. Richard L. Kohls and Joseph N. Uhl, *Marketing of Agricultural Products*, 6th ed. (New York: Macmillan, 1985), p. 357.

43. Geoffrey Lamb and Linda Muller, *Control, Accountability, and Incentives in a Successful Development Institution: The Kenya Tea Development Authority*, World Bank Staff Working Paper 550, Washington, D.C., 1982.

44. For a description of working capital requirements of processors, see C. Magnus and J. Upper, "Kanoun Cannery Financial Analysis Case Study," EDI 320/003, World Bank, Economic Development Institute, Washington, D.C., 1982, and J. Stockard and others, "Greenbelt Cannery Ltd. Exercise," EDI 550/022, World Bank, Economic Development Institute, Washington, D.C., 1978.

45. J. M. Krochta and B. Feinberg, "Effects of Harvesting and Handling on the Composition of Fruits and Vegetables," in Robert S. Harris and Endel Karmas, eds., *Nutritional Evaluation of Food Processing*, 2d ed., (Westport, Conn.: AVI, 1975), p. 98.

46. James G. Brown with Deloitte & Touche, *Agroindustrial Investment and Operations*, EDI Development Study (Washington, D.C.: World Bank, forthcoming).

47. For a practical approach to farm-level financial analysis, see Maxwell L. Brown, *Farm Budgets: From Farm Income Analysis to Agricultural Project Analysis* (Baltimore, Md.: Johns Hopkins University Press, 1979); J. Price Gittinger, *Economic Analysis of Agricultural Projects*, 2d ed. (Baltimore, Md.: Johns Hopkins University Press, 1982); C. Peter Timmer, Walter P. Falcon, and Scott R. Pearson, *Food Policy Analysis* (Baltimore, Md.: Johns Hopkins University Press, 1983), chapter 3.

48. Kohls and Uhl, *Marketing of Agricultural Products*, pp. 16–17.

49. O'Mara, *"Pricing and Marketing Policies to Intensify Rice Agriculture,"* p. 83.

50. Timmer, Falcon, and Pearson, *Food Policy Analysis*, p. 169.

51. Jenkins and Lai, *Trade, Exchange Rate, and Agricultural Pricing Policies in Malaysia*, pp. 41–42.

52. Raisuddin Ahmed, "Pricing Principles and Public Intervention in Domestic Markets," in John E. Mellor and Raisuddin Ahmed, eds., *Agricultural Price Policy for Developing Countries* (Baltimore, Md.: Johns Hopkins University Press, 1988), pp. 66–68.

53. Raisuddin Ahmed and Narendra Rustagi, "Marketing and Price Incen-

tives in African and Asian Countries: A Comparison," in Elz, *Agricultural Marketing Strategy and Pricing Policy,* p. 114.

54. James E. Austin, "State-Owned Enterprises: The Other Visible Hand," in Ray A. Goldberg, ed., *Global Agribusiness Now and in the Year 2000* (Boston: Harvard Business School Press, forthcoming).

55. Ahmed, "Pricing Principles," p. 73.

56. Ravi Gulhati, *Impasse in Zambia: The Economics and Politics of Reform,* EDI Development Policy Case Series, Analytical Case Study 2 (Washington, D.C.: World Bank, 1989) p. 22.

57. David Sahn, ed., *Seasonal Variability in Third World Agriculture: The Consequences for Food Security* (Baltimore, Md.: Johns Hopkins University Press, 1989).

58. Jenkins and Lai, *Trade, Exchange Rates, and Agricultural Pricing Policies in Malaysia,* pp. 92–93.

59. Gustavo Viniegra Gonzalez, "Generating and Disseminating Technology," in James E. Austin and Gustavo Esteva, eds., *Food Policy in Mexico: The Search for Self-Sufficiency* (Ithaca, N.Y.: Cornell University Press, 1987), pp. 138–41.

60. John C. Abbott, "Alternative Agricultural Marketing Institutions," in Elz, *Agricultural Marketing Strategy and Pricing Policy,* p. 17.

61. For more details on this case, see Kenneth L. Hoadley, "The Nicaraguan Cotton Case" (Managua: Instituto Centroamericano de Administración de Empresas, 1974).

62. Frank C. Child and Hiromitsu Kaneda, "Links to the Green Revolution: A Study of Small-scale, Agriculturally Related Industry in the Pakistan Punjab," *Economic Development and Cultural Change* 23, no. 2 (January 1975), pp. 249–75.

63. For such a perspective, see Joyce Lewinger Moock, ed., *Understanding Africa's Rural Households and Farming Systems* (Boulder, Colo.: Westview, 1986).

64. Singh provides a succinct literature review and analysis of the efficiency issue in "Small Farmers in South Asia," pp. 16–36.

65. Rodrigo A. Medellin E., "The Peasant Initiative," in Austin and Esteva, *Food Policy in Mexico,* pp. 148–71.

66. Eliot Berg, "Obstacles to Liberalizing Agricultural Markets in Developing Countries," in Elz, *Agricultural Marketing Strategy and Pricing Policy,* pp. 22–27.

67. James E. Austin and Michael Buckley, "Food Marketing Public Enterprises: Mexico Versus Venezuela," in K. L. K. Rao, ed., *Marketing Perspectives of Public Enterprises in Developing Countries* (Ljubljana, Yugoslavia: International Center for Public Enterprises, 1986), pp. 166–93.

68. An instructive discussion of agricultural marketing constraints in rural Africa can be found in Uma Lele, *The Design of Rural Development: Lessons from Africa,* 3d printing (Baltimore, Md.: Johns Hopkins University Press, [1975] 1979), pp. 100–15.

69. Internal World Bank report.

70. Abbott, "Alternative Agricultural Marketing Institutions," p. 14.

71. Michael Halse, "Operation Flood: An Introduction to the Study Papers

on the Indian Dairy Development Program," Case Study 577-100, Harvard University, Graduate School of Business Administration, Boston, 1976.

72. Wen-fu Hau, "Development of Integrated Cooperative Export Marketing System for Bananas in Taiwan," seminar on Marketing Institutions and Services for Developing Agriculture, The Agricultural Development Council, Inc., Washington, D.C., September 10–12, 1974.

73. James E. Austin, *Managing in Developing Countries: Strategic Analysis and Operating Techniques* (New York: The Free Press, 1990), p. 134.

74. Land O' Lakes, Inc., *1989 Annual Report* (Minneapolis, Minn., 1989), p. 16.

## Chapter 5

1. For a detailed analysis of these operations, see James G. Brown with Deloitte & Touche, *Agroindustrial Investment and Operations*, EDI Development Study (Washington, D.C.: World Bank, forthcoming).

2. FAO (Food and Agriculture Organization of the United Nations), "Postharvest Losses in Quality of Food Grains," Food and Nutrition Paper 29, Rome, 1984, p. 10.

3. Louis T. Wells, Jr., and Ehsan-ul-Haque, "Milkpak," in James E. Austin with Tomás Kohn, *Strategic Management in Developing Countries: Case Studies* (New York: The Free Press, 1990), pp. 359–75.

4. Arnold von Ruemker, "Reappraisal of Himachal Pradesh Apple Processing and Marketing Project (India) Case Study," EDI Case Study Exercise Series, AC-156-p, revised, World Bank, Economic Development Institute, Washington, D.C., January 1977.

5. D. G. Coursey, "Traditional Tropical Root Crop Technology: Some Interactions with Modern Science," *IDS Sussex Bulletin* 13, no. 3 (June 1982), p. 16.

6. For a fuller discussion of public and private divergences and economic cost-benefit methodology in agroindustry projects, see Brown with Deloitte & Touche, *Agroindustrial Investment and Operations*; also, see James E. Austin, *Managing in Developing Countries: Strategic Analysis and Operating Techniques* (New York: The Free Press, 1990), pp. 156–66 and appendix D.

7. C. Peter Timmer, "Choice of Technique in Rice Milling on Java," *Bulletin of Indonesian Economic Studies* 9, no. 2 (July 1973), pp. 57–76; reprinted as a Research and Training Network Reprint (New York: Agricultural Development Council, Inc., September 1974).

8. Martin Greeley, "Farm-level Post-harvest Food Losses: The Myth of the Soft Third Option," *IDS Sussex Bulletin*, 13, no. 3 (June 1982), pp. 51–60.

9. For a fuller discussion of gender analysis and technology, see Mary B. Anderson, "Technology Transfer Implications for Women," in Catherine Overholt, Mary Anderson, Kathleen Cloud, and James Austin, eds., *Gender Roles in Development Projects: A Casebook* (West Hartford, Conn.: Kumarian Press, 1985), pp. 57–78.

10. James Pickett and Robert Robson, *Manual on the Choice of Industrial Technique in Developing Countries* (Paris: Organization for Economic Cooperation and Development, 1986), p. 40.

11. Howard Pack, "The Substitution of Labour for Capital in Kenyan Manufacturing," *The Economic Journal* 86 (1976), p. 56.

12. James E. Austin, "Leather Industry in India," in Austin with Kohn, *Strategic Management in Developing Countries*, p. 260.

13. The analyst should verify the availability of parts and servicing (relative to costs and quality) of any imported versus local equipment, whether the imported equipment is new or secondhand.

14. Louis T. Wells, Jr., "Economic Man and Engineering Man," in Robert Stobaugh and Louis T. Wells, Jr., eds., *Technology Crossing Borders: The Choice, Transfer, and Management of International Technology Flows* (Boston: Harvard Business School Press, 1984), pp. 47–68.

15. For a discussion of these technology issues, see Austin, *Managing in Developing Countries*, pp. 234–61.

16. U.S. Federal Energy Administration, Office of Industrial Programs, *Energy Use in the Food System* (Washington, D.C.: U.S. Government Printing Office, 1976).

17. U.S. Bureau of Census, *Annual Survey of Manufactures* (Washington, D.C.: U.S. Department of Commerce, 1986).

18. R. Paul Singh, "Energy Accounting in Food Process Operations," *Food Technology* 32, no. 4 (1978), p. 40.

19. International Federation of Institutes for Advanced Study (Energy Analysis Workshop on Methodology and Conventions, 1974), in "Energy Accounting as a Policy Analysis Tool," Report to the Committee on Science and Technology, U.S. House of Representatives (Washington, D.C.: U.S. Government Printing Office, 1976).

20. For a more complete analysis, see World Bank, *Alcohol Production from Biomass in the Developing Countries* (Washington, D.C., September 1980).

21. M. Wayman and S. R. Parekh, *Biotechnology of Biomass Conversion* (Englewood Cliffs, N.J.: Prentice Hall, 1990), pp. 231–58.

22. International Labour Organisation, "Labour and Social Problems Arising out of Seasonal Fluctuations of the Food Products and Drink Industries," Second Tripartite Technical Meeting for the Food Products and Drink Industries, Report 2, Geneva, 1978.

23. John M. Connor, Richard T. Rogers, Bruce W. Marion, and Willard F. Mueller, *The Food Manufacturing Industries: Structure, Strategies, Performance, and Policies* (Lexington, Mass.: Lexington Books, 1985), p. 39.

24. See James E. Austin, "Can Nutrition Sell?," *The Professional Nutritionist* 8, no. 3 (September 8, 1976), pp. 12–15; Austin, "Marketing Nutrition," *Cereal Foods World* 22, no. 11 (November 1977), pp. 567–71; and Austin, *Confronting Urban Malnutrition: The Design of Nutrition Programs*, World Bank Staff Occasional Paper 28 (Baltimore, Md.: Johns Hopkins University Press, 1980), pp. 36–43.

25. A. M. Altschul and R. W. Planck, "Effects of Commercial Processing of Cereals on Nutrient Content: Rice and Rice Products," in R. S. Harris and H. W. von Boesecke, eds., *Nutritional Evaluation of Food Processing*, 1st ed. (New York: John Wiley and Sons, 1960), p. 204.

26. M. C. Kik, *Arkansas Agricultural Experimental Station Bulletin* (1957), p.

589; C. M. Lyman and others, *Journal of Agricultural Food Chemistry* 4 (1956), p. 1008.

27. C. H. Edwards and others, *Journal of Agricultural Food Chemistry* 3 (1955), p. 953.

28. Altschul and Planck, "Effects of Commercial Processing," p. 204.

29. R. J. Dimler, "Effects of Commercial Processing of Cereals on Nutrient Content: Milling, Part A: Wheat," in Harris and von Boesecke, *Nutritional Evaluation of Food Processing*, 1st ed., pp. 197–204.

30. D. B. Lund, "Effects of Blanching, Pasteurization, and Sterilization on Nutrients," in Robert S. Harris and Endel Karmas, eds., *Nutritional Evaluation of Food Processing*, 2d ed. (New York: John Wiley and Sons, 1975), p. 205.

31. Lund, "Effects of Blanching," p. 205.

32. For a further discussion of fortification, see James E. Austin, ed., *Global Malnutrition and Cereal Fortification* (Cambridge, Mass.: Ballinger Publishing Co., 1979); and Austin, *Confronting Urban Malnutrition*, pp. 71–75.

33. Nevin Scrimshaw and others, *High-Protein Product Development in Thailand* (Cambridge, Mass.: Massachusetts Institute of Technology, International Nutrition Planning Program, 1973).

34. For further discussion of the technological options and the potential and problems of nutritious formulated foods, see Jerianne Heimendinger, Marian Zeitlin, and James E. Austin, *Nutrition Intervention in Developing Countries: Formulated Foods*, (Cambridge, Mass.: Oelgeschlager, Gunn, and Hain, 1980); and Alan Berg, "Industry's Struggle with Malnutrition," *Harvard Business Review* 50, no. 1 (January–February 1972), pp. 130–41.

35. In general, trucks are more economical for short hauls, railroads for medium hauls, and ships for long hauls. Air transport is particularly appropriate for high-value products and those for which speed is critical.

36. G. N. Puri and Frank Lamson-Scribner, "Technical Aspects of Appraisal," EDI Report CN439, World Bank, Economic Development Institute, Washington, D.C., May 1976; see also UNIDO (United Nations Industrial Development Organization), *Manual for the Preparation of Industrial Feasibility Studies*, Sales no. E.78.II.B.5 (New York, 1978), pp. 54–97; and S. Soderman, *Industrial Location Planning* (New York: Halsted, 1975).

37. Antonio Custer and James E. Austin, "Industrias del Maiz, S.A.," in Austin with Kohn, *Strategic Management in Developing Countries*, p. 123.

38. Robert Bates, *Rural Responses to Industrialization* (New Haven, Conn.: Yale University Press, 1976), p. 252.

39. United Nations, *Industrial Location and Regional Development*, Proceedings of an Interregional Seminar, August 1968, Sales no. 71.II.B.18 (New York, 1971).

40. Edward Felton and Ralph Sorenson, "Republic Flour Mills, Inc.," Case Study ICH 12M30 (Manila: Inter-University Program for Graduate Business Education, 1966).

41. N. N. Potter, *Food Science*, 4th ed. (Westport, Conn.: AVI, 1986), p. 288.

42. For a description of some of these procedures, see J. Orlicky, *Material Requirements Planning* (New York: McGraw-Hill, 1975); O. W. Wright, *Production and Inventory Management in the Computer Age* (Boston: Cahny Books,

1974); and D. C. Whybark and J. G. Williams, "Material Requirements Planning under Uncertainty," *Decision Sciences* 7, no. 4 (October 1976), pp. 595–606.

43. E. R. Pariser and others, *Post-Harvest Food Losses in Developing Countries* (Washington, D.C.: National Academy of Sciences), pp. 47–109.

44. C. Rha, *Theory, Determination, and Control of Physical Properties of Food Materials* (Boston: D. Reidel Publishing Company, 1975), pp. 212–15.

45. Robert M. May, "Food Lost to Pests," *Nature* 267 (June 23, 1977).

46. Y. V. Wu and G. E. Inglett, "Effects of Agricultural Practices, Handling, Processing, and Storage on Cereals," in Endel Karmas and Robert S. Harris, eds., *Nutritional Evaluation of Food Processing*, 3rd ed. (New York: AVI, 1988), p. 101; L. Zeleny, "Effects of Commercial Storage on the Nutrient Content of Processed Foods: Cereal Grains," and A. M. Altschul and R. W. Planck, "Effects of Commercial Processing of Cereals on Nutrient Content: Rice and Rice Products," both in Harris and von Boesecke, *Nutritional Evaluation of Food Processing*, 1st ed., pp. 353 and 204, respectively.

47. FAO, "Post-harvest Losses," p. 10.

48. Zeleny, "Effects of Commercial Storage," p. 353.

49. V. L. Frampton, "Effect of Commercial Processing of Oilseeds and Oils on Their Composition; Part A: Effect of Processing on Composition of Oilseeds," in Harris and von Boesecke, *Nutritional Evaluation of Food Processing*, 1st ed., p. 238.

50. W. J. Wolf, "Effects of Agricultural Practices, Handling, Processing, and Storage on Legumes and Oilseeds," in Karmas and Harris, *Nutritional Evaluation of Food Processing*, 3rd ed., p. 119.

51. A. M. Altschul and others, *Oil and Soap* 20 (1943), p. 258.

52. A. M. Altschul, in A. E. Baily, ed., *Cottonseed and Cottonseed Products* (New York: Interscience Publishers, 1948).

53. H. W. Ockeerman, "Effects of Agricultural Practices, Handling, Processing, and Storage on Meat," in Karmas and Harris, *Nutritional Evaluation of Food Processing*, 3rd ed., p. 153.

54. D. K. Salunkhe and B. B. Desai, "Effects of Agricultural Practices, Handling, Processing, and Storage on Vegetables," and S. Nagy and W. F. Wardowski, "Effects of Agricultural Practices, Handling, Processing, and Storage on Fruits," both in Karmas and Harris, *Nutritional Evaluation of Food Processing*, 3rd ed., pp. 23 and 73, respectively.

55. Henry Arthur, *Commodity Futures as a Business Management Tool* (Boston: Harvard University, Graduate School of Business Administration, Division of Research, 1971).

56. Connor and others, *The Food Manufacturing Industries*, p. 67; Richard L. Kohls and Joseph N. Uhl, *Marketing of Agricultural Products*, 6th ed. (New York: Macmillan, 1985), p. 216.

57. Rudolf Heiss and Karl Eichner, "Packaging Requirements for Foodstuffs," in Rudolf Heiss, ed., *Principles of Food Packaging* (Rome: Food and Agriculture Organization of the United Nations, 1970), pp. 22–31.

58. Rudy de Man, "A Multinational View of Trends and Needs in Food Packaging," *Food Review* (August/September 1988), pp. 15–17.

59. The following examples are drawn from Dana B. Ott, "Trends in Food Packaging," *Journal of Home Economics* 80, no. 3 (Fall 1988), pp. 36–43.

60. D. H. Dewey, "Controlled Atmosphere Storage of Fruits and Vegetables," in S. Thorne, ed., *Developments in Food Preservation* (Englewood Cliffs, N.J.: Applied Science Publications, 1983), p. 1.

61. T. S. Lioutas, "Challenges of Controlled and Modified Atmosphere Packaging: A Food Company's Perspective," *Food Technology* 42, no. 9 (1988), p. 78.

62. Ott, "Trends in Food Packaging," p. 42.

63. These elements are also important for small-scale industries (ssi's) and will frequently require external assistance. The UNIDO (United Nations Industrial Development Organization) Expert Group has said such assistance is critical to ssi success; see UNIDO, *Industrialization and Rural Development* (New York: 1978), pp. 9–16.

64. See United Nations, *Programming and Control of Implementation of Industrial Projects in Developing Countries*, ID/SER.L/1, Sales no. 70.11.B.18; and United Nations, *The Initiation and Implementation of Industrial Projects in Developing Countries: A Systematic Approach*, ID/146, Sales no. 75.11.B.2 (New York, 1970 and 1975, respectively).

65. UNIDO, *Manual for the Preparation of Industrial Feasibility Studies*, pp. 108–09.

66. See also Economic Development Foundation, *Manual on Plant Layout and Material Handling* (Tokyo: Asian Productivity Organization, 1971); and Siegmar Frey, *Plant Layout* (Munich: Hansen, 1975).

67. Potter, *Food Science*, pp. 133–39.

68. D. A. Coorlett, Jr., "Refrigerated Foods and Use of Hazard Analysis and Critical Control Point Principles," *Food Technology* 43, no. 2 (1990), p. 91; F. L. Bryan, "Application of HAACP to Ready-to-Eat Chilled Foods," *Food Technology* 44, no. 7 (1990), p. 7.

69. A. S. Menon, "Salmonellae and Pollution Indicator Bacteria in Municipal and Food Processing Effluents and the Cornwallis River," *Canadian Journal of Microbiology* 31, no. 7 (July 1985), pp. 598–603.

70. Larry A. Esvelt, "Wastewater Reuse in the Food Processing Industry," in E. Joe Middlebrooks, ed., *Water Reuse* (Ann Arbor, Mich.: Ann Arbor Science Publishers, 1982), p. 577.

71. Esvelt, "Wastewater Reuse," pp. 591–94.

72. J. R. Campos, E. Foresti, and R. D. P. Camacho, "Anaerobic Wastewater Treatment in the Food Processing Industry: Two Case Studies," *Water Science Technology* 18, no. 12 (1986), pp. 87–97.

73. As reported by A. Maheswaran, in "The Food Processing Industry and the Environment with Emphasis on Palm Oil Production," UNEP (United Nations Environment Programme) *Industry and Environment* (October/November/December 1985), pp. 2–9.

74. Edward L. Felton, Jr., and Ray A. Goldberg, "The Broiler Industry of Guyana," Case Study 4-373-015, Harvard University, Graduate School of Business Administration, Boston, 1972.

# Appendix A: Checklist of Critical Questions for Agroindustrial Project Analysis

IN THIS APPENDIX the "salient points for project analysis" listed at the end of chapters 3–5 are combined into a single and somewhat fuller checklist. It is hoped that this inventory of pertinent, analytical questions will not only serve to review the issues discussed in this book but will also furnish the practicing analyst with a useful tool for assessing agroindustrial projects in the field. The organization of the questions parallels the organization of the book in its chapter and section headings.

## The Marketing Factor

### Consumer Analysis

*Who are the potential consumers?*
- [ ] What are their economic characteristics: income levels? variability?
- [ ] What are their sociocultural characteristics: ethnicity? language? class? education?
- [ ] What are their demographic characteristics: regional location? urban or rural? age? sex?
- [ ] What are the market segments?
- [ ] What are the possible forms of processed product?
- [ ] What are the product's positioning options among these segments?
- [ ] What do the segments imply for the marketing plan?

*Why would consumers buy the product?*
- [ ] What physiological, sociological, or psychological needs would the product meet?
- [ ] What are the expressed reasons for purchasing: sensory appeal? sustenance? status? convenience? necessity?
- [ ] What is the relative importance of the needs and reasons?
- [ ] What are the implications of these reasons for the distribution options and the marketing plan?

*How would consumers buy the product?*
- [ ] Which individuals would make the purchase decision and what are their roles in the decisionmaking unit?
- [ ] What are the appropriate methods for disseminating information to each member of the decisionmaking unit?

- [ ] Would the purchases be on impulse or planned?
- [ ] Would the purchases be made frequently or seldom?
- [ ] Would the purchases be seasonal?
- [ ] Where would the purchases be made?
- [ ] What are the implications of the buying process for the marketing plan?

*What market information and methods of data collection are needed?*
- [ ] What are the data needs?
- [ ] What are the data sources: primary? secondary?
- [ ] What methods of data collection were used: formal? informal?
- [ ] How valid is the research design for data collection?
- [ ] How reliable are the data sources and collection methods?
- [ ] What is the cost of collecting additional data?
- [ ] Do the benefits expected from the incremental information outweigh the additional costs of data collection?
- [ ] Will small-scale industries need assistance to conduct market research?

## Analysis of the Competitive Environment

*What is the product's market structure?*
- [ ] Who are the competitors: public or private? regional, national, or international? old or new?
- [ ] What are the possibilities and likely effects of new entrants or substitute products?
- [ ] What is the chance of raw material suppliers' integrating forward, or of distributors' integrating backward?
- [ ] How many competing firms are there?
- [ ] Where are the competitors located relative to markets and raw materials?
- [ ] What size are the competitors' assets and sales?
- [ ] What is each firm's market share?
- [ ] How have these shares changed over recent years?
- [ ] How serious are the barriers to entry?
- [ ] Do economies of scale, absolute cost advantages, vertical system control, brand franchises, and switching costs act as barriers to entry?
- [ ] What is the basis of competition in the industry?
- [ ] What is the nature of cost advantages?
- [ ] What are the possibilities of controlling costs?
- [ ] Are efficiency gains possible by reconfiguring resources or activities?
- [ ] What opportunities exist to gain cost advantages through procurement operations?
- [ ] What cost reductions can be achieved through economies of scale and increased capacity utilization?
- [ ] What are the cost effects of the plant location decision?
- [ ] To what extent do cost advantages make price advantages possible?
- [ ] How sensitive are consumers to price?
- [ ] How prevalent is price discounting?
- [ ] How sensitive are consumers to product quality?
- [ ] How do consumers define quality and value?

☐ What are the bases for product differentiation?
☐ How sensitive are consumers to brand names?
☐ What kind of special services are given to distributors or retailers, and how often?
☐ Can differentiation be achieved through raw material or processing ingredients?
☐ Are differentiating innovations possible in product design, processing technology, or packaging?
☐ What stage of its life cycle is the product in, and what implications does that stage hold for cost advantages or product differentiation?
☐ What is the cost of achieving differentiation?

*How do government policies and actions affect the competitive environment?*
☐ What effect will import or export duties or quotas have on competition?
☐ Will an overvalued exchange rate increase import competition, create cost advantages through cheaper imported inputs, or hurt export competitiveness?
☐ Will an undervalued exchange rate have the opposite effects?
☐ Will an undervalued exchange rate attract foreign investment and new competitors?
☐ What are the competitive implications of subsidies to consumers, producers, exporters?
☐ What are the competitive effects of state-owned enterprises operating in the industry?
☐ What are the competitive consequences of regulatory measures such as antitrust, food safety, capacity licensing, and patents?

## The Marketing Plan

*Was the product adequately designed?*
☐ What product characteristics do consumers want?
☐ Which characteristics are most important?
☐ Does the cost of quality improvements keep the product within the consumer's price range?
☐ Have the product's concept and prototype been tested with consumers?
☐ Do small-scale industries need government assistance with product design?
☐ What were the results of the product's design tests?
☐ Were further adjustments to the design made?
☐ Was the final product market tested?
☐ What were the results?
☐ Does the end product meet consumer needs?

*Was the appropriate pricing strategy adopted?*
☐ Is cost-plus pricing feasible?
☐ Are prices regulated?
☐ How is the markup calculated?
☐ Is penetration pricing needed to overcome entry barriers?

☐ Would low prices expand the market enough to offset the lower profit margins?

☐ Would predatory or preemptive pricing be legally or socially responsible?

☐ Would loss-leader pricing expand the sales volume of other company products enough to offset the sacrifice of the loss leader?

☐ Is the product sufficiently new, differentiated, and lacking in competition to permit a skimming price strategy?

☐ Is there an industry price leader?

☐ If so, what are the benefits of following or deviating from the leader's pattern?

☐ What are the effects of controlled or subsidized prices?

☐ How do you manage price negotiations with the government?

☐ Can the project make products whose prices are not controlled?

☐ What are the implications of price policies, levels, and exchange rates in neighboring countries for the competitive pricing decisions here?

☐ Will the pricing strategy work, given the competitors' strategy?

☐ How does the firm expect the pricing strategy to change over time?

*Was the right promotional strategy formulated?*

☐ What is the market-segment audience?

☐ What differences are there among members of the decisionmaking unit?

☐ Will promotion be directed toward end consumers as a "pull" strategy?

☐ Will promotion be directed toward distributors as a "push" strategy?

☐ Is the promotional message consistent with analyses of the consumers and the competitive environment?

☐ What are the consumers' informational needs?

☐ What information is being supplied by competitors?

☐ What does the firm expect the promotional message to do?

☐ Will the consumer misinterpret the message or misuse the product?

☐ How will increased consumption affect the nutritional well-being of low-income consumers?

☐ Will the promotion stimulate primary or secondary demand?

☐ Would branding increase selective demand?

☐ Are quality-control procedures at the processing and procurement stages adequate to permit branding?

☐ Is the promotional vehicle an indirect communication or direct, personal selling?

☐ Are the promotional vehicles consistent with the characteristics of the selected audience?

☐ What portion of the audience will be reached by the vehicles and how frequently?

☐ What is the cost of promotional vehicles relative to their coverage?

☐ Would the cost-benefit ratio of the promotion improve if a combination of vehicles were used?

*Will the distribution system adequately link the manufacturer to the marketplace?*

☐ What is the structure of the distribution system? length of the channels?

☐ How many distributors are at each level of the channels?

☐ What kinds of distributors are at the wholesale and retail levels?

- [ ] Who is performing the logistical functions (transport, assembly, repackaging, storage, inventory management)?
- [ ] Who is performing the service functions (financing, promotion, information collection)?
- [ ] Should the firm use the existing institutions for distribution or perform some functions directly through forward vertical integration?
- [ ] Can small-scale industries realize economies by performing these functions collectively?
- [ ] To what extent will integration permit the firm to realize cost advantages of differentiation?
- [ ] What are the cost, quality, and dependability of existing distribution services?
- [ ] Are the distributors capable and willing to meet the consumers' needs?
- [ ] Where is the power in the distribution channels?
- [ ] Why is the power there?
- [ ] How will the power distribution affect the project?
- [ ] What capital and managerial resources would the firm require for forward integration?
- [ ] What are the social, political, or legal barriers to integration?
- [ ] Has the distribution system adopted intensive, selective, or exclusive retail outlets?
- [ ] Is that choice consistent with the characteristics of the product, the market segment, and the consumers' buying processes?

*Are the elements of the marketing mix integrated into a viable marketing plan?*
- [ ] Are the marketing elements internally consistent?
- [ ] How will the marketing plan for this product affect other products in the company's line?
- [ ] Is the marketing plan compatible with the company's financial, organizational, production, and procurement plans?
- [ ] What does the firm expect the competitive response to the marketing plan to be?
- [ ] How will the marketing effort respond to the competitive response?


## Demand Forecasting

*Are the forecasts based on sound data?*
- [ ] Are the data sources consistent?
- [ ] Are the units of measure standardized?
- [ ] Are the data disaggregated sufficiently to project market-segment demand and total demand?
- [ ] Have all the relevant secondary data sources been used?
- [ ] Was market research used to generate primary data?
- [ ] How were the data collected?
- [ ] Are the data representative?
- [ ] Have the data been verified?
- [ ] What are the underlying assumptions of the data projections?

☐ How sensitive are sales and profit estimates to changes in the assumptions?

*Are the forecasting methods appropriate?*
☐ Who provided the judgmental estimates?
☐ What was the basis of their expertise?
☐ Can other relevant opinions be gathered?
☐ If trend projections were made, how representative were the historical series?
☐ Are the financial data in real or current terms?
☐ Were seasonal, secular, cyclical, or random variations in the series considered?
☐ Were moving averages or exponential weighting techniques employed?
☐ If a regression analysis was used, was it simple or multiple, arithmetic or logarithmic?
☐ Were estimates made of price and income elasticity of demand?
☐ If an econometric model was used, what were the variables?
☐ What causal relationships are assumed in the model?
☐ Are these assumptions reasonable?
☐ Is the accuracy of the projection acceptable, given the risk and uncertainty?
☐ How much could the accuracy be increased by using a more sophisticated technique?
☐ Would the incremental accuracy justify the added cost?
☐ Is the previously used forecasting method still appropriate?
☐ How do the possible forecasting techniques rank in cost, accuracy, skill requirements, data requirements, and speed?

## The Procurement Factor

### Adequate Quantity

*What was the total production pattern?*
☐ What were the production levels? By region? For the past five years?
☐ How variable was output?
☐ What factors affected the variability?

*What is the usage pattern of the area planted?*
☐ How much variation has there been in planted area?
☐ How much land is economically arable but uncultivated?
☐ What trends are there toward opening up new land for planting?
☐ How do government policies affect land expansion?
☐ How productive is the new land relative to the old?
☐ What are the irrigation trends and double-cropping possibilities?
☐ What is the extent of farm mechanization and its effects on land expansion and farm size?
☐ To what extent have farmers shifted among crops?
☐ How much shifting is agronomically feasible?

☐ How much shifting is economically feasible?
☐ What are the nutritional consequences of crop shifts?
☐ How much land or labor has urbanization or industrialization absorbed?
☐ What effect will land-reform programs have on the area planted?

*What is the crop yield?*
☐ How variable have yields been? Why have they varied?
☐ What is the quality of the land?
☐ What is irrigation's effect on yields?
☐ To what extent do farmers use agrochemicals?
☐ To what extent do they use improved seed varieties?
☐ What barriers (for example, credit, price, distribution, knowledge) prevent increased usage of these inputs?
☐ How can these barriers to usage be overcome?
☐ Do the farmers know how to use these inputs?
☐ Do they receive technical assistance? How much? Of what kind? From whom?

*How profitable is the crop?*
☐ How profitable is the crop for the farmer?
☐ How does that differ from returns on other crops?
☐ What does it cost the farmer to produce the crop?
☐ How does that differ from costs of other crops?
☐ How risky is the crop for the farmer?

*What is the possible impact of biotechnology on supply?*
☐ Can it affect yields? disease resistance or detection? cycle?
☐ Has it been field tested?
☐ What is the state of biotechnology research and availability of technology?
☐ What are the actual and likely roles of molecular, cell, and whole plant biotechnologies?
☐ What are the possible effects of production costs?
☐ What are government's policies toward biotechnology?

*How sensitive is supply to production changes?*
☐ How would a change of 20 percent (and more) in area planted affect total supply?
☐ What price incentive is required to increase acreage?
☐ How would a change of 20 percent (and more) in yields affect total supply?
☐ What would it cost to increase the yield?
☐ What is the probability of increases in area or yield?

*Is the raw material a by-product of another agroindustry?*
☐ What is the supply of the primary product from which the by-product is derived?
☐ What is the market demand for the primary product?
☐ Are external supplies of the primary or by-product available through imports if domestic shortfalls occur?
☐ Are there alternative forms of the raw material?

*What is the on-farm consumption?*
☐ What percentage of the crop is consumed on the farm?
☐ How would increased output or higher prices affect the amount flowing into the commercial channels?
☐ How would increased off-farm sales affect the nutritional well-being of the farm families? of landless laborers?

*How is the product consumed?*
☐ Is the raw material consumed fresh or processed?
☐ What are the proportions and trends for usage?
☐ How complementary are the product's uses in fresh and processed forms?

*What is the animal versus human usage?*
☐ Is the raw material consumed by animals and humans?
☐ What are the proportions and trends for usage?
☐ What are the government's priorities for usage?

*What are the industrialization options for the raw material?*
☐ How many end products are produced from the raw material?
☐ What is the demand for these various uses?
☐ What are the price differentials for the raw material among these different uses?

*Is there competition in procurement among similar agroindustries?*
☐ How many firms procure the same raw material?
☐ Are they foreign-based processors or domestic agroindustries?
☐ How much raw material do they purchase?
☐ How does their buying power compare with that of the project?
☐ How do local or foreign government policies affect procurement competition?

*What are the probable crop losses?*
☐ How much of the harvested crop is lost because of rodent or insect damage, poor handling, or inadequate storage?
☐ What measures could reduce these losses?
☐ Do proposed production schemes have adequate on- and off-farm storage facilities?

## Acceptable Quality

*What are the market's quality requirements?*
☐ What market segments will be served?
☐ How quality conscious are they?
☐ What characteristics do they use to define quality?
☐ What do they pay for different levels of quality?

*What is the quality of the farm supply?*
☐ What seed varieties are used?
☐ Will the resultant characteristics of the raw material be consistent with the quality needs of the processed product?

☐ What other quality-oriented inputs are used?
☐ How might biotechnology affect quality?
☐ Do farmers have adequate knowledge of these inputs to achieve the desired levels of quality?
☐ Will technical assistance be needed? Of what kind? From whom?

*How does handling and transport affect quality?*
☐ Have harvesting and transport personnel been trained in handling techniques that will minimize damage to produce?
☐ Will transport methods and delays damage the produce?
☐ What nutrient losses and adverse changes in appearance will occur?

*How does storage affect quality?*
☐ What are the storage facilities and fumigation practices?
☐ Will they prevent damage to produce (including nutrient loss)?

*What government grading and health standards exist?*
☐ What are the requirements for the raw materials?
☐ What are the requirements for the processed goods?
☐ What are the implications of these requirements for the procurement and processing specifications?

*What inputs or services can increase quality control?*
☐ Should the processing plant provide seeds, agrochemicals, storage, drying, or other services?
☐ What would be the cost?
☐ How much would quality improve?
☐ What would be the economic benefits of these measures?

*What quality specifications and inspection procedures should be instituted?*
☐ Are quality standards for the raw material specified?
☐ Are there means to communicate these quality standards to the farmers?
☐ Are there procedures for crop inspection?
☐ Are there adequately trained inspection personnel?

*What quality control would result from backward integration?*
☐ How much additional quality control would be gained if the processor integrated backward to assume the production, storage, transport, and handling functions?
☐ How do these benefits compare with the cost and with the alternatives for quality control?

## Appropriate Timing

*What is the seasonal harvesting pattern?*
☐ When is the crop harvested (or the animal slaughtered)?
☐ Would different seed varieties (or livestock breeds) lengthen or spread the flow of raw material to the plant?
☐ Would staggered planting (or altered feeding patterns) lengthen or spread the flow of raw material to the plant?

☐ What would it cost to adjust the flow period?
☐ How do the costs compare with the benefits of a more even flow?

*What facilities are required by the seasonal pattern?*
☐ What drying (or corral) capacity will be needed to absorb the harvest (or animals)?
☐ What will be the peak of the raw material inventory?
☐ How much storage capacity will be needed for peak inventory?
☐ Can the firm rent space for peak inventory, thereby reducing the overall investment?

*How perishable is the raw material?*
☐ When must the crop be harvested (or animal be slaughtered) to avoid deterioration of quality?
☐ How soon after harvest must the crop be processed to avoid aesthetic or nutritional damage?

*What facilities are necessitated by the raw material's perishability?*
☐ Are there adequate harvesting, transport, and storage services?
☐ Can these services meet the constraints of the material's period of perishability?
☐ Can special treatments (for example, freezing, precooling, waxing) reduce perishability?

*When and for how long will the raw material be available?*
☐ Is the crop (or breed) new to the area?
☐ How long a trial period is needed to ensure agronomic suitability (or acclimatization)?
☐ How long is the planting-to-harvest period (or breeding cycle)?
☐ How will farmers be financed during this period?
☐ Will the agroindustry have to finance the farmers?
☐ Do cultural practices threaten the viability of the crop (or livestock)?
☐ What is the yield pattern over the life span of the crop (for perennial crops and breeding animals)?
☐ How will this pattern affect the flow of the raw material?
☐ What is the risk of suppliers' switching among crops or land uses?
☐ Are there multiple sources of the raw material?

## Reasonable Cost

*How do supply and demand affect the cost of raw material?*
☐ How strong is the demand from competing users of the raw material?
☐ How will the project affect raw material demand and prices?
☐ What are the supply projections under varying prices?

*What are the farmers' opportunity costs?*
☐ What are the land's alternative uses?
☐ How profitable are these activities?

*How do structural factors affect costs?*
☐ What margins do the intermediaries between farmer and factory receive?

☐ Would it be cost effective and organizationally and politically feasible for the factory to perform these intermediary functions?
☐ What are the working capital requirements?

*How do logistical services affect raw material costs?*
☐ What are the farmers' transport charges?
☐ What portion of the price on delivery is the transport charge?

*How does governmental involvement affect raw material costs?*
☐ Has or will the government make infrastructure investments (roads, storage, irrigation, public markets) that will lower production or marketing costs?
☐ Are services or inputs subsidized?
☐ How will import duties or exchange rates affect costs?
☐ Are imports of the raw materials allowed?
☐ How will the marketing activities of state-owned enterprises affect raw material prices?

*Should spot prices be used?*
☐ What are the prevailing spot prices?
☐ How have they varied annually and across years?
☐ Do competitors use spot prices?
☐ How does price variability affect working capital requirements?

*Are multiple sources a potential pricing mechanism?*
☐ Can the plant use multiple crops for the raw material?
☐ How comparable are crops' price levels and variability?
☐ What is the lowest cost combination?
☐ What organizational or technical problems for processing do multiple sources cause?

*How do support prices affect pricing?*
☐ Is there a governmental minimum support price for the crop?
☐ What percentage of the crop flow is affected by this program?
☐ How comparable are the support price and the spot price?
☐ If support prices are pan-temporal, what effect will they have on storage economics and patterns?
☐ If pan-territorial, how will they affect the economics of sourcing from different geographical areas?
☐ Do the support prices offer quality differentials?
☐ Who has access to the support prices?

*Is contracting a desirable pricing mechanism?*
☐ Are production contracts currently used by farmers?
☐ What should the contract terms be for quantity, quality, delivery, technical and financial assistance, and price?
☐ How long a period should the contract cover?
☐ Will the farmers comply with the contract terms?

*Are joint ventures feasible and desirable?*
☐ Are farmers interested in investing in the plant?

☐ Will such investment increase the certainty of supply or lower the raw material costs?
☐ What socioeconomic benefits would investment bring to the farmers?

*Would backward integration lower the costs of raw material?*
☐ Should the plant integrate backward and undertake transport or production or both?
☐ Would that lower the raw material costs?

*What does the sensitivity analysis of raw material costs reveal?*
☐ How would a 20 percent (and more) change in raw material costs affect profits and return on investment?
☐ How likely are such changes?

## Organization of the Procurement System

*What are the number, size, and location of the operators in the structure of the existing system?*
☐ How many producers, transporters, and buyers operate in the existing system?
☐ What are the implications of these numbers for the organization and control of a procurement system?
☐ What percentage of total marketed produce does each participant handle?
☐ How do their production techniques and needs differ?
☐ How differently must the plant interact with large and small suppliers?
☐ Where are the suppliers located?
☐ What implications does the geographical dispersion of producers have for plant location, logistical control, and the vulnerability of agronomic supply?

*What is the suppliers' crop mix?*
☐ What crops do the farmers grow?
☐ Do they specialize?
☐ To what extent do they shift among crops?

*What are the patterns of land ownership?*
☐ How much land is owned, rented, or sharecropped?
☐ How will differences in ownership affect farmers' relations with the processing plant?
☐ How mobile are the farmers?

*What are the routes, timing, and adequacy of the raw material's flow?*
☐ What are the raw material's flow channels?
☐ How much flows through these channels?
☐ When does it flow through?
☐ Can the flow meet the project's requirements?

*What does the analysis of power relationships reveal?*
☐ How much power does each participant in the system have?
☐ How is it spread?

☐ What is the basis of power for each participant?
☐ What is the basis and strength of the project's power?

*Should processors integrate vertically backward?*
☐ How much will control of quantity, quality, and timing improve with integration?
☐ How far back should the producers integrate?
☐ How much additional fixed investment will be required to integrate?
☐ How much additional working capital is required?
☐ How might integration reduce the project's flexibility in obtaining sources of raw material?
☐ What are the economic and operational risks of a decrease in this flexibility?
☐ How will integration affect variable and fixed costs?
☐ How will integration affect the plant's break-even point?
☐ Is integration politically feasible or socially desirable?

*Are there producers' organizations?*
☐ How organized are producers?
☐ What are the goals and activities of existing producers' organizations?
☐ What are the barriers to organization?
☐ What incentives can the agroindustry provide to facilitate organization?
☐ How can the producers' organization be a vehicle for communication between factory and farmer?
☐ How can the producers' organization transmit services or quality-control functions?
☐ How can the producers' organization aid in economic bargaining?

*Should farmers integrate vertically forward?*
☐ What are the financial and managerial requirements for such integration?
☐ What are the benefits?

## The Processing Factor

### Selection of Processing Technology

*Is the processing technology consistent with the qualitative requirements of the marketplace?*
☐ Will the technology match the quality standards of the selected market segments?
☐ Will the incremental revenue from higher quality justify the increased investment in technology?
☐ Will the technology for the local market meet consumer requirements in the export market?

*What constraints are imposed on technology selection by the technical requirements of the transformative process?*
☐ How many forms of technology can meet the requirements of the process?
☐ Do these requirements dictate a minimum economic scale of operation?

☐ Are the sales forecasts consistent with this required minimum volume?

☐ Do government health or safety standards require specific processes and technologies?

*Which technology has the lowest socioeconomic costs?*

☐ What are the relative costs of alternative mixes of capital and labor?

☐ Do the private and social costs of these factors differ?

☐ Are there component processes in the technological package that could operate more economically manually?

☐ Could small-scale industries perform any of the functions within the agroindustrial system?

☐ Can new technologies be developed that will be more appropriate to the country's factor endowment?

☐ Can costs of technology be minimized by buying secondhand equipment?

☐ What are the estimated energy requirements of alternative technologies relative to energy costs, supply, and sources?

☐ Can energy sources be derived from biomass?

☐ How significantly will the chosen technology economize on raw materials?

☐ How do government policies affecting labor, capital, raw material, and energy costs influence the economics of the technology choice?

☐ Are such policies likely to change?

*How will the technology affect use of project capacity?*

☐ To what extent can the technology be adjusted to process other products and lengthen the project's operating period?

☐ What are the costs and benefits of such an adjustment?

*How well does the technology fit with the firm's managerial and technical skill capability?*

☐ Will supervisory demands be excessive?

☐ Will technical demands be excessive?

☐ How can the technology be adjusted to reduce these demands?

*What are the technology's nutritional effects?*

☐ How will processing affect the quality and quantity of the food product's proteins, carbohydrates, fats, vitamins, and minerals?

☐ How can the technology be adjusted to minimize nutrient loss?

☐ Can the technology improve the product's nutritional value through fortification, nutrient concentration, or by-product usage?

## Plant Location

*Do the raw material, market, and transport factors support the proposed location?*

☐ How perishable and fragile is the firm's product?

☐ Will the processing increase or decrease the weight or volume of the raw material?

☐ How significant are transport costs and what are the foreseeable changes?

☐ If supplies or markets are scattered, how do the transport savings from multiple plants compare with the economies of scale from a single plant?

☐ How significant are transport costs relative to total product value?
☐ How adequate are the supply and quality of existing transport facilities?
☐ Should the plant develop its own transport services?

*Is there an adequate labor supply at the location?*
☐ Are the plant's requirements for unskilled labor compatible with the local supply?
☐ Can the plant recruit skilled technicians and professional managers at the proposed location?
☐ Will the plant need to offer special recruiting incentives?

*Is the infrastructure at the location acceptable?*
☐ How does the plant's incremental demand for electricity and steam compare with the projected supply?
☐ How many power supply interruptions have occurred in the past and how serious were they?
☐ What will the energy services cost?
☐ How does the plant's incremental demand for cooling, processing, and potable water compare with the actual and potential quantity and quality of the supply?
☐ What will the water cost?
☐ What are the effluent requirements and does the infrastructure adequately avoid pollution?
☐ Are there adequate fire-protection facilities?
☐ Is the transport infrastructure acceptable?
☐ Are the housing, educational, health, and recreational facilities adequate for plant personnel?
☐ How does the cost of remedying infrastructural deficiencies compare with site advantages?

*What will the plant's land cost?*
☐ How do the prices for a square meter of land compare among various sites?
☐ What is the rate of the land's appreciation?
☐ Can the firm purchase adequate land to allow for future expansion?
☐ Will future urbanization create transport congestion and increase costs?

*What will be the developmental effects of the location?*
☐ What direct and indirect employment will be generated?
☐ How will the project's location affect the income of low-income groups?
☐ What developmental benefits will the plant bring to the region?
☐ Are fiscal or other governmental incentives available?

## Inventory Management

*What are the best storage capacities for raw materials and finished goods?*
☐ How quickly must the product be processed?
☐ Does processing make storage of the product easier?
☐ Can the product be partially processed to reduce the investment for the inventory of finished goods and extend the plant's use of its capacity?

☐ What are the comparative spatial and qualitative requirements for the inventory of the raw material and the finished goods?

☐ Is inventory capacity adequate for processing supplies and spare equipment parts?

*Are the physical facilities adequate?*
☐ What are the potential quantitative and qualitative losses in the inventories of raw material and finished goods?

☐ What are the economic costs and benefits of adjusting facilities for inventory handling and storage to reduce these losses?

☐ Are the storage facilities effectively located relative to suppliers of raw material and distributors of finished goods?

*Have the requirements for working capital and the inventory price risks been adequately analyzed?*
☐ What are the working capital needs for seasonal procurement of the raw material?

☐ Is it possible to hedge against price risks on an existing futures market?

☐ What are the advantages and disadvantages of buying raw materials from a wholesaler throughout the year rather than stockpiling them at harvest time?

☐ Is it possible to achieve price protection for inventory through advance contracts?

## Packaging and Other Processing Inputs

*What functions will packaging perform?*
☐ Will it protect product quality?
☐ Will it provide convenience for users?
☐ What image will it convey?
☐ What information will it transmit?
☐ Will it enable cost savings in processing or distribution?
☐ Will it create value through differentiation?

*Which packaging should be used?*
☐ What are the requirements of the consumer and the distribution channels?
☐ Are there unmet needs that could be satisfied with a different type of packaging?
☐ What requirements are imposed by the intrinsic nature of the product?
☐ How do transportation infrastructure conditions affect packaging requirements?
☐ What packaging characteristics are determined by government regulations?
☐ What are the strengths and weaknesses of different packaging technologies?
☐ How can the technologies enhance the product's value to the consumer?
☐ What are the materials, operating, and investment costs of packaging alternatives?
☐ What are the ecological considerations for the packaging alternatives?

*Where should the plant procure its ancillary supplies (packaging, ingredients, chemicals)?*
☐ Can supplies be obtained locally in adequate quantity and quality when needed and at a reasonable cost?
☐ If supplies are imported, what are the foreign exchange requirements, delivery delay risks, additional transport costs, and import duties?
☐ How can the processor help develop local suppliers' capabilities?
☐ What is the economic, technical, and managerial feasibility of the plant's integrating to produce its own supplies?

## Programming and Control

*Is there a clear and systematic implementation plan?*
☐ Are each of the postinvestment and preproduction steps delineated?
☐ Have programming techniques such as Gantt charts, Critical Path Method (CPM), or Project Evaluation and Review Technique (PERT) been used?

*Has project engineering been diagrammed?*
☐ Have general functional layouts been made?
☐ Have flow diagrams of materials been designed?
☐ Have production line diagrams been specified?
☐ Have transport, utility, communications, and manpower layouts been set forth?

*Does a master schedule for procurement and processing exist?*
☐ Has the seasonal availability of the raw material been considered?
☐ Has the possibility of multiple shifts been explored?
☐ Have alternative uses of the production capacity been examined?

*Have systematic quality-control procedures for raw materials, work in process, and finished goods been instituted?*
☐ Is there an inspection system for the raw material as it is being grown?
☐ Are contamination levels, packaging integrity, temperature, and chemical composition controlled?
☐ Are sampling procedures designated?
☐ Do laboratory testing facilities exist?
☐ Can nutritional quality be verified?
☐ Are corrective procedures specified?

*Have adequate environmental protection measures been planned for?*
☐ Have safety risks to employees from contaminants and hazardous materials and processes been ascertained and minimized?
☐ Have emission controls been instituted ?
☐ Have design measures been taken to maximize in-process reuse and to minimize effluent load?
☐ Are biological treatment technologies available for treating effluent?
☐ Can wastes be converted to other positive uses?
☐ Are facilities and processes in compliance with government environmental control regulations?

## By-Products

*How much revenue do by-products generate?*
- [ ] What are the outputs?
- [ ] Are there unsold by-products that have an economic or nutritional value?
- [ ] What are the price levels and variations of the by-products?
- [ ] Do the by-product sales provide any countercyclical or seasonal balancing to variations in primary product prices?
- [ ] Would integration into the businesses that use the by-products be feasible and desirable?

*Can the by-products be used as energy sources for the processing operations?*
- [ ] What additional investment would be required to convert the by-product to an energy source?
- [ ] Can the energy be used to meet the agroindustry's own fuel needs?
- [ ] Can the energy from by-products be sold outside the agroindustry?

# Appendix B:
# Biotechnology Glossary

THIS GLOSSARY IS INTENDED to provide nonscientists with definitions of terms they may encounter in analyzing or discussing biotechnologies related to agroindustry projects. The definitions in this glossary are taken primarily from the U.S. Congress Office of Technology Assessment's *Commercial Biotechnology: An International Analysis* (Washington, D.C.: U.S. Government Printing Office, 1984). Other sources include Jean L. Marx, ed., *A Revolution in Biotechnology* (New York: Cambridge University Press, 1988); and National Research Council, *Genetic Engineering of Plants: Agricultural Research Opportunities and Policy Concerns* (Washington, D.C.: National Academy Press, 1984).

**Aerobic**: Acting or living only in the presence of oxygen.

**Amino acids**: These constitute the building blocks of proteins.

**Anaerobic**: Acting or living in the absence of oxygen.

**Anther culture**: A form of tissue culture using pollen sacs to produce homozygous parents (purebred lines).

**Bacteria**: Any of a large group of microscopic organisms lacking a nucleus, which may exist as free-living organisms in soil, water, and organic matter or as parasites in live plants and animals.

**Bacterial virus**: A virus that multiplies in bacteria; certain types are used as vectors in rDNA experiments.

**Biocatalyst**: An enzyme that plays a fundamental role in living organisms or in industrial processes by activating or accelerating a process.

**Bioconversion**: A chemical conversion by means of a biocatalyst.

**Biodegradation**: The breakdown of substances by biological processes.

**Biological oxygen demand**: The amount of oxygen used to meet the metabolic needs of aerobic organisms in water containing organic compounds; term is used in relation to biological waste treatment processes.

**Biomass**: All organic matter grown by the photosynthetic conversion of solar energy.

**Bioprocess**: Processes using complete living cells or their components to carry out physical or chemical changes.

**Bioreactor**: Container for bioprocessing, usually involving fermentation reactions.

**Biosynthesis**: Production of a chemical compound by a living organism by means of synthesis or degradation.

**Biotechnology**: Techniques using living organisms or their components to make or modify a product; recombinant DNA and cell fusion are examples of such techniques.

**Callus**: A mound of undifferentiated plant cells that is an initial step in plant regeneration by tissue culturing. A tiny piece of tissue is taken from a plant and put in a petri dish with hormones and nutrients that cause the cells to grow, divide, and form the callus. The callus is then transferred to a regeneration medium in which the cells differentiate into roots and shoots, which grow into plants.

**Catalyst**: A substance (often an enzyme in biotechnology) that induces a chemical reaction to proceed under different conditions than otherwise possible (such as at milder temperatures but at a faster rate).

**Cell**: The smallest structural unit of living matter able to function independently; it is a mass of protoplasm surrounded by a semipermeable membrane.

**Cell culture**: The growth in vitro (that is, in laboratory dishes) of cells isolated from multicellular organisms.

**Cell differentiation**: The process by which descendants of a common parental cell achieve a sustainable specialized structure and function.

**Cell fusion**: The formation of a single hybrid cell with nuclei and cytoplasm from different cells.

**Cell line**: Cells that attain the ability to multiply indefinitely in vitro.

**Chloroplasts**: The cellular organelles in which photosynthesis occurs.

**Chromosomes**: The rodlike structures, composed mostly of DNA and protein, in a cell's nucleus that store and transmit genetic information; each species contains a characteristic number of chromosomes.

**Clone**: A group of cells or organism genetically identical and produced asexually from a common ancestor.

**Cloning**: Replication of segments of DNA, usually genes.

**Coding sequence**: The region of a gene that encodes the sequence of the amino acid of a protein.

**Cosmid**: A vector used in DNA cloning consisting of plasmid and phage sequences.

**Culture medium**: A nutrient system used in tissue and cell culturing to multiply the organism.

**Cytoplasm**: The outside portion of a cell surrounding the nucleus.

**DNA**: Deoxyribonucleic acid—a linear polymer that is the carrier of genetic information present in chromosomes. A DNA strand consists of many individual building blocks (nucleotides) linked together into a large molecule. All inherited characteristics have their origin in the individual's DNA.

**DNA probe**: A DNA sequence used to detect the presence of a particular nucleotide sequence.

**Dominant gene**: The inheritance of a single copy of this gene will confer its specified trait.

*E. coli*: A bacteria species often used experimentally as a host for rDNA.

**Embryo culture**: A tissue culture method to achieve wide crosses between species, such as wheat-rye or pea-peanut-bean.

**Gene**: The basic unit of heredity, which is an ordered sequence of nucleotide bases comprising a DNA segment; it encodes the trait passed on to the next generation.

**Gene amplification**: An increase in gene number for a specified protein to enable its production at increased levels.

**Gene cloning**: The reproduction through recombinant DNA technology of an individual foreign gene in bacterial or other cells.

**Gene expression**: The process in which a particular cell's genetic directions are decoded and processed into a final functioning product, which is usually a protein.

**Gene library**: A set of cell clones containing a DNA fragment from a specific source.

**Gene splicing**: The process of inserting an isolated gene into a plasmid vector. The same restriction enzyme used to cut the gene from the donor cell can be used to cut open the plasmid into which the foreign gene is inserted. The plasmid carries the new gene into a host cell, where the plasmid replicates, the new gene expresses itself, and the host cell is transformed.

**Genetic engineering**: The application of rDNA technology to create organisms with specific traits.

**Gene transfer**: The introduction by genetic or physical manipulation of foreign genes into host cells to achieve specific characteristics in offspring.

**Genome**: The genetic endowment of an individual or organism.

**Germ cell**: The reproductive male and female cells (egg and sperm).

**Germplasm**: The total genetic variability available to a specific species.

**Host**: A cell whose metabolism is used for growth and reproduction of plasmid, a virus, or other form of foreign DNA.

**Host-vector system**: Compatible combinations of host and vector (for example, bacterium and plasmid) that allow stable introduction of foreign DNA into cells.

**Hybrid**: The progeny of genetically dissimilar parents.

**Hybridoma**: The cell resulting from the fusion of a myeloma cell and a lymphocyte cell and producing, in culture, monoclonal antibodies.

**In vitro**: In glass, referring to the container in which tissue or cell culturing takes place, often a petri dish.

**Meristem culture**: A type of tissue culture using the apex bud, often used with heat therapy to produce disease-free clones of tubers and roots.

**Microencapsulation**: Process of surrounding cells with a permeable membrane.

**Monoclonal antibodies (MAbs):** Homogeneous antibodies derived from a single clone of cells and recognizing only one chemical structure; they are, therefore, highly useful as disease diagnostics.

**Monocots:** Plants with single first embryonic leaves, simple stems and roots, and parallel-veined leaves, such as cereal grains.

**mRNA:** Messenger ribonucleic acid carries the transcribed genetic code from the DNA to the ribosomes where it directs protein synthesis.

**Mutagenesis:** The induction by chemical or physical means of mutation in the genetic material of an organism to improve its production capabilities.

**Nitrogen fixation:** Conversion by a limited number of microorganisms of atmospheric nitrogen to ammonia, which is essential to growth.

**Nucleus:** The spherical body inside a cell that contains the chromosomes.

**Organelles:** Parts of a cell performing specialized functions, such as nuclei, which contain the genetic material, chloroplasts, which conduct photosynthesis, and mitochrondia, which provide energy.

**Pathogen:** A disease-producing agent such as bacterium or virus.

**Plasmid:** An extrachromosomal, self-replicating, circular segment of DNA often used as a vector for cloning DNA in bacterial host cells.

**Protoplast:** Cells with their walls removed; protoplast fusion is the joining by chemical or electrical induction of two protoplasts from different cells to create hybrid plants.

**Recombinant DNA (rDNA):** The combining in vitro of pieces of DNA from different organisms to produce a hybrid DNA.

**Regeneration:** The laboratory culturing process of growing a whole plant from a cell or clump of cells (callus).

**Resistance gene:** A gene that is able to resist certain environmental stress, such as exposure to salt or herbicides.

**Restriction enzymes:** Bacterial enzymes able to cut DNA at specific DNA sequences; automated methods for protein sequence analysis facilitate the detection of desired genes to be cut by the restriction enzymes.

**Ribosomes:** Intracellular particles, consisting of proteins and ribosomal RNA, that serve as the site of photosynthesis.

**RNA:** Ribonucleic acid—any nucleic acid containing ribose; generally found in the cytoplasm of cells.

**Somatic cells:** Any of an organism's cells except the germ cell.

**Somatic embryogenesis:** A culturing process whereby protoplasts are grown in a nutrient and hormonal suspension, where the cell walls are reformed and embryolike structures are generated. These structures produce tiny plants, which are then planted in soil for regeneration.

**Somoclonal variation:** Genetic variation occurring in the culturing process of cells, which may produce desirable new characteristics.

**Ti plasmid:** Plasmid from *Agrobacterium tumefaciens* sometimes used as a vector to introduce new genes into plants.

**Transcription**: The first step in gene expression consisting of the synthesis of mRNA on a DNA template, producing an RNA sequence complementary to the DNA sequence.

**Translation**: The second step in gene expression in which the genetic code in the nucleotide base sequence of mRNA directs the synthesis of a specific amino acid order to produce a protein.

**Transfer RNA (tRNA)**: This type of RNA picks up amino acids, carries them to the ribosomes, and aligns them on the mRNA so they can be joined together to form a protein.

**Vector**: A DNA molecule (such as a plasmid or virus) used to introduce foreign DNA into host cells.

# Appendix C: Illustrative Costs of Food-processing Technologies

THIS APPENDIX PROVIDES the reader with additional information on the costs and operating characteristics of three common food-processing technologies: drying, freezing, and canning. The listed prices of equipment and costs of labor and energy should, of course, be updated and made site-specific by any analyst wishing to estimate costs of a particular project. The data do, however, indicate the relative orders of magnitude of the costs of different technological options and a methodology for making such calculations.

The appendix contains three descriptive tables: C-2, which presents information on different types of dryers (sun, cabinet, tunnel, continuous conveyor, belt trough, freeze, pneumatic conveyor, spray, drum, bin, and kiln); C-3, which covers various freezing methods (air-blast, fluidized bed, liquid immersion, spray, and plate); and C-4, which covers different methods of canning (still retort, hydrostatic cooker, hydrolock system, direct flame sterilizer, aseptic sterilizer, sterilmatic retort, and orbitant).

The author expresses appreciation to Dr. S. S. H. Rizvi and assistants, who updated the literature review used to prepare this appendix. Dr. Sam Young helped in developing the original version of the appendix.

## Methodology for Calculating Costs

The next section presents detailed cost calculations for most of the technologies in tables C-2, C-3, and C-4. Explanations of these calculations are not given with the tables, nor are all sources of data identified, because of space constraints. Since all costs were derived in a similar fashion, however, one example can illustrate the methodology.

Let us consider the estimated costs and the performance data for cabinet dryers. Cost estimates are based on 1970 data from H. F. Porter, "Gas-Solid Systems," in Robert H. Percy and Cecil H. Chilton, *Chemical Engineers' Handbook*, 5th ed. (New York: McGraw-Hill, 1973), pp. 30-1 to 30-121. These data showed that f.o.b. (free-on-board) costs of cabinet dryers ranged from $12 per cubic foot (for dryers larger than 300 cubic feet) to $40 per cubic foot (for dryers with 100 cubic feet). Costs included aluminized steel housing with four inches of insulation, a circulating fan, and an air heater. Control instruments added $200–800, trays cost $2–4 per square foot, and trucks or racks cost $200–400. The 1970 installed cost was then calculated at 50 percent over f.o.b. to arrive at the following:

| Dryer volume (cubic feet) | 1970 f.o.b. dryer cost (dollars) | 1970 f.o.b. cost of trays, trucks, controls (dollars) | 1970 installed cost (dollars) |
|---|---|---|---|
| 100 | 4,000 | 750 for trays (250 square feet at $3 per square foot) 300 for one truck/rack 400 for controls | 8,175 |
| 400 | 4,800 | 3,000 for trays (1,000 square feet at $3 per square foot) 900 for three trucks 800 for controls | 14,200 |
| 800 | 9,600 | 6,000 for trays (2,000 square feet at $3 per square foot) 1,800 for six trucks 800 for controls | 27,300 |

The 1970 cost data were then updated using the 1990 M & S Equipment Cost Index (*Chemical Engineering* 97, no. 6, p. 190) to produce the following:

| Dryer volume (cubic feet) | Capacity (pounds of raw material daily) | 1990 installed cost (dollars) | 1990 operating cost (dollars) | |
|---|---|---|---|---|
| | | | Daily | Per pound of raw material |
| 100 | 1,500 | 24,430 | 90.7 | 0.060 |
| 400 | 6,000 | 42,450 | 211.5 | 0.035 |
| 800 | 12,000 | 81,610 | 374.6 | 0.031 |

Capacity estimates were derived from the following assumptions:
- The dryer capacity is fifty 5-square-foot trays per 100 cubic feet, or 750 pounds per 100 feet.
- Each tray is loaded with three pounds of raw material per square foot, or fifteen pounds per tray.
- Raw material contains 75 percent moisture (generally speaking, meat products contain 55–81 percent moisture, vegetables contain 75–90 percent moisture, and fruits contain 80–95 percent moisture), and most of this moisture is removed during drying at an overall drying rate of 0.2 pounds of water evaporated per square foot hourly, or one pound per tray per hour.
- At 75 percent moisture, raw material weighing 750 pounds contains 560 pounds of water, and, at a rate of one pound per tray per hour, a 100-cubic-foot dryer holding fifty trays will take eleven hours for drying and half an hour for loading and unloading.
- Two twelve-hour cycles are completed daily.
- "Raw material" refers to prepared material ready for drying.

The 1990 operating cost estimates are derived according to the following assumptions:
- Two person-hours are required to load and unload fifty trays or one truck in each twelve-hour drying cycle.
- Two and three-quarters pounds of steam or its equivalent in energy are required to evaporate one pound of water.

- The annual maintenance cost is 3–5 percent of the installed cost for a 300-day year.
- One-third person-hour is required to supervise the machine during drying in each twelve-hour drying cycle.
- Unskilled labor earns an hourly wage of $6.
- Three shifts maintain twenty-four–hour operation.
- No amortization has been taken into consideration.

From these assumptions, daily 1990 operating costs, excluding energy costs, can be disaggregated as follows:

| Dryer volume (cubic feet) | Trays (number) | Labor (hours) | Maintenance cost (dollars) |
|---|---|---|---|
| 100 | 50 | 72 | 3.25 |
| 400 | 200 | 144 | 5.66 |
| 800 | 400 | 240 | 10.88 |

The component 1990 daily energy costs are tabulated as follows:

| Dryer volume (cubic feet) | Energy cost (dollars) |
|---|---|
| 100 | 15.47 (= 1,125 pounds of water evaporated × 2.75 pounds of steam × $5 per 1,000 pounds of steam) |
| 400 | 61.88 (= 4,500 pounds of water evaporated × 2.75 pounds of steam × $5 per 1,000 pounds of steam) |
| 800 | 123.75 (= 9,000 pounds of water evaporated × 2.75 pounds of steam × $5 per 1,000 pounds of steam) |

## Detailed Cost Calculations

This section presents the cost calculations used to compute the estimates in tables C-2, C-3, and C-4.

### Cabinet Dryer

1. Installed cost

| Dryer volume (cubic feet) | Installed cost (dollars) 1970 | 1990 |
|---|---|---|
| 100 | 8,175 | 24,430 |
| 400 | 14,200 | 42,450 |
| 800 | 27,300 | 81,610 |

*M & S Equipment Cost Index

| Year | Cost index |
|---|---|
| 1970 | 303.0 |
| 1990 | 905.8 |

so, ratio $= \dfrac{905.8}{303.0} = \underline{\underline{2.989}}$

2. Operating cost

   a) Labor cost

| Dryer volume (cubic feet) | Labor time (hours) | Dollars per hour | Labor cost |
|---|---|---|---|
| 100 | 12 | 6 | 72 |
| 400 | 24 | 6 | 144 |
| 800 | 40 | 6 | 240 |

   b) Maintenance cost, 1990

$$= \text{(installed cost)} \times \text{(annual maintenance cost)} \div \text{(days operated}$$
$$\text{(3–5\%)} \qquad \text{per year)}$$
$$\text{(300)}$$
$$= 24{,}430 \times 0.04 \div 300$$
$$= \underline{\underline{3.25}} \text{ for dryer volume of 100 cubic feet}$$

c) Energy cost

The same as that in 1970.

Therefore,

*Daily operating cost in 1990*

$$= 72 + 3.25 + 15.5 = \underline{\underline{90.7}} \text{ for dryer volume of 100 cubic feet}$$

*Operating cost ÷ pounds of raw material*

$$= 90.7 \div 1{,}500 = \underline{\underline{0.060}} \text{ for dryer volume in cubic feet}$$

## Tunnel Dryer

1. Installed cost, 1990

$$= \text{(installed cost in 1977)} \times \left(\frac{905.8}{500}\right)^{*}$$
$$= 58{,}000 \times 1.81$$
$$= \underline{\underline{105{,}072}}$$

*From M & S Equipment Cost Index

| Year | Cost index |
|---|---|
| 1990 | 905.8 |
| 1977 | 500.0 |

2. Operating cost, 1990

   a)   Maintenance cost

       = (installed cost) × (annual maintenance cost) ÷ (days operated
          per year)
       = 105,000 × 0.04 ÷ 300 = 14

   b)   Energy cost, 1990

       = (water evaporated) × (2.75 pounds of steam) × ($5 per 1,000
          pounds of steam)
       = (16,534 × 0.75) × 2.75 × (5 ÷ 100)
                          → 75% water
       = 170.5

   c)   Labor cost, 1990

       = (total operating cost in 1977) − (energy cost in 1977)
          − (maintenance cost in 1977)
       = (0.024 × 16,534) − 170.5 − (58,000 × 0.004 ÷ 300)
       = 218.5

       Labor time (hours) = 218.594 = 54.6 ~ 54 hours

       Therefore,
       Labor cost in 1990 = 54 × 6 = 324

*Operating cost in 1990* = 14 + 170.5 + 324 = 508.5 daily

*Operating cost per pound of raw material* = 508.5 ÷ 16,534 = 0.030

*Operating cost per pound of water removed* = 508.5 ÷ (16,534 × 0.75)
                                       = 0.041

## All Dryers

Table C-1 presents operating costs for eight different types of dryers.

### Conventional Air-Blast Freezer

1. Maintenance cost, 1990

       = (installed cost) × (annual maintenance cost) ÷ (days operated per year)
       = 337,000 × 0.04 ÷ 300
       = 44.9

**Table C-1.** *Operating Cost for Dryers, 1990*

| Dryer type | Dryer volume | Labor time (hours) | Operating cost (dollars) | | | |
|---|---|---|---|---|---|---|
| | | | Daily | Per pound of raw material | Per pound of water removed | As a percentage of labor cost |
| Cabinet | 1,500 pounds | 12 | 90.7 | 0.060 | 0.080 | 74 |
| | 6,000 pounds | 24 | 211.5 | 0.035 | 0.047 | n.a. |
| | 12,000 pounds | 40 | 374.6 | 0.031 | 0.041 | n.a. |
| Tunnel | 7½ tons | 54 | 508.5 | 0.030 | 0.041 | 63 |
| | 15 tons | 101 | 920.5 | 0.027 | 0.037 | 65 |
| Continuous conveyor | 15 tons | 18 | 479.1 | 0.0144 | 0.019 | 22 |
| | 92 tons | 108 | 2,843.6 | 0.0140 | 0.0186 | 4 |
| Freezer | 320 pounds | 12 | 79.5 | 0.248 | 0.331 | 90 |
| | 4,409 pounds | 24 | 210.4 | 0.0477 | 0.063 | 68 |
| Pneumatic conveyor | 90 tons | 12 | 919.3 | 0.0046 | 0.015 | 5 |
| Rotary | 16 tons | 22 | 306.9 | 0.0087 | 0.029 | n.a. |
| | 75 tons | 24 | 913.6 | 0.0055 | 0.018 | n.a. |
| Spray | 11 tons | 42 | 581.6 | 0.0239 | 0.0319 | n.a. |
| | 144 tons | 84 | 3,977.0 | 0.0125 | 0.0167 | n.a. |
| Drum | 1½ tons | 24 | 188.9 | 0.0571 | 0.0761 | n.a. |
| | 32 tons | 24 | 926.5 | 0.0131 | 0.0175 | n.a. |

n.a.   Not available.

2. Energy cost, 1990

$= (0.9¢ \text{ per pound of product}) \times (132,275 \text{ pounds}) \div 100$
$= \underline{\underline{1,190.4}}$

3. Labor cost, 1990

$= (\text{operating cost in 1977}) - (\text{maintenance cost}) - (\text{energy cost})$
$= (132,275 \text{ pounds} \times 0.0183) - (186,000 \times 0.04 \div 300) - (1,190.4)$
$= 1,205.4$

Therefore,
Labor time (hours) $= 1,205.4 \div 4 = 301 \text{ hours}$

Labor cost in 1990 $= 301 \times 6 = \underline{\underline{\$1,806}}$
Therefore,
*Total operating cost*
$= 44.9 + 1,190.4 + 1,806 = \underline{\underline{3,041.3}}$

*Operating cost per pound of raw material*
$= 3,041.3 \div 132,275$
$= \underline{\underline{0.0229}}$

## Operating Cost for Freezer, 1990

| | Raw material processed (tons) | Labor time (hours) | Operating cost (dollars) | |
| --- | --- | --- | --- | --- |
| Freezer type | | | Daily | Per pound of raw material |
| Conventional air-blast | 60 | 301 | 3,041.3 | 0.0229 |
| Air-blast tunnel and conveyor tunnel | 60 | 93 | 1,838.2 | 0.0138 |
| Liquid immersion (freon) | 60 | 98 | 3,758.7 | 0.0284 |
| Spray | | | | |
| LN | 60 | 247 | 7,195.4 | 0.0543 |
| CO$_2$ | 60 | 161 | 5,361.5 | 0.0405 |
| CO$_2$ with recovery | 60 | 22 | 2,112.2 | 0.0159 |
| Plate | 60 | 110 | 1,675.7 | 0.0126 |

## *Operating Cost for Aseptic Sterilizer for Canning*

1. Maintenance

$$= 2,047,000^{lb} \times 0.04 \div 300$$
$$= \underline{\underline{272.9}}$$

2. Labor

$$= 20 \text{ hours} \times \$6$$
$$= \underline{\underline{120}}$$

3. Energy

$$= (440,917^{lb} \times 0.0018) - (1,130,000 \times 0.04 \div 300) - (20^{hr} \times 4)$$
$$= \underline{\underline{562.9}}$$

*Total operating cost*
$$= 272.9 + 120 + 562.9$$
$$= \underline{\underline{955.8}}$$

*Operating cost per pound of raw material*
$$= 955.8 \div 440,917$$
$$= \underline{\underline{0.0021}}$$

**Table C-2.** *Comparison of Selected Dryers*

| Dryer | Mode and scale of operation | Capital cost, 1990[a] | Operating cost, 1990[b] | Comment |
|---|---|---|---|---|
| Sun | Batch operation for small- to large-scale production of dried grains, seeds, spices, fruits, fish, and other piece-form foods as a means of preservation; large-scale production limited by need for large area, lack of ability to control drying process, possible degradation due to biochemical or microbiological reactions, insect infestation, and so forth | Negligible (for racks, trays, and the like) | High labor requirement but free energy; no maintenance problems; nonpolluting, renewable, abundant energy source | Loss of products from adverse change in weather during drying season can be substantial; not suited to areas with cool or humid climate (or both); more destructive than mechanical dehydration to provitamin A carotenes, vitamin C, and (possibly) riboflavin; adding sulfite to fruits and vegetables to prevent browning causes large losses of thiamine but is beneficial to provitamin A and vitamin C retention; long drying time contributes to nutrient losses and bacterial spoilage; products (such as dried fruits) have special accepted organoleptic characteristics difficult to reproduce in mechanical drying; sun drying generally will not lower moisture content below about 15 percent, which is too high for storage stability of numerous food products; requires considerable space |
| Cabinet | Batch operation for small-scale production (1–20 metric tons daily) of dried vegeta- | $23,000 for ³⁄₄ ton, $43,000 for 3 tons, $81,000 for 6 tons daily | High labor requirement for loading/ unloading; labor cost is 65–75 percent of | Long drying time because of slow removal of water (0.2 pounds per hour per square foot) contributes to high losses of nutrients and lower organ- |

| | Applications | Equipment cost | Operating and labor cost | Product quality |
| --- | --- | --- | --- | --- |
| | bles, fruits, meat products, egg whites; air-convection tray dryer can process almost any form of food (solids, liquids, or slurries) | | total operating cost; relatively low maintenance cost (simple operation): $0.031–0.060 per pound raw material (75 percent moisture), $0.041–0.080 per pound water removed | oleptic quality: long drying time and relatively low drying temperature sometimes present sanitary problems; suited to small-scale batch production of different products or as back-up dryer for sun drying during adverse weather |
| Tunnel | Semicontinous operation for large-scale (10–50 tons daily) production of dried vegetables, fruits, meats, other piece-form foods; can process various solid foods with minor changes in operations | $105,000 for 7½ tons, $204,000 for 15 tons daily | Relatively high labor requirements for loading/unloading trucks; labor cost is 65 percent of total operating cost; relatively low maintenance cost; $0.027–0.030 per pound raw material (75 percent moisture), $0.037–0.041 per pound water removed | Long drying time contributes to higher losses of nutrients and lower organoleptic quality than more advanced drying methods; sanitary problems are sometimes encountered; especially suitable for drying prunes; in concurrent process, rapid initial drying and slow final drying can cause case hardening, internal splits, and porosity as centers finally dry; in countercurrent flow, initial product temperature and moisture gradients will not be as great, and the product is less likely to undergo case hardening or other surface shrinkage, leaving wet centers |

*(Table continues on the following page.)*

237

**Table C-2** (continued)

| Dryer | Mode and scale of operation | Capital cost, 1990[a] | Operating cost, 1990[b] | Comment |
|---|---|---|---|---|
| Continuous conveyor | Continuous operation for medium- to large-scale production of dried piece-form foods; best for large volumes of one product; not suited to different products in one plant | $226,000 for 15 tons, $376,000 for 30 tons, $507,000 for 46 tons, $780,000 for 92 tons daily | Low labor costs but skilled personnel required for operation and maintenance; labor cost is 5–20 percent of total operating cost; more efficient cost than cabinet or tunnel dryers; $0.0140–0.0144 per pound raw material at 75 percent moisture, $0.018–0.019 per pound water removed | Shorter drying times produce products with higher nutrient retention, better organoleptic quality, and fewer sanitary problems than those from tunnel or cabinet drying; handles the product gently; permits free passage of air through the bed; offers closely controlled process conditions at each stage of the drying cycle, optimizing both product quality and energy utilization |
| Belt-trough | Continuous operation for medium- to large-scale production of piece-form foods; best for large volumes of one product; piece sizes must be small and uniform for efficient drying | 2–3 times conveyor-dryer cost, based on conveyor surface, for comparable output | Similar to conveyor dryer | Similar to conveyor dryer; fast drying time (3–4 times faster than conveyor dryer); produces high-quality products with good nutrient retention |

238

| | | | | |
|---|---|---|---|---|
| Freeze | Batch operation for small- to medium-scale production; best for small volumes of piece-form foods sensitive to dehydration and with high market value (such as spices, coffee, and juices); can process almost any form of food (solids, liquids, or slurries) | $32,000 for 320 pounds, $61,000 for 1,120 pounds, $157,000 for 2 tons daily[c] | Relatively labor-intensive because of batch loading/unloading (similar to cabinet dryers); $0.047–0.248 per pound raw material (75 percent moisture), $0.063–0.331 per pound water removed | The low processing temperatures, the relative absence of liquid water, and the rapid transition of the material from a fully hydrated to a nearly completely dehydrated state minimize the degradation that normally occurs in ordinary drying processes, including nonenzymatic browning, protein denaturation, and enzymatic reactions; in general, freeze drying can produce dried products with the best organoleptic quality, delicate flavors, colors, good texture and appearance, and highest retention of nutrients; freeze-dried products suffer negligible shrinkage compared with other dried products and enjoy high consumer acceptance; however, freeze drying is expensive because of its slow drying rate and its use of a vacuum chamber |
| Pneumatic conveyor | Batch or continuous operation for large-scale drying of powder or granules with | $217,000 for 90 tons, $246,000 for 120 tons, $297,000 for 200 | Low labor costs but skilled personnel required for maintenance and operation; | This dryer is used for materials that can be carried by high-velocity air (such as flour, grains, powder); because drying time is short, loss of nu- |

*(Table continues on the following page.)*

239

**Table C-2** *(continued)*

| Dryer | Mode and scale of operation | Capital cost, 1990[a] | Operating cost, 1990[b] | Comment |
|---|---|---|---|---|
| Pneumatic conveyer *(continued)* | low moisture content; best for operations requiring conveyance and classification during drying | tons, $378,000 for 480 tons daily[d] | $0.0046 per pound raw material; $0.015 per pound water removed | trients is negligible, and little adverse organoleptic change takes place; usually requires recirculation of dry product to make suitable feed; suitable for processing heat-sensitive, easily oxidized, explosive, or flammable materials that cannot be exposed to process conditions for extended periods; steam-tube and direct-heat types are universally applicable |
| Rotary | Batch or continuous operation for medium- to large-scale drying of relatively free-flowing and granular solids, such as grains | $221,000 for 16 tons, $329,000 for 28 tons, $478,000 for 48 tons, $657,000 for 75 tons daily[d] | Low labor costs but skilled personnel required for maintenance and operation; $0.0055–0.0087 per pound raw material; $0.018–0.029 per pound water removed | Similar to, but requiring less floor space than, pneumatic conveyor |
| Spray | Continuous operation for medium- to large-scale drying of fluids, slurries, and pastes; | $597,000 for 11 tons, $896,000 for 32 tons, $1,165,000 for | Low labor costs but skilled personnel required for maintenance and operation; | Product is usually powdery, spherical, and free-flowing; high temperatures can be used with heat-sensitive materials; product properties and quality |

| | | | |
|---|---|---|---|
| | best for drying one product in large volumes; consists of three process stages; atomization, spray-air mixing and moisture evaporation, separation of dry product from the exit air | 64 tons, $1,494,000 for 144 tons daily[e] | $0.0125–0.0229 per pound raw material; $0.0167–0.0319 per pound water removed | are more effectively controlled; heat-sensitive foods, biologic products, and pharmaceuticals can be dried at atmospheric pressure and low temperatures; because the operating gas temperature may range from 150 to 600°C, the efficiency is comparable to that of other types of direct dryers; spray drying can produce products comparable in organoleptic quality and nutrition with those produced by freeze drying |
| Drum | Continuous operation for small- to medium-scale drying of fluids, slurries, and pastes; best for one product; may be chosen in cases where crystallization and liquid/solid separation are not feasible | $81,060 for 1½ tons, $126,000 for 5 tons, $181,000 for 8 tons, $413,000 for 32 tons daily[e] | Same as for spray drying; $0.013–0.057 per pound raw material, $0.017–0.076 per pound water removed | In general, drum-dried products are inferior in organoleptic and nutritive quality to spray-dried products because of scorching and other problems; drum-dried milk, however, is often preferred over spray-dried milk for candy making (because of higher free fat content and heat-induced stabilization against oxidation) and for sausage making (because of higher water absorption); because of its flaking characteristics, drum drying is extensively used to make potato flakes and similar products; drum drying |

*(Table continues on the following page.)*

**Table C-2** (continued)

| Dryer | Mode and scale of operation | Capital cost, 1990[a] | Operating cost, 1990[b] | Comment |
|---|---|---|---|---|
| Drum (continued) | | | | usually involves much smaller capital investment than spray drying, which may be advantageous when the drying operation is small, seasonal, or dependent on raw materials whose availability is not secure |
| Bin | Batch operation for finish drying (that is, to reduce moisture from 10 to 3 percent) of previously dried products; best for piece-form foods containing low moisture (such as grains, dried potato flakes) | One-half to one-third that of a cabinet dryer of similar size | One-half to one-third that of a cabinet dryer, per pound water removed | During finish drying, most moisture is removed and the rest is redistributed among the almost dry products; this lowering and redistribution is very important to the storage stability of dried foods |
| Kiln | Batch operation for small- to medium-scale drying of apple rings, hops, green fodder, and the like; used to dry food | Same as for bin dryers | Same as for bin dryers | Because of the long drying time required, the nutritional and organoleptic quality of the products is probably inferior to that obtained by cabinet drying and comparable to that obtained by sun drying; sanitary prob- |

242

lems occur; still in use for apple slices; this kind of drier will not reduce moisture to below about 10 percent

solids in areas where sun drying is impractical because of high humidity, cold climate, or both

a. Dollar figures have been rounded to the nearest thousand.

b. Operating costs are obtained from previous tabulations (see text) and have been rounded to the nearest thousandth of a dollar (mill, or tenth of a cent); operating costs listed do not include amortization.

c. Cost of freezing equipment not included.

d. Raw material is assumed to contain only 30 percent moisture.

e. Liquid raw material contains 75 percent moisture.

*Sources:* Estimates for dryers are based on 1962 cost data from Brown and others, "Drying Methods and Driers," in W. B. Van Aredel and M. J. Copley, eds., *Food Dehydration*, vol. 2 (Westport, Conn.: AVI Publishing Co., 1964); and updated by data from M & S Equipment Cost Index in *Chemical Engineering* 97, no. 6 (June 1990). p. 190; N. N. Potter, *Food Science*, 4th ed. (Westport, Conn.: AVI Publishing Co., 1986), p. 246; C. M. Vantland, "Selection of Industrial Dryers," *Chemical Engineering* 91, no. 3 (March 5, 1984), p. 54; A. S. Mujumdar, *Handbook of Industrial Drying* (New York: Marcel Dekker, Inc., 1987), pp. 133–516.

**Table C-3.** *Comparison of Selected Freezers*

| Freezer | Mode and scale of operation | Capital cost, 1990[a] | Operating cost, 1990 | Comment |
|---|---|---|---|---|
| Conventional air-blast | Batch operation for small- to large-scale production of frozen boxed foods (such as vegetables), poultry, fish; versatile in the variety of products it can process | $336,000 for 60 tons daily | High labor requirement for loading/ unloading; $0.0229 per pound raw material | Capable of freezing almost anything that can be fit into them; because of slow freezing time,[b] high labor costs, low organoleptic quality of products, and high drip losses during thawing (which can cause nutrient losses), these freezers are being replaced by more advanced technology; they can, however, be economically used to freeze foods containing high solids (meats, for example) that are not highly sensitive to freezing damages and that have relatively low market value |
| Air-blast tunnel and conveyor tunnel | Batch or continuous operation for me- dium- to large-scale production of frozen whole poultry, fish, fish fillets, and the like (can freeze any- thing that can fit on conveyor or tray); | $637,000 for 60 tons daily | High labor require- ment for batch opera- tion; labor require- ment lower for con- tinuous operation but still high compared to fluidized-bed freez- ing; $0.0138 per pound raw material | Faster than conventional air-blast freezers but still slower than other methods; most frequently used for high-solid foods not highly sensitive to freezing damages that cannot be adequately or economically frozen by more advanced methods (for example, whole poultry, boned fish fillets, whole fish); relatively long freezing |

| | Description | Cost | Labor | Comments |
|---|---|---|---|---|
| | best for continuous operation; the air moves counter-current to the product on trays or on a mesh belt that moves through an insulated tunnel | | | time makes evaporation losses from unpackaged foods significant (alleviated by wrapping foods in thin plastic) |
| Fluidized bed | Continuous operation for medium- to large-scale production of peas, shrimp, cut vegetables, and other small, individually frozen foods; method can process only foods that can be fluidized by air; more efficient heat transfer and more rapid rates of freezing; less product dehydration and less frequent defrosting of equipment | $637,000 for 60 tons daily | Low labor requirement but skilled personnel required for operation and maintenance | Best suited to continuous production of one product in large volumes (technical complexities occur in readjusting machine for different products); to achieve efficient freezing, raw material must consist of uniform pieces that are not easily ripped apart by high-velocity air; fast freezing makes product quality comparable to that from liquid-immersion freezing and spray freezing; individually frozen pieces have high consumer utility |

*(Table continues on the following page.)*

**Table C-3** (continued)

| Freezer | Mode and scale of operation | Capital cost, 1990[a] | Operating cost, 1990 | Comment |
|---|---|---|---|---|
| Liquid immersion (brine) | Batch or continuous operation for small- to large-scale production of frozen canned foods or whole fish | Data unavailable (but much cheaper than freon immersion freezer) | Relatively high labor requirement for batch operation; cost probably similar to that of conventional air-blast freezer | Best suited to freezing foods not adversely affected by brine (for example, canned juice or whole fish); fast freezing rate because of good contact between brine and foodstuff and because brine is a better medium for heat transfer than air; used extensively to freeze canned, concentrated fruit juices and whole fish (in factory boats); good for poultry, especially during initial stage of freezing (to impart a uniform white color to the surface) |
| Liquid immersion (freon) | Continuous operation for small- to large-scale production of individually frozen foods such as shrimp, scallops, onion rings | $963,000 for 60 tons daily | High operating cost because of loss of expensive freezant; $0.0284 per pound raw material | Best suited to individual freezing of delicate foods that have high market value and cannot be adequately frozen by other methods; extremely rapid freezing rates yield products with high organoleptic quality; individually frozen pieces have high consumer utility; large-scale operation is required to offset high capital cost |
| Spray | Continuous operation for small- to large-scale production of | $192,000 for 60 tons daily (if liquid nitrogen | High operating costs, especially in system without freezant re- | Relatively low capital cost without freezant recovery system makes these freezers best-suited to small- and |

| | | | | |
|---|---|---|---|---|
| | individually frozen foods such as fish, poultry, meat patties; adaptable to various production rates and product sizes; small space requirement; heat transfer by convection | or carbon dioxide is used); $963,000 for 60 tons daily (if liquid or solid carbon dioxide is used with recovery system) | covery (liquid nitrogen and carbon dioxide are very expensive): $0.0543 per pound raw material (if liquid nitrogen is used); $0.0405 per pound (if carbon dioxide is used with recovery system) | medium-scale, seasonal production of high-quality products with high market value; probably produces highest quality of freezing methods; because of the high capital cost of the recovery system, spray freezers with freezant recovery systems are economically feasible only if large-scale production can be assured throughout the year; individually frozen pieces have high consumer utility; more rapid freezing rates can be achieved even though the liquid may be at a higher temperature than that normally used in air blast |
| Plate | Batch operation of small- to medium-scale production of packaged frozen foods such as fish fillets, meats, fruits; heat transfer by conduction; double-contact plate freezers are commonly used for freezing foods in retail packages; operation is automatic | $673,000 for 60 tons daily | High labor costs for loading/unloading food materials; $0.0126 per pound of raw material; modern plate freezers are highly automated and labor requirements minimal; such automation, however, makes a plate freezer more costly | Good contact between cold plates and packaged food materials gives this method the fastest freezing rate for packages filled with food materials; because of the pressure applied on the plates, uniform, well-shaped products with minimum voids can be manufactured; not suited to freezing packages with much dead air space; used extensively to produce "fish sticks" (bits and pieces, as well as fillets, of fish are into large slabs with application of pressure in plate freezer; the frozen |

*(Table continues on the following page.)*

**Table C-3** (continued)

| Freezer | Mode and scale of operation | Capital cost, 1990[a] | Operating cost, 1990 | Comment |
|---------|------------------------------|------------------------|----------------------|---------|
| Plate (continued) | with a stack of horizontal cold plates with intervening spaces to accommodate single layers of packaged product; an economical method that minimizes problems of product dehydration, defrosting of equipment, and package bulging | | | slab is sawed into desired sizes and batter is applied; the ready-to-fry product is frozen again) |

a.  Cost estimates are based on 1976 data from J. R. Behnke, "Freezing: End-Product Quality Is as Important an Investment as Operating Costs in Freezing System," *Food Technology* 30, no. 12 (1976). p. 32, and 1971 data from A. W. Ruff "Freezing Systems: Investment and Operating Costs," *Food Engineering* 43, no. 9 (September 1971). p. 76; updated with data from M & S Equipment Cost Index in *Chemical Engineering* 97, no. 6 (June 1990), p. 190.

b.  A comparison of freezing times for small fruits and vegetables by different freezing methods and the product form they require follows: conventional air-blast (10-ounce packages), 3–5 hours; plate (10-ounce packages), $\frac{1}{2}$–1 hour; air-blast conveyor tunnel (individual pieces in bulk), 20–30 minutes; fluidized bed or tray (individual pieces in bulk), 5–10 minutes; cryogenic (individual pieces in bulk), $\frac{1}{2}$–1 minute. Data are from C. L. Rasmussen and R. L. Olson, "Freezing Methods as Related to Costs and Quality," *Food Technology* 26, no. 12 (1972). p. 32.

**Table C-4.** *Comparison of Selected Types of Canning Equipment*

| Canning method | Mode and scale of operation | Capital cost, 1990[a] | Operating cost, 1990 | Comment |
|---|---|---|---|---|
| Still retort | Batch operation for small- to medium-scale production of canned or bottled foods; versatile in the variety of products able to process | $25,000 for 8–16 tons daily; $28,000 for 12–24 tons daily | High labor requirement for loading and unloading; low maintenance cost; $0.0029–0.0077 per pound raw material | Can process a variety of can sizes and products; the sterilization time, however, is long and the canned products have poor organoleptic quality and low nutrient retention compared with products of more advanced methods; oldest and probably most commonly used equipment for commercial sterilization; use of laminated, flexible pouches instead of cans or bottles can significantly reduce sterilization time and improve product quality |
| Hydrostatic cooker | Continuous operation for large-scale production of canned or bottled foods; most suited to processing one particular food product in large volume | $1,146,000 for 100–200 tons daily | Skilled labor required for operation and maintenance; low manual labor requirement; $0.0019–0.003 per pound raw material | Suited to handling containers susceptible to thermal shock (such as glass bottles); shorter sterilization time than still retort (particularly for nonviscous food materials) because of agitating motion of the conveyor during sterilization; accordingly, yields products with better organoleptic and nutritive quality than those from still retorts; rather complicated engineering |

*(Table continues on the following page.)*

**Table C-4** *(continued)*

| Canning method | Mode and scale of operation | Capital cost, 1990[a] | Operating cost, 1990 | Comment |
|---|---|---|---|---|
| Hydrolock system | Similar to hydrostatic cookers | Not available (probably similar to that for hydrostatic cookers) | Not available (similar to that for hydrostatic cookers) | Similar in performance to hydrostatic cookers; also suited to processing laminated flexible pouches |
| Direct-flame sterilizers | Continuous operation for large-scale production of canned vegetables (particularly mushrooms); can process only small cans because of build-up of internal pressure during heating | Not available | Not available (similar to that for hydrostatic cookers) | These sterilizers are suited to processing nonviscous foods in small containers; because of short sterilization time (shorter than hydrolock or hydrostatic systems), produces products with very good organoleptic quality and nutrient retention |

| | | | | |
|---|---|---|---|---|
| Aseptic sterilizer | Continuous operation for large-scale production of canned, bottled or laminated pouch-packaged fluid foods | $2,047,000 for 200 tons daily | Low manual labor requirements but skilled labor required for operation and maintenance; high maintenance cost; 0.0021 per pound raw material | Extremely short sterilization time; yields best organoleptic quality and nutrient retention among all canning methods, but can process only fluid foods |
| Sterilmatic retort and orbitant | Continuous operation for medium- to large-scale production of canned foods | Not available | Not available (similar to that for hydrostatic cookers) | Similar to hydrostatic cookers |

a. Cost estimates are based on data from the following sources: for still retort, A. K. Robbins and Co.; for hydrostatic cookers, F. K. Lawler, "The French Build Efficient Canneries," *Food Engineering* 32, no. 3 (March 1960), p. 64; for aseptic sterilizers, "Aseptic Milk Makes N. American Debut," *Food Engineering* 47, no. 9 (September 1975), p. 15. Estimates are updated with data from M & S Equipment Cost Index in *Chemical Engineering* 97, no. 6 (June 1990), p. 190.

# Index

Advertising, 62–65

Agrarian reform projects, 89–90, 123

Agribusiness, 9, 188 n21. *See also* Agroindustry

Agriculture, agroindustry and, 4–5, 9–13, 188 nn22–23

Agroindustrial projects. *See* Analytical framework (agroindustry); Marketing analysis; Processing; Procurement system

Agroindustry: aid flows for, 14; agriculture and 4–5, 9–13, 188 nn22–23; analytical framework for, 4, 14, 17–38, 190 n13; backward linkages and, 5; biotechnology and, 93, 95–96; characteristics of, 1–4, 187 n1; definition of, 1; employment and, 8–9, 13, 188 n19; environmental protection and, 173–74, 178–80, 181; exports and, 9–13, 188 n22; as a force for economic development, 4–14, 188 nn19, 22; growth of, 6, 14; inventory management and, 141, 164–67, 169–70; nutritional issues and, 13–14, 16; plant location and, 141, 159–64. *See also* Processing

Alcohol. *See* Ethanol; Gasohol

Analytical framework (agroindustry), 4, 14; institutional linkages and, 17, 28–29, 31, 34–37; international linkages and, 17, 37–38; macro-

micro policy linkages and, 17, 23, 25, 28; production chain linkages and, 17–23. *See also* Marketing analysis; Processing; Procurement system

Anand Cooperative, 129

Animal feed, 102, 117, 166. *See also* Livestock

Animal pests, 105, 111, 165–66

Biomass, 150

Biotechnology, 93, 95–96

Brands: franchise and, 51; product promotion and, 64–65; product quality and, 53, 108

Brown, James G., x, 16, 18

Buying process (consumers), 46–47

By-products, 112; as energy sources, 181, 186; processing and, 140, 180–81, 182, 186

Canning, 148; nutrition and, 159

Capacity (manufacturing): 151–52

Capital: inventory management and, 169–70; labor and, 146–49; for procurement and storage of raw material, 109, 126–27

Carbohydrates: in cereal grains, 166; effect of processing on, 153

Causal demand forecasting models, 76–78

Cereals, 165–67

*Chaya*, 42

Collective organizations. *See* Producer organizations

Community participation, 5

Compañía Nacional de

The World Bank
Economic Development Institute

Agroindustries are enterprises that process agricultural raw materials—crops and livestock—and transform them into consumable goods found in markets and homes. In developing countries especially, agroindustries not only supply needed food and fiber products, they save consumers labor, create employment opportunities, stimulate innovations in farm production and manufacturing, spur improvements in the infrastructure, and produce valuable exports. Thriving agroindustries, then, are a catalyst for economic development.

This book provides a field-tested analytical framework for designing effective agroindustrial projects. Written for private agribusiness managers, officials in the public sector, and analysts in development agencies, *Agroindustrial Project Analysis* has been called "a landmark reference." This second edition preserves the strengths of the first while incorporating the lessons of recent experience and fresh examples.

A new chapter has been added elaborating the systems approach to agroindustrial analysis, and that conceptual approach is emphasized throughout. Expanded chapters on the three main components of agroindustrial activity—procurement of raw materials, processing, and marketing—identify the elements vital for success. Critical questions for practitioners to ask are found at the ends of chapters and in a detailed checklist at the end of the book. This edition also includes a new glossary of biotechnology terms and updated information on the costs and operating characteristics of common food-processing technologies.

JAMES E. AUSTIN holds the Chapman professorship at the Harvard University Graduate School of Business Administration. An internationally renowned management expert in agroindustry and development, he has published extensively and frequently advises governments, international organizations, and private businesses.

The Johns Hopkins University Press

Cover design by ~~C~~ ellehamer

ISBN 0-8018-4530-0